1. Ely Cathedral, from the south-east

THE
MEDIEVAL FENLAND

BY

H. C. DARBY

Fellow of King's College, and
Professor of Geography in the University
of Cambridge

David & Charles
Newton Abbot

0 7153 5919 3

First published in 1940

Reprinted by permission of The Cambridge
University Press 1974

Printed in Great Britain
by Redwood Burn Limited, Trowbridge & Esher
for David & Charles (Publishers) Limited
South Devon House   Newton Abbot   Devon

To
BERNARD MANNING

CONTENTS

The Face of Places, and their Forms decay;
And that is solid Earth, that once was Sea:
Seas in their turn retreating from the Shore,
Make Solid Land, what Ocean was before.

OVID, Metamorphoses, liber xv.

(Dryden's translation.)

EDITOR'S PREFACE

DR DARBY's position as an historical geographer makes an editor's task when introducing him in the character of an economic historian easy, almost otiose. It is only the pressure of our schemes for teaching and examination that has made these two labels necessary for any one man, or couple of men. He is a very imperfect economic historian who is not also a tolerable geographer; and I cannot picture to myself a useful historical geographer who has not a fair working knowledge of economic history. But I think it likely that geographers with Dr Darby's technical equipment as an historian are rare. The evidence of that equipment—one which any mere historian will respect—is to be found in the text and the footnotes of this book. The same historian might also perhaps covet the geographical equipment.

For many years it has been a dream of mine, and of some other people in Cambridge, that the story of the Fenland should be rewritten here on a foundation of thorough documentary and geographical knowledge. William Cunningham knew his Fens, as an Archdeacon in these parts must, and he made contributions to their history; but he was never able to attempt a complete narrative. Others of us talked about it; but we lacked the time, or it might be some part of the equipment, or the resolution in attack. The book that was dreamed of never got written.

"Such a book", if I may adapt John Wesley's Preface to the 1779 edition of Wesley's hymns, "you have now before you. It is not so large as to be either cumbersome or expensive; and it is large enough to contain such a variety of" historical material "as will not soon be worn threadbare. It is large enough to contain all the important truths" of early Fenland history; and its companion volume, which has the same merits, will serve equally well for the later history. There is really no more that an editor need say.

J. H. CLAPHAM

PREFACE TO SECOND EDITION

When this book first appeared in 1940, one reviewer said that 'perhaps the most striking single new generalization to emerge from this is the tremendous change in the prosperity of the Fenland between Domesday and the early fourteenth century. In a short two hundred and fifty years the silt Fenland is shown to change from country far inferior to the upland to land a good deal more prosperous than the upland'.[1] The generalization was based upon a comparison of the statistics of the Domesday Book with those of the Lay Subsidies of the early fourteenth century. Since this comparison was made, a great deal of work has been done on both these sources. Domesday geography has been more fully explored,[2] and the Lay Subsidy of 1334 has been mapped by Dr R. E. Glasscock.[3] The results of this new work, in so far as it relates to the Fenland and neighbouring districts, can be seen in Figs A and B, for 1086 and 1334 respectively; the information on both maps has been calculated in terms of the same unit areas. The contrast between them is indicated by Fig C which, so to speak, summarises the changes of two and a half centuries, and shows the great improvement in the siltlands.

In the meantime, Prof. H.E. Hallam has shown how these changes came about, particularly in his outstanding study of the Lincolnshire Fenland entitled *Settlement and Society: A Study of the Early Agrarian History of South Lincolnshire* (Cambridge, 1965). The wealth of detail he has assembled indicates how numerous were the enclosures on both the seaward and the fenward side of the silt belt during the twelfth and early thirteenth centuries, and also along the upland margins of the Fenland. These changes he discusses

[1] H. Godwin in *The New Phytologist*, 39 (1940), 237–8.
[2] H. C. Darby, *The Domesday Geography of Eastern England* (Cambridge, 3rd edn., 1971).
[3] R. E. Glasscock, "England *circa* 1334", being chapter 4 of H. C. Darby (ed), *A New Historical Geography of England* (Cambridge, 1973).

against their social and demographic background. There is, as yet, no corresponding study for the Norfolk siltlands.

Another study that must be mentioned is Dr Joan Thirsk's *Fenland Economy in the Sixteenth Century* (University College of Leicester, 1953). This gives a picture of the Lincolnshire fens at the end of the Middle Ages, and shows the parts played by salt-marsh, arable, pasture and meadow in the economy of the region.

I am much indebted to Mr G. R. Versey for drawing the three new maps.

H.C.D.

New Year's Day, 1973

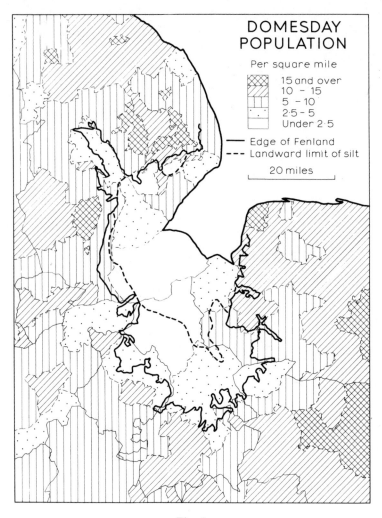

Fig. A

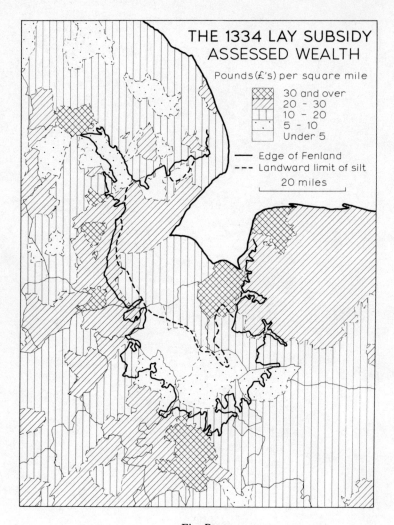

THE 1334 LAY SUBSIDY
ASSESSED WEALTH

Pounds (£'s) per square mile

30 and over
20 - 30
10 - 20
5 - 10
Under 5

——— Edge of Fenland
- - - Landward limit of silt

20 miles

Fig. B

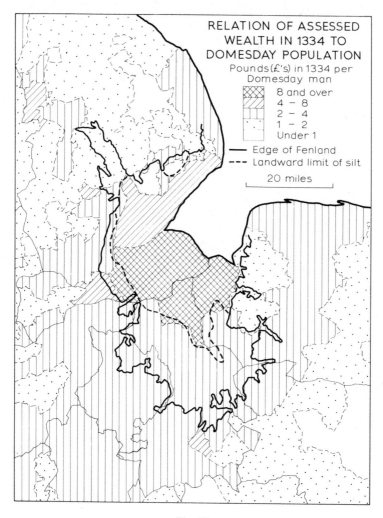

RELATION OF ASSESSED
WEALTH IN 1334 TO
DOMESDAY POPULATION
Pounds(£'s) in 1334 per
Domesday man
8 and over
4 – 8
2 – 4
1 – 2
Under 1
—— Edge of Fenland
---- Landward limit of silt
20 miles

Fig. C

PREFACE

OVER sixty years have passed since there appeared a general survey of the Fenland. Published in 1877, S. B. J. Skertchly's *The Geology of the Fenland* was an outstanding contribution, with wider implications than its title might suggest. In the following year, S. H. Miller and S. B. J. Skertchly together produced *The Fenland Past and Present*. Ten years earlier had come the first edition of W. H. Wheeler's *History of the Fens of South Lincolnshire* (1868), which was greatly enlarged in 1896. These are not the only accounts of the area to be written within the last half-century: Miss Neilson's *Terrier of Fleet, Lincolnshire* (1920) is a notable contribution to the medieval story; while summaries of the history of the draining have been made in connection with other topics, and many reports have dealt with drainage problems. But the fact remains that there is no recent work outlining the economic development of the Fenland as a whole.

Despite the scarcity of its modern literature, the fascination of the theme cannot be denied. The thirteen hundred square miles of Fenland constitute a very distinctive region in the English plain, and the vast horizon of the fen has made an appeal to the imagination of many people. This book, together with its companion volume, *The Draining of the Fens*, is an attempt to outline the changing conditions of the region. The division into two parts reflects the two phases in the exploitation of the fens—the pre-drainage period, and the post-drainage period, each with a distinctive economy.

There are many topics this outline does not elaborate. No great reference has been made, for example, to the constitutional history of the sewer courts. Due partly to intention and partly to circumstance, these two studies are economic and geographical in character. The narrative begins, by way of introduction, before the Domesday Survey; but, as the text makes clear, these earlier years still await their archaeological unfolding. A conclusion is reached, in *The Draining of the Fens*, with the year 1900, but an epilogue summarises the legacy of difficulty that 250 years of draining (from, say, 1653 onwards) bequeathed to the twentieth century. This legacy constitutes the core of the problems that are with us to-day.

It is with great pleasure that I acknowledge here the help I have received. This book has been written in the most delightful surroundings at King's College, overlooking the "Backs" that are themselves a product of reclamation, and that border a stream soon to enter the Fenland proper. This setting was made possible by my election to the Open Fellowship, founded by his parents, in memory of Sidney Hellman Ehrman, sometime research student of the College. Upon completion, the manuscript was awarded the University Prize in Economic History endowed by the late Ellen McArthur. It is my first duty therefore, "in piam memoriam", to thank these two benefactions—one at King's College, and the other in the University.

Among those who have been most helpful, I owe particular thanks to Dr Clapham. His help as editor of this series is only a part of my debt to him; one of the strongest memories I have of this book is that of his many kindnesses. To Professor Debenham I also owe a great debt, for it was in his Department of Geography, and with his encouragement, that the idea for an account of the Fenland grew up. There are also many people whose help has been technical. Professor F. M. Stenton has given me much advice about sources. Major Gordon Fowler read through the manuscript and made many suggestions; and, too, I have had the benefit of his important publications on fenland topography, mentioned on the appropriate pages below. Others who have given me suggestions after reading the manuscript are: Mr John Saltmarsh, Mr C. F. Tebbutt, Dr W. M. Palmer and Professor M. M. Postan. For help and suggestions, I am also indebted to Miss N. M. O'Farrell, Dr P. H. Reaney and Mr C. M. G. Woodgate. I must also thank the numerous authorities who have given me facilities or have allowed me to make use of material in their possession. This material is acknowledged on the relevant pages below. All the maps have been drawn by Mr L. D. Lambert; permissions to reproduce material on certain maps are acknowledged on p. xiv. Finally, came the kindness of the University Press whose officials were to make the last stages of this book not a labour but a delightful experience.

To this list I must add the name of Mr B. L. Manning of Jesus College. This book, together with *The Draining of the Fens*, has grown from work originally carried out under his direction. Too often have I trespassed upon his time and patience. I wish that these two volumes could be better tokens to convey to him my appreciation.

H. C. DARBY

KING'S COLLEGE
CAMBRIDGE
St Govan's Day 1939

MAP ACKNOWLEDGEMENTS

I am indebted for the following permissions:

For Figs. 1, 2, 4, 5, 12, and portions of Figs. 6, 7, 8, 10, 13, 14, 15 and 16 to the Controller of H.M. Stationery Office and the Director General of the Ordnance Survey.

For Fig. 13 to the British Academy and the Oxford University Press.

For Fig. 14 to Major Gordon Fowler and the Editor of the *Geographical Journal*.

H. C. D.

MAPS & DIAGRAMS

LIST OF PLATES

1. Ely Cathedral, from the south-east   *Frontispiece*

By permission of Mr G. H. Tyndall of Fulbourn. In the foreground is the River Ouse which runs very close to the island of Ely at this point (see Fig. 14). For a more distant view, see plate 7.

2. Aerial Photograph: Romano-British evidence at Throckenholt.   *facing p.* 6

By permission of Major G. W. G. Allen, F.S.A. Mr C. W. Phillips has kindly provided the following note: "Air-photograph showing a system of Romano-British fields and their connecting droveways at Throckenholt (near Parson Drove). The ancient features appear by soil colouration in all places except in the middle of the photograph where an unploughed grass field shows them in relief." See p. 4 below. Map reference: O.S. One Inch Popular Edition, sheet 65, squares E 3 and 4.

3. The Sea Bank at Newton near Wisbech   *facing p.* 7

By permission of Miss Lilian Ream, The Borough Studios, Wisbech. The view was taken from the landward side of the bank, looking eastwards; on the other side lay the estuary of the Nene. See footnote 4, p. 4 below.

4. Aerial Photograph: The Little Ouse Roddon   *facing p.* 10

By permission of Major Gordon Fowler. The meanders of the Little Ouse roddon (see Fig. 15) approach the Littleport-Shippea Hill road shown running across the photograph. See p. 6 below. Map Reference: O.S. One Inch Popular Edition, sheet 75, square D 12.

5. St Guthlac goes to Crowland   *facing p.* 11

From the British Museum Harleian MS. Y. 6. See p. 8 below. For a description of the plate, see W. de Gray Birch, *Memorials of St Guthlac* (1881), p. xli. The MS. is probably 12th century in date.—See W. G. Searle, *Ingulf and the Historia Croylandensis* (1894), p. 37.

CHAPTER ONE

INTRODUCTION: THE PRE-DOMESDAY FENLAND

THE main story of the formation of the Fenland depression is fairly clear. There was a time, before the Quaternary Ice Age, when the Chalk Uplands of Lincolnshire were continuous with those of Norfolk, stretching across what is now the Wash. Through gaps in this chalk escarpment, the early representatives of the modern rivercourses flowed eastward to join, possibly, the ancestor of the Rhine and the Thames, before reaching a northern sea. This ridge disappeared under the action of two forces.[1] The rivergaps, enlarged by the normal processes of erosion, reduced the one-time escarpment to little more than a line of isolated outliers, while the submergence of the land completed the work, so that the sea gained access to a western plain—the gentle dip slopes formed by the outcrops of older, but softer and easily denuded, Jurassic clays. Thus, the Fenland, by origin, was essentially a flooded plain, which had for its limits the harder rocks around—chalk to the north and south, and resistant Jurassic rocks in the west (see Fig. 1). The surface of this Jurassic plain was uneven, and its higher portions projected above the general level to become the "islands" of the historical period—Ely, March, and so on. The whole region emerged from the complicated events of the various phases of the Ice Age with its islands capped with boulder clay but with its basin character unchanged. All subsequent time has witnessed the filling up of this basin by the various agents of sedimentation, leaving the Wash of the present day as the remnant of a much larger indentation of the sea.

[1] For the geology there is the long-standing account by S. B. J. Skertchly, *The Geology of the Fenland* (1877). See also: (1) W. H. Penning and A. J. Jukes-Brown, *The Geology of the Neighbourhood of Cambridge* (1881); (2) *The Geology of Parts of Cambridgeshire and Suffolk*, a co-operative work published in 1891 (Mem. Geol. Survey).

The post-glacial deposits are of two kinds.[1] On the seaward side, the fen deposits are "silts and clays laid down under conditions of greater or less salinity". On the landward side, they are composed "largely or wholly of peat, which has formed as a result of an accumulation of fresh water". This expanse of peat covers nearly one half of the whole of the Fenland separating the marine silt belt from the solid upland around (see Fig. 2). The thickness of the peat varies from a few inches to ten feet or more;[2] but, of course, these modern figures do not give an indication of the pre-drainage thickness before shrinkage and wastage had done their work.[3] Alterations in the relative levels of land and sea have produced an inter-digitation of deposits when seen in vertical section—peats on the one hand, clays and silts on the other.

The boundary of the depression, thus formed and partly filled, may be defined by a line running from Firsby through Tattershall to Lincoln, and then southward by Billinghay and Peterborough to Earith, whence it curves eastward through Cottenham and Burwell, and so northward through Denver to King's Lynn. The regularity of this outline is broken by the extension of fen up the valleys whose rivers emerge from the surrounding upland. The extreme length of the Fenland,

[1] For a summary, see H. Godwin, "The Post-Glacial Deposits of Fenland", in *The Cambridge Region*, ed. by H. C. Darby (1938), pp. 17–18. The two quotations that follow are from this account.

For longer accounts, see (1) H. Godwin and M. H. Clifford, "Studies of the Post-Glacial History of British Vegetation", *Phil. Trans. Roy. Soc. London* (Series B), ccxxix, 323 (1938). (2) H. Godwin, in *V.C.H. Cambs*, i, 49 (1938).

[2] See S. B. J. Skertchly (1877), *op. cit.* pp. 132–3: "The greatest thickness attained by the peat, so far as I have ascertained, is 18 feet, in the parish of Earith....A like thickness was pierced in the parish of Warboys. ...In the arm which stretches up to Lincoln and forms the valley of the Witham the peat occasionally attains a thickness of from six to eight feet....From Heckington to Deeping Fen the peat is thin, seldom attaining a greater thickness than three feet, and is more frequently less than a foot....The average thickness of the peat in the Bedford Level may be taken at about six feet, but it is very variable."

[3] See H. C. Darby, *The Draining of the Fens* (1940), pp. 104 and 231.

between Lincoln and Quy, is about 73 miles; the extreme breadth, between Peterborough and Brandon, is about 36 miles. The total area is approximately 1306 square miles.

The condition of the Fenland during Roman times has aroused considerable discussion from time to time. The Car

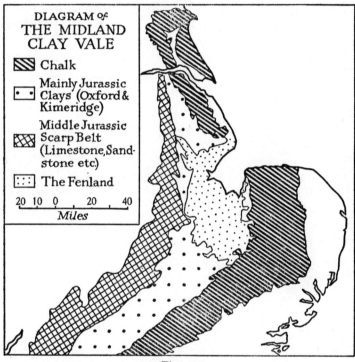

DIAGRAM of
THE MIDLAND
CLAY VALE

☒ Chalk

▣ Mainly Jurassic Clays (Oxford & Kimeridge)

☒ Middle Jurassic Scarp Belt (Limestone, Sandstone etc.)

▦ The Fenland

20 10 0   20   40
        Miles

Fig. 1

Dyke, the coastal sea-banks, the Peterborough-Denver cause-way, the various scattered finds—all have been productive of speculation and theory.[1] But the whole problem of the Roman Fenland has been placed in an entirely new setting by the development of a new instrument of research—aerial photo-

[1] See Cyril Fox, *The Archaeology of the Cambridge Region* (1923), pp. 179–80 and pp. 222 *et seq.* See also E. J. A. Kenny, "A Roman Bridge in the Fens", *Geographical Journal*, lxxxii, 434 (1933). See "Note on Roman Literary Evidence", p. 20 below.

graphy. The pioneer work of Mr O. G. S. Crawford has
yielded fruitful results when applied to this area. By taking
a sequence of photographs across a given stretch of country,
it is possible to fit together a "mosaic" in one complete
photograph. Several of these mosaics have been made for
various fen localities, but until a complete survey has been
made, an entire picture of the Roman Fenland cannot be
given.[1] It is evident, however, that in Romano-British times
(50 B.C. to A.D. 450) some of this country,[2] at any rate, was
occupied by cultivators, who tilled the soil in small rectangular or irregularly shaped fields upon a system of agriculture which is associated with the Celtic fringe of Britain,
and which was quite unlike the open-field system of the
Anglo-Saxon invaders.[3] All this, of course, stands in great
contrast to later conditions in the Fenland. To explain the
transition is one of the major problems that await solution.
The alternative answers are: (i) that the Romans, with their
highly developed political organisation and engineering skill,
practised artificial drainage with conspicuous success; and
that their works fell out of repair after their occupation was
over:[4] (ii) that the deterioration was the result of natural

[1] In 1932, the Fenland Research Committee was formed to investigate
the problems of the fens. For a summary of the early work of the
committee see J. G. D. Clark, "Recent Researches on the Post-glacial
Deposits of the English Fenland", *The Irish Naturalists' Journal*, v, 144
(1934).

[2] Particularly on the silt areas and on certain islands; "the region of
maximum farming activity" seems to have been upon the silt lands of
south-eastern Lincolnshire—see C. W. Phillips, "Romano-British Times"
in *The Cambridge Region*, ed. by H. C. Darby (1938), p. 92.
    For a sample of the evidence, see plate 2.

[3] See J. G. D. Clark and C. W. Phillips in the catalogue to the *Fenland
Survey Exhibition*, p. 29 (Heffer, Cambridge, 1934).

[4] But, so far, no signs of such works have been found. Of the so-called
"Roman" sea-bank, C. W. Phillips writes: "While not categorically
denying that some parts of this bank may have had a Roman origin it
must be pointed out there is not a shred of evidence for this...a medieval
origin seems to be indicated." See "The Present State of Archaeology
in Lincolnshire, Part II", *Archaeological Journal*, xci, 123, 124 (1934).
Apparently the "Roman Bank" was always called "sea bank" (*fossatum
maris*) until Sir William Dugdale, without any authority, suggested that

Fig. 2

S. B. J. Skertchly, in *The Geology of the Fenland* (1877), p. 129, noted that the precise boundaries of the peat and silt were "very obscure, for the peat thins out insensibly along its borders".

agencies—a silting up of watercourses or, more particularly, a basic land subsidence in post-Roman times.[1] Both answers may be correct. In the present state of knowledge it is unsafe to be dogmatic because too many associated problems await investigation.

One of the keys to a solution lies in the study of extinct watercourses. The existence of extinct watercourses, called "roddons", in the Fenland has been demonstrated by Major Gordon Fowler.[2] Today, these watercourses appear in the form of banks of silt meandering above the surface of the peat fen. They were formed as the natural levées of tidal streams, and their present character is due to wasting of the peat that subsequently formed over their flanks.[3] Air photographs, taken under favourable conditions, show them up well (see plate 4), and it has been definitely established that many roddons were active streams in Romano-British times.

However rich the Roman Fenland, and whatever the cause of its transformation, the fact is that by Anglo-Saxon times

it might be Roman—*History of Imbanking and Drayning* (1772), pp. 173–5. Later writers, following this lead, assumed it to be Roman. For a photograph of the sea bank, see plate 3. See also C. W. Phillips, "Roman Ferry across the Wash", *Antiquity*, vi, 342 (1932).

[1] Evidence suggests that submergence took place comparatively rapidly during or just after the Roman Occupation. Discoveries in the Thames estuary show that the level of the land has sunk about 15 feet relatively to that of the sea—T. E. Longfield, *The Subsidence of London*. Ordnance Survey Professional Paper, new series, no. 14 (1933). See (1) the discussion in *Abstracts of the Proceedings of the Geological Society of London*, no. 1260, p. 73 (March 3rd, 1933); (2) H. H. Swinnerton, "The Post-Glacial Deposits of the Lincolnshire Coast", *Quart. Journ. Geol. Soc.* lxxxvii, 360 (1931). Many other papers, too, discuss the evidence for other parts of the coast. See the references in *An Historical Geography of England before* A.D. 1800, ed. by H. C. Darby (1936), pp. 61–2, 94.

[2] See the following papers by Gordon Fowler: (1) "The Old River Beds in the Fenlands", *Geographical Journal*, lxxix, 210 (1932); (2) "Fenland Waterways, Past and Present. South Level District. Part I", *Proc. Cambridge Antiquarian Society*, xxxiii, 108 (1933); Part II, *ibid.* xxxiv, 17 (1934); (3) "The Extinct Waterways of the Fens", *Geog. Journ.* lxxxiii, 30 (1934). See also Fig. 14 below.

[3] H. Godwin, "The Origin of Roddons", *Geog. Journ.* xci, 241 (1938).

2. Aerial photograph: Romano-British evidence at Throckenholt

Mr C. W. Phillips has kindly provided the following note: "Air-photograph showing a system of Romano-British fields and their connecting droveways at Throckenholt (near Parson Drove). The ancient features appear by soil colouration in all places except in the middle of the photograph where an unploughed grass field shows them in relief."

Lilian Ream

3. The Sea Bank at Newton near Wisbech

Taken from the landward side of the bank, looking eastwards; on the other side lay the estuary of the Nene

the region shows a startling change. An index of the relative intensity of the Anglo-Saxon settlement is provided by the size of the hundreds. Those of the southern Fenland are anything from two to four times as large as those of the surrounding upland. The following are typical:

Fenland		Upland	
Ely	44,420 acres	Humbleyard (Norf.)	23,000 acres
Wisbech	70,790 ,,	Whittlesford (Camb.)	10,928 ,,

The figures of the "Tribal Hidage", probably an eighth-century document, likewise indicate lightness of settlement.[1] In 731, Bede, writing of the late seventh century, said that when the Ely folk desired stone they "went on board ship because the country of Ely is on every side encompassed with the sea or marshes, and has no large stones".[2] And at the end of the same chapter Bede declared: "Ely is in the province of the East Angles, a country of about six hundred families, in the nature of an island, enclosed as has been said before, either with marshes or with waters, and therefore it has its name from the great plenty of eels taken in those marshes."[3] Mention of the "six hundred families" serves as a reminder that although most of the peat fen must have been waste, it is unlikely to have been completely without value

[1] *Cartularium Saxonicum*, ed. W. de Gray Birch, i, 414 (1885).
An addition to the Anglo-Saxon Chronicle, dated ostensibly in 657, declares that Wulfhere, king of Mercia, gave to the monastery of Peterborough "these meres and lakes, *Scælfremere* and *Witlesmere*, and all the others which lie thereabouts" (see p. 26 below). But the passage is a twelfth-century fabrication.

[2] Bede, *Historia Ecclesiastica*, lib. iv, cap. 19. Bede also said (iv, 6) that Peterborough was "in the country of the Girvii". And "the Girvii", wrote the twelfth-century Ely chronicler, "are all the southern Angles that inhabit the great marsh in which the island of Ely is situated".— *Liber Eliensis*, ed. by D. J. Stewart (1848), p. 4. But it must be admitted that he wrote a long time after the event (see footnote 4 on p. 10 below).
The twelfth-century Peterborough chronicler (Hugo Candidus) also has some relevant remarks: "In the country of the Gyrvii there is a famous monastery, hitherto called Medeshamstede, but now usually Burch: the Gyrvii being those which inhabit near the fens because *gyr* in English is the same as *palus profunda* (a deep fen) in Latin."—"Historiae Coenobii Burgensis," p. 1, in *Historiae Anglicanae Scriptores Varii*, ed. by J. Sparke (1723). [3] See p. 29 below.

even at this time. As Professor Stenton writes: "The local names of the Fens are very difficult, but they do at least show that the whole of this country had been explored, was being exploited, and had been named far back in the Anglo-Saxon period. In this respect the history of the Fens is not unlike that of the Sussex Weald."[1] But even so, it is not difficult to understand that many parts in the eighth century could still be described as a "wide wilderness",[2] devoid of settled habitation.[3] And an eighth-century monk, Felix, tells how:

There is in Britain a fen of immense size, which begins from the river Granta [*Grante*] not far from the city, which is named Grantchester [*Granteceaster*]. There are immense marshes, now a black pool of water, now foul running streams, and also many islands, and reeds, and hillocks, and thickets, and with manifold windings wide and long it continues up to the north sea.... Guthlac...inquired of the inhabitants of the land where he might find himself a dwelling place in the wilderness. Whereupon they told him many things about the vastness of the wilderness. There was a man named Tatwine, who said that he knew an island especially obscure, which oft-times many men had attempted to inhabit, but no man could do it on account of manifold horrors and fears, and the loneliness of the wide wilderness.[4]

And when St Guthlac came to Crowland,[5] he found the place infested with devils of various kinds. The incredible nature of these tales is irrelevant to the argument; the spirit which

[1] In a letter. In this connection, the account of the limits of the grant to Peterborough set forth in the Anglo-Saxon Chronicle under the year 657 is illuminating in its detail—though this entry is clearly of a late date. See footnote 1, p. 7 above.

[2] Felix, *Life of St Guthlac* (Anglo-Saxon version), ed. by C. W. Goodwin (1848), p. 21. The legend of Crowland tells how the wild birds of the wilderness came to St Guthlac, and how he fed them according to their kind. *Ibid.* pp. 51–7.

[3] *Codex Exonensis*, ed. by B. Thorpe (1842), pp. 115, 120, 156, 158; ed. by I. Gollancz (1895), pp. 117, 123, 159, 161.

[4] *Guthlac* (Goodwin), p. 21. Grantchester refers not to the village of that name but to Cambridge. The Latin version has "haut procul a castella quod dicunt gronta" with variants of *gronta*, *bricc* added over the line; and *nomine gronte*. See *Memorials of St Guthlac* (Latin version), ed. by W. de Gray Birch (1881), p. 17. Another edition is *The Guthlac Roll*, ed. by Sir George Warner (Roxburghe Club, 1928).

[5] See plate 5.

created them is an indisputable fact. They show something of what the barrier of the fens meant in the lives of people at this time. Only familiarity with the region in its most sombre aspects can do justice to the fears of these early settlers. Many centuries did not assuage their terror; and at last the horror of the fen passed into tradition—so deeply was it grounded in the Saxon mind. Nor were all the horrors imaginary. They had indeed a very substantial foundation; for the Fenland was a pestilential place "oft-times clouded with moist and dark vapours".[1] Many are the references to the unhealthy nature of the region.[2] Ague and malaria with their hallucinations made the life of the fenman very miserable; and it is little wonder that St Guthlac "was greatly troubled within him about the undertaking he had begun, namely to dwell there alone in the wilderness".[3] Abbo of Fleury in the tenth century mentioned "vast fens and swamps".[4]

Taken together, the evidence suggests that the Fenland became a frontier region between East Anglia and Mercia; that it was the resort of brigands and bandits; and that the Isle of Ely was a border state whose local ruler gave his allegiance to the king of East Anglia or of Mercia according to the political conditions of the time.[5] Apparently nothing, or little, was done towards the draining of the country for many hundreds of years.

But the seeds of some changes were already being sown. There was at any rate one ameliorating social influence during these early times. Christianity was replacing paganism in England. Looking back, the thirteenth-century chronicler, Roger of Wendover, saw it as a time "when religion shone

---

[1] *Guthlac* (Birch), p. 17.

[2] *Codex Exon.* pp. 120, 123 of Thorpe's edition. But see I. Gollancz, *op. cit.* pp. 123, 125.

[3] *Guthlac* (Goodwin), p. 29.

[4] *Memorials of St Edmund's Abbey*, ed. by T. Arnold, i, 6 (Rolls Series, 1890).

[5] See H. C. Darby, "The Fenland Frontier in Anglo-Saxon England", *Antiquity*, vii, 185 (1934). This discusses the suggested survival of a British population in the Fenland; but one can only come to the conclusion that the evidence may be uncertain (pp. 192–94).

with so bright a light that kings and queens, princes and dukes, earls, barons and churchmen alike inflamed with the desire of the heavenly kingdom became monks, recluses, voluntary exiles forsaking all to follow their Lord".[1] The Fenland benefited greatly by this piety, for "these marshes afforded, to not a few congregations of monks, desirable havens of lonely life where the solitude could not fail the hermits".[2] The chroniclers record how Guthlac "longed for the wilderness"[3] and established Crowland in 716; how Etheldreda, laying aside "all worldly cares",[4] founded a nunnery in the isolation of Ely in 673; how, about the year 662, in a neighbouring fen, the island of Thorney provided a "holy refuge" to those wishing "to follow a hermit's life";[5] and how Peterborough was founded[6] upon the edge of the fen about the year 655.

The coming of the Scandinavians in the ninth century rudely interrupted much of this peaceful development. Place-name distributions bear ample testimony to the negative part played by the fen region in the Danish settlement. No county map bears clearer traces of the Danes than that of Lincolnshire. About one-fourth of its village-names present the cha-

---

[1] *Flores Historiarum*, ed. by H. R. Luard, i, 281 (Rolls Series, 1886).

[2] *Memorials of St Edmund's Abbey*, ed. by T. Arnold, i, 6 (Rolls Series, 1890).

[3] *Guthlac* (Goodwin), p. 18. See W. Dugdale, *Monasticon Anglicanum*, ii, 90 *et seq.* (1819).

[4] Bede, iv, 19; and *Liber Eliensis*, p. 26. Professor F. M. Stenton writes: "Much is told of the earlier history of the Ely estates in the Anglo-Norman compilation known as the *Historia Eliensis*. That the compiler of this work had ancient records before him is certain. He can often be traced in the act of rendering an Old English text into twelfth-century Latin.... But until the compiler's work has received critical discussion his narratives will always remain subject to a measure of suspicion, and at present they can only be used with caution as materials for the history of the eastern midlands in the tenth century."—*V.C.H. Huntingdonshire*, i, 328 (1926).

[5] See R. H. Warner, *History of Thorney Abbey* (1879), p. 18.

[6] Anglo-Saxon Chronicle, anno 655; a late addition to the chronicle. It was believed that St Botolph sought out the desolation of Boston in 650; but St Botolph's site may now be identified with Iken in Suffolk.—F. S. Stevenson, "St Botolph (Botwulf) and Iken", *Proc. Suffolk Inst. Arch. and Nat. Hist.* xviii, 29 (1924).

Gordon Fowler

4. Aerial photograph: The Little Ouse Roddon

The meanders approach the Littleport-Shippea Hill road shown running across the photograph

5. St Guthlac goes to Crowland
(British Museum Harleian MS. Y. 6)

racteristic Danish suffix -by, and there are many other Danish terminations as well. In the western counties of Nottingham, Leicester, Northampton and Rutland, Scandinavian names are fairly plentiful. But the fens which bordered the Witham, the' Welland, and the Nene seem to have marked a limit for the Danish settlers.[1] On the other side of the Fenland, in Norfolk, there is a further sprinkling of Danish names, not as numerous as in Lincolnshire, but still considerable; enough, in fact, to emphasise the vacant gap formed by the Fenland and by the counties immediately behind it—Cambridgeshire, Huntingdonshire and Bedfordshire. There are, of course, some Danish names in the Fenland, but the two most characteristic suffixes, -by and -thorpe, are absent. Lincolnshire Holland, however, has "a few Scandinavianised names as Kirton, Skirbeck, Scrane, or names in *toft*, as Brothertoft, Fishtoft, Wigtoft, also Bicker, which seems to be OScn *bȳkiarr* 'village marsh'. Elloe wapentake has no Scandinavian name at all. Very likely the Danish settlements in Holland mostly belong to a somewhat later period".[2] The Isle of Ely, to the south, also has no parish name of Scandinavian origin. There, "the evidence suggests the naming of minor places in a more or less settled time, and the substitution of English terms by similar, corresponding Scandinavian ones".[3]

[1] For a general account of the Danes in Lincolnshire see the discussions by E. Ekwall in (1) *Introduction to the Survey of English Place-Names*, ed. by A. Mawer and F. M. Stenton (1929), p. 83; (2) *An Historical Geography of England before* A.D. 1800, ed. by H. C. Darby (1936), p. 144.

M. A. S. Beddoe, in a *Memoir of the Anthropological Society* in 1869, stated of Lincolnshire (p. 252) that as far as the borders of the fens were concerned, the Danish element in the physical appearance of the people was particularly strong. Isaac Taylor wrote, in *Words and Places* (1902), p. 111: "The fens which border the Witham, the Welland, and the Nen effectually guarded the southern frontier of the Danish settlers; and this natural boundary they do not seem to have crossed in any considerable numbers." In this connection it is interesting to note that, in Lincolnshire, the fen wapentake of Elloe had the lowest number of sokemen in the Domesday Survey.

[2] E. Ekwall in *An Historical Geography of England before* A.D. 1800, ed. by H. C. Darby (1936), p. 144.

[3] P. H. Reaney in *The Cambridge Region*, ed. by H. C. Darby (1938), p. 102.

In the Anglo-Saxon Chronicle[1] there is mention of the "great heathen army" on either side of the marsh, in East Anglia, in Northumbria and in Mercia. And, though they did not settle in the Fenland, the Danes certainly raided some of the fen monasteries. The pseudo-Ingulph has much to say about the plundering of Crowland.[2] Little reliance can be placed upon this account, but it may incorporate some core of truth. The *Liber Eliensis*, although written about three centuries after the event, also records something that may approximate to the truth itself. So great was the depth of the waters around Ely that the Danes had easy access to the island, and, after burning the monastery, went away loaded with spoil.[3] And, under the year A.D. 870, a late addition to the Anglo-Saxon Chronicle records how the Danes "came to Medeshamstede [Peterborough], and burned and beat it down, slew abbot and monks, and all that they found there. And that place, which was before full rich, they reduced to nothing".[4]

During most of the tenth century, the Scandinavian peril was in abeyance, and in the monastic revival associated with the name of Edgar (A.D. 969–75) many religious houses were founded or refounded upon the fen islands. The chronicles again describe how Ramsey was founded in 969;[5] how Ely

[1] Under the years A.D. 866–80.

[2] *Ingulph's Chronicle of the Abbey of Croyland*, ed. by H. T. Riley (1854), pp. 40 *et seq*. For a critical note on this, see footnote 4, p. 43 below.

[3] *Liber Eliensis*, pp. 81–2: "Hujus siquidem communis tribulationis et miseriae nullatenus expers fuit Elyensis insula, praesertim cum paludes et aquae quibus circumcingitur in mare porigantur, sit ab ipsis aestuantis aequoris fluctibus quarumlibet navium ad eandem insulam non difficilis accessus." See J. Bentham, *History and Antiquities of the Conventual and Cathedral Church of Ely* (1812), pp. 67–9.

[4] Matthew Paris gives a list of the monasteries so plundered: "Crulandia, Thornheia, Ramesia, Hamstede, quod nunc Burgum Sancti Petri dicitur, cum insula Helyensi et coenobio olim famosissimo feminarum."—*Chronica Maiora*, ed. by H. R. Luard, i, 393 (Rolls Series, 1872). But this is of no value for the ninth century, and Matthew has clearly slipped up in making Ramsey an early monastery.

[5] *Chronicon Abbatiae Ramsiensis*, ed. by W. D. Macray, p. 47 (Rolls Series, 1886). See W. Dugdale, *Monasticon Anglicanum*, ii, 546 ff. (1819). The Anglo-Saxon Chronicle records the restoration of Peterborough in 963.

was restored in 970;[1] and Thorney in 972;[2] and how, in the year 980, the nunnery at Chatteris was established;[3] how, in short, the Fenland began to be famous as a home of monastic foundations.

During the onslaught of the Scandinavians in the late tenth and early eleventh centuries, the Fenland suffered once more.[4] Under the year A.D. 1010, the Anglo-Saxon Chronicle records that, after defeating an English army near Thetford, the Danes ravaged the neighbourhood for three months, penetrating even into the "wild fens".[5]

But the last pictures of the Danes in the Fenland are pleasant enough. King Canute (1017–35) loved Ely well, and attended services in its monastery. But he could not always row across. To keep the Feast of the Purification on one occasion, he had to go by sledge over frozen waters.[6]

[1] *Liber Eliensis*, p. 154. See W. Dugdale, *Mon. Ang.* i, 457 ff. (1817).

[2] See W. Dugdale, *op. cit.* ii, 593 ff. (1819).

[3] See W. Dugdale, *ibid.* ii, 614 ff. (1819).

[4] The early and untrustworthy portion of Ingulph's chronicle (see footnote 4, p. 43 below) tells a story of the ravaging of the villages along the fen border, and of the defence of the fenmen upon the island refuges, protected by reeds and rushes, and aided by unusual floods. For what it is worth, Ingulph's account of the defence of Crowland reads: "It happened, fortunately, that this year the inundations had increased to an unusual degree in consequence of the frequent showers, and consequently rendered the neighbouring fens, as also the marsh-lands adjoining thereto, impassable. Accordingly, all the population repaired thither, and infinite multitudes flocked to the spot; the choir and the cloisters were filled with monks, the rest of the church with priests and clerks, and the whole abbey with laymen; while the cemetery was filled night and day with women and children under tents. The stoutest among them, as well as the young men, kept watch among the sedge and alder-beds upon the mouths of the rivers; and every day, not to speak of other expenses, one hundred monks sat down to table."—*Ingulph*, p. 114.

[5] Later, in the reign of Edward the Confessor (1042–66), Matthew Paris relates how the abbot of St Albans hearing fresh rumours of another Danish incursion sent some relics of his monastery to Ely because of its safety: "Erat enim eorum insula intransmeabilibus circundata paludibus, et arundinetis; unde hostium incursus nequaquam timuerunt." *Gesta Abbatium Monasterii Sancti Albani*, ed. by H. T. Riley, i, 34 (Rolls Series, 1867).

[6] *Liber Eliensis*, p. 203.

The ancient song preserved in the *Liber Eliensis*[1] shows how completely he had wiped out the memory of his youth:

> Merry sang the monks in Ely
> As King Canute rowed thereby.
> Row knights, near the land,
> And hear we these monks sing.

And there also is the tradition[2] that Canute, in crossing from Ramsey to Peterborough, was once in danger owing to a storm on Whittlesey Mere, and that in consequence he caused a channel (subsequently known as King's delph) to be constructed to the north-east of the mere.

But it is impossible to attempt any reconstruction of the economy of the Fenland during Anglo-Danish times. There is no substantial body of evidence. Hints and fragments alone remain. But these hints and fragments are sufficient to show that, although the Fenland was but scantily peopled, and although much of it was marsh and water, yet even its waters were not without value; already its characteristic activities were not lacking in organisation and control. The references to fisheries in the foundation charter of Ramsey Abbey;[3] a possible division of the fens near Ely in the late tenth century;[4] another possible division of some of the Huntingdonshire fens, among the villages around, early in the eleventh century;[5]

---

[1] *Liber Eliensis*, p. 202. For a discussion of this verse, see the note by W. W. Skeat in C. W. Stubbs, *Historical Memorials of Ely Cathedral* (1897), pp. 49–52.

[2] W. Dugdale, *Imbanking and Drayning* (1772), p. 363. A 1334 confirmation of a charter (1052–56) of Edward the Confessor contains the form *Cnoutesdelfe kynges* which is suggestive.—*Ramsey Cartulary*, ed. by W. H. Hart and P. A. Lyons, ii, 80 (Rolls Series, 1886). Matthew Paris, in the *Chronica Maiora*, ed. by R. Luard, i, 509 (Rolls Series, 1872), says: "Idemque [Rex Canutus] viam in marisco inter Ramesheiam et burgum, quod Kingesdelf dicitur, ut periculum magnorum stagnorum vitaretur, eruderavit."

For a discussion see A. Mawer and F. M. Stenton, *The Place-Names of Bedfordshire and Huntingdonshire* (1926), p. 185.

[3] See p. 29 below.   [4] See p. 74 below; see also p. 44.

[5] The foundation charter of Sawtry Abbey granted by Simon, Earl of Northampton (1146), stated that the country around had belonged to his predecessors since the time of King Canute: "et sicut idem Cnut rex ipsum mariscum singulis villis juxta mariscum in illa parte positis proprium

Fig. 3

The present-day coastline is shown; in all probability the Domesday coastline lay considerably behind this. The villages bordering the coast were situated upon a bed of silt that separated the peat fen from the sea (see Fig. 2). The only settlements within this peat area were upon the islands. Adjacent to the middle portion of the Fenland, on the east, lay the Breckland that likewise had unoccupied tracts of country.

the assignments of property in a pre-Conquest Thorney document;[1] "the many fens at *Well*" which Bishop Æthelwold "bought from Ælfsige and from Ufi for 13 ores"[2]—when scattered details of this nature are weighed against the evidence of desolation, the result may be some very general idea of the condition of the Fenland in pre-Conquest times.

Summing up the results of the settlements of both the Anglo-Saxons and the Danes came the Domesday Inquest in 1086. The distribution of Domesday settlements (Fig. 3) reflected the topographical differences of the Fenland. This was the framework for the economy of the region during all subsequent time. Settlement was prohibited on the peat area because here the soil provided no stable foundations on which to build. Even those portions that escaped winter flooding were subject to an annual heaving motion as the swelling peat absorbed more and more water.[3] Consequently, not one Domesday village was located in all the area. The settlements were all upon the islands. But the silt area, bordering the Wash, was composed of a substance more solid than fen peat,

mariscum dividi jussit et constituit per Turkillum Danensem."—W. Dugdale, *Mon. Ang.* v, 522 (1825). Another charter of about the same time said: "sic enim Turkillus per regem Cnud constituit, ut nulla villata in alterius marisco foderet vel falcaret sine licentia; villis enim singulis juxta mariscum positis, per jussum regis Cnut ipse mariscum divisit."—*Ibid.* v, 524; and *Ramsey Cartulary*, ed. by W. H. Hart and P. A. Lyons, i, 164 (Rolls Series, 1884).

[1] See A. J. Robertson, *Anglo-Saxon Charters* (1939), pp. 253–7. This contains many references to eels; see also footnote 5, p. 29 below. Miss Robertson regards the date of the main portion of the document as being soon after the refounding of Thorney Abbey in 972 (p. 503). The last entry starts suggestively enough: "This is the rent of the fen at Fordham and at Hilgay...." But there are many gaps in the text, and, says Miss Robertson, the handwriting of this latter part "seems to be of a later date" (p. 503). For an account of a portion of the document see W. W. Skeat, "Two Anglo-Saxon Fragments of the Eleventh Century", *Proc. Camb. Philol. Soc.* (1903), p. 12.

[2] A. J. Robertson, *Anglo-Saxon Charters* (1939), p. 73. The date of the charter is after the restoration of Peterborough by Æthelwold in A.D. 963 (*ibid.* p. 325). See footnote 5, p. 12 above.

[3] See H. C. Darby, *The Draining of the Fens* (1940), p. 27.

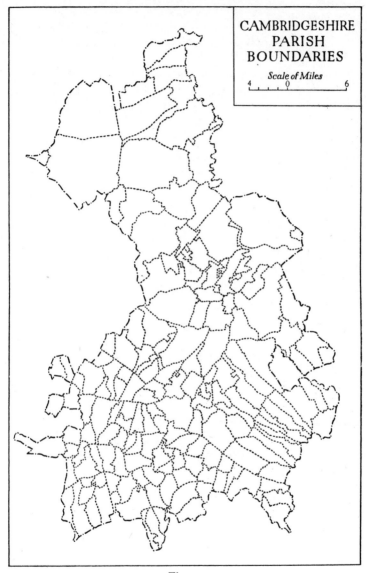

CAMBRIDGESHIRE
PARISH
BOUNDARIES

Scale of Miles

4   0   6

Fig. 4

The group of small parishes in the southern Fenland
are those of the island of Ely

and offered better opportunities for continuous settlement. The distribution of village sites in Domesday times shows this silt region as a belt of uniformly occupied territory joining the uplands of Norfolk and Lincoln; probably the eleventh-century coastline lay not far beyond the line of the villages. On the inland edge of the Fenland lay another line of settlements—the margin of the upland settlements around.

The configuration of present-day parish boundaries in many parts of England preserves, in a fossilised form, vestiges of older arrangements. But in the Fenland, parish boundaries were greatly complicated by intercommoning practices,[1] and frequently their present-day features are due to comparatively late adjustments. But even so, they cannot fail to throw some light upon early conditions, and the contrast between the shapes of parishes in the silt and peat regions respectively is most striking. In the peat area of Cambridgeshire (Fig. 4), the village itself is usually situated in the midst of a fairly square or oblong parish territory; the effect is block-like.[2] In the silt zone the area of the parish usually extends in a narrow belt across from salt-marsh to peat fen; the effect is strip-like.[3] This is certainly the case in Lincolnshire (Fig. 5); and it is also prevalent in Norfolk where, however, its presence is sometimes obscured by the fact that two or three contiguous double-name villages bearing the same general name (and entered under one heading in the Domesday Book) may have different qualifying appellations on the modern map.[4] The late date of some of these arrangements does not alter the fact that they may embody an indication of the original disposition of village rights. And these hints may be used quite legitimately to supplement the evidence that is

[1] See p. 67 below.
[2] The settlement itself is on an island, and the village territory is spread about it.
[3] Each village includes three types of land: salt-marsh, raised silt and peat fen.
[4] Wiggenhall St Mary the Virgin; St German; St Peter; St Mary Magdalen. Tilney cum Islington; All Saints; St Lawrence. Terrington St Clement; St John. Walpole St Peter; St Andrew. See Fig. 13.

LINCOLNSHIRE
PARISH BOUNDARIES

Miles
2 0   12

Fig. 5

available concerning the pattern of the medieval economy of the region. But, alas, the pre-Domesday evidence relating to the Fenland is, at best, very little.

NOTE ON ROMAN LITERARY EVIDENCE

The literary evidence is very general and very scanty. The page references in the following summary refer to the *Monumenta Historica Britannica*, edited by H. Petrie and J. Sharpe (1848). "Many parts of the British country being constantly flooded by the tides of the ocean become marshy" (p. lxiv), and in their conquest of these regions the Romans encountered much difficulty. Xiphilinus related (p. lx) how the Britons "inhabit mountains wild and waterless, and plains desert and marshy" and how in war "they are capable of enduring hunger and thirst, and hardships of every description", for "when hiding in the marshes they abide there many days with their heads only out of water". And Plutarch noted how the enemy attacked "certain leaders who had strayed into a place which was marshy" (p. lxviii). Dion Cassius, too, recorded how the Romans "wandered into the pathless marshes, and lost many of their soldiers" (p. liv). Herodian, speaking of Severus, declared that "he more especially endeavoured to render the marshy places stable by means of causeways, that his soldiers treading with safety might easily pass them and, having firm footing, might fight to advantage. For many parts of the British country, being constantly flooded by the tides of the ocean, become marshy. In these the natives are accustomed to swim and traverse about as high as their waists" (pp. lxiii–lxiv).

It is, of course, impossible to say whether any of these references refers to the great Fenland. They are recorded here as a matter of interest.

CHAPTER TWO

OCCUPATIONS

IT is sometimes difficult, as we look over the broad expanse of arable land and meadow which meets our eye today, to think ourselves back to the medieval aspect of the Fenland; to what a twelfth-century monk called "the great marsh in which the island of Ely is situated".[1] The character of the district in these early times may best be judged from the words of those who saw it. Hugo Candidus, a monk of Peterborough, writing about 1150, thus described the district near which he lived:

From the flooding of the rivers, or from their overflow, the water, standing on unlevel ground, makes a deep marsh and so renders the land uninhabitable, save on some raised spots of ground, which I think that God set up for the special purpose that they should be the habitations of His servants who have chosen to live there....*Burch* [Peterborough] is founded in the land of the Gyrvii, where the same marsh begins on its eastern side, to extend for sixty miles or more. This marsh, however, is very useful for men; for in it are found wood and twigs for fires, hay for the fodder of cattle, thatch for covering houses, and many other useful things. It is, moreover, productive of birds and fish. For there are various rivers, and very many waters and ponds abounding in fish. In all these things the district is most productive.[2]

Even so, Hugo's list of fenland activities was not complete, and to it must be added the items of turbaries and salt pans. But, still, his picture does show us the chief features of the country; and the main characteristics of life in the fens did not change very rapidly. Nearly five hundred years later, the description given by Michael Drayton in the *Polyolbion* of 1622 agrees substantially with that of the monk Hugo.[3] During

---

[1] *Liber Eliensis*, p. 4.

[2] "Historiae Coenobii Burgensis", p. 2, in *Historiae Anglicanae Scriptores Varii*, ed. by J. Sparke (1723).

[3] M. Drayton, *Polyolbion* (1622), p. 442. See H. C. Darby, *The Draining of the Fens* (1940), p. 26.

this span of the centuries, the Fenland, as much as any district
in the English plain, constituted an area of characteristic
occupations and peculiar practices arising from the nature of
its terrain. Here, regional custom, the *consuetudo loci*, was of
paramount importance in the development of an individual
economy, and in the maintenance of a local habit of life quite
different from that in the normal medieval community.

The fens themselves were of varying usefulness. Some were
quite flooded, and formed great lakes; others were flooded in
winter but available for pasture in summer; others were
fairly dry during ordinary years; the islands themselves were
but little different from the surrounding upland. Consequently, the activities of the region fell into three main
groups:

(1) Those belonging to the marsh itself—fishing and fowl-
    ing; the gathering of reeds and rushes; and the making
    of salt along the sea-shore.

(2) Those associated with the intermediate zone (usually,
    but not always, above the water-level) and consisting
    mainly of the production of hay, of the grazing of
    animals, and of the cutting of turves.

(3) Finally, there was the more usual arable farming on
    the islands, or in the permanently drained portions of
    the fen.

These three kinds of activity must be considered separately.

MARSH PRODUCTS

Fisheries. The most casual glance through the Domesday
Book[1] will show how frequently fisheries are mentioned,
sometimes in connection with the mill-pond, sometimes
separately. They were particularly important along all the
great rivers of the country, but it was in the Fenland that they
attained the status of a characteristic industry. Indeed, some

[1] The edition of the Domesday Book used (and referred to as D.B.) is
Domesday Book seu Liber censualis Wilhelmi Primi regis Angliae, vols. i–ii (ed.
by Abraham Farley), 1783; vols. iii–iv (ed. by Henry Ellis), 1816.

writers have suggested that this abundance of fish was among the motives that promoted early monastic settlement within the marsh.[1] Whether this was true or not, the fishery by the eleventh century had come to occupy an important place in the life of the fenland monastery as well as in that of the fenland village. The most important fishing centres in Cambridgeshire[2] seem to have been at Doddington, Littleport, Soham, Stuntney, and Wisbech.[3] The Soham entries are particularly informative:

(1) *folio* 189: de piscaria iii millia et quingentae anguillae.... Ibi vii piscatores reddentes regi presentacionem piscium ter in anno secundum quod possunt.
(2) *folio* 190b: una navis quae piscatur in mara per consuetudinem.
(3) *folio* 192: ibi est unus piscator habens i sagenam[4] in lacu eiusdem villae.
(4) *folio* 195b: 1 millenum et dimidium anguillarum, et in mara de Saham i sagenam consuetudine.

At Doddington[5] there was a fishery returning 27,150 eels; from Littleport[5] came 17,000 eels; from Stuntney,[5] 24,000 eels; and, in addition to these renders, there were money payments as well. For Wisbech there are six separate entries, five consisting exclusively of eels:

(1) *folio* 192: de piscariis mille et quingentae anguillae.
(2) *folio* 192: ii piscatores reddunt abbati xiiii millia anguillarum et de presentatione xiii solidos et iiii denarios.
(3) *folio* 192: 1 piscatorem reddentem v millia anguillarum.
(4) *folio* 192b: viii piscatores reddentes v millia et cclx anguillarum.
(5) *folio* 193: iii piscatores reddentes iiii millia anguillarum.
(6) *folio* 196b: vi piscatores reddentes iii millia anguillarum et dimidium, et v solidos.

[1] E.g. W. Dugdale, *Imbanking and Drayning* (1772), p. 179.
[2] See Fig. 6.
[3] See H. C. Darby, "The Domesday Geography of Cambridgeshire", *Proc. Camb. Antiq. Soc.* xxxvi, 50–2 (1936).
[4] One of the Swaffham entries mentions *de theloneo retis vi solidi* (D.B. i, 190 b). In the *Inquisitio Comitatus Cantabrigiensis*, ed. by N. E. S. A. Hamilton (1876), p. 13, the corresponding entry is *de appulatione navium vi solidi.*
[5] D.B. i, 191 b.

The Cambridgeshire entries for Whittlesey are two in number and comparatively small in amount:

(1) *folio* 191 b: de gurgite ii solidi.
(2) *folio* 192b: de gurgite iiii solidi et de piscibus praeter hoc xx solidi.

But this is explained by the fact that Whittlesey Mere itself was in the county of Huntingdon. Among the Huntingdonshire folios it was entered[1] under the lands of the abbey of Thorney thus:

In *Witelsmare* the abbot of Ramsey has one boat [*navis*], and the abbot of Peterborough one boat, and the abbot of Thorney two boats. One of these two boats, and two fisheries, and two fishermen, and one virgate of land, the abbot of Peterborough holds from the abbot of Thorney, and for these he gives pasture sufficient for 120 pigs, and if pasture fails he feeds and fattens 60 pigs with corn. Moreover he finds timber for one house of 60 ft., and rods for the enclosure [*curia*] round the house. He also repairs the house and the enclosure if they are in decay. This agreement was made between them in King Edward's time.

The fisheries and meres [*marae*] of the abbot of Ramsey in Huntingdonshire are valued at £10, those of the abbot of Thorney at 60s., those of the abbot of Peterborough at £4.

An idea of the nature of this watery tract can be obtained from another description that comes also from the early Middle Ages:[2]

[1] D.B. i, 205. For a repetition of the Domesday account, see the Red Book of Thorney, f. 374b (Cambridge University Library, Additional MSS. 3021). For later details of Whittlesey Mere, see *V.C.H. Huntingdonshire*, iii, 186 (1936).

[2] From the end of the *Chronicon Petroburgense*, which contains a list of the manors and other possessions of the abbey, and which concludes with an account of Whittlesey Mere. The date of the main list is 1125–28, but, from the appended list of prelates who were present, the Whittlesey instrument may have been written between 1020 and 1023. This was edited by Thomas Stapleton, and published by the Camden Society in 1859 (Old Series, no. 47, Appendix, pp. 182–3), and is printed as the last part of the "Liber Niger Monasterii S. Petri de Burgo".

For a pre-Domesday reference to ships and nets at Whittlesey Mere, see "Assignments of property to Thorney Abbey" in *Anglo-Saxon Charters*, by A. J. Robertson (Cambridge University Press), p. 253. The date of the document is probably late tenth century.

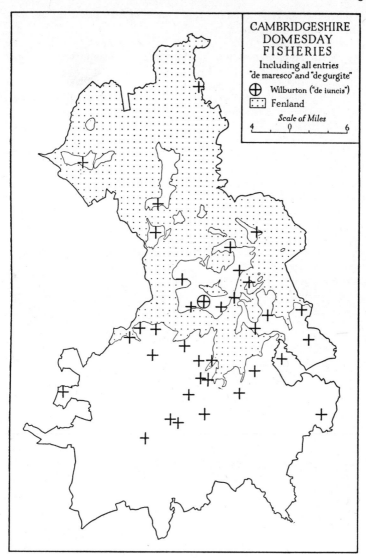

Fig. 6

From H. C. Darby, "The Domesday Geography of Cambridgeshire", *Proc. Camb. Antiq. Soc.* xxxvi, 51 (1936). The Wilburton entry (D.B. i, 192) is *de iuncis xvi denarii*—"sixteen pence from the rushes". See footnote 2, p. 32.

How the pool that is called *Witelesmere,* with its fisheries, marshes, and waters is bounded.

In the north part of the pool is a water by name *Merelade* going out of the river *Nen,* where is the northern boundary of the pool itself. This [Merelade], with its marshes, adjoins it [the mere] having at the end one fishery called *Æthemuthe.* In the east part are two pools called *Wellepol* and *Trendmære.*[1] Between these pools is a narrow water two furlongs long, called *Trendmære Bece,* having in it two fisheries. There is also a narrow water one mile long called *Falet,* having in it one fishery. In that part between *Witlesmere* and *Kyngesdelf,* where is the eastern boundary, there is a marshy space three miles broad, having in it a narrow water called *Thescuf,* and a wood called *Ragreholt.* In the south part is a narrow water three furlongs long, called *Scælfremære Bece,* having in it two fisheries. At the end of this is a pool called *Scælfremære,* having at its southern region a narrow water called *Ubbemære-lade,* half a mile long. At the head of this, that is at the end of the pool, is one fishery. Halfway along this water [*Ubbermære-lade*], is a place on the opposite side in the marsh called *Aldwines Barwe,* where is the southern boundary. In the west part is a narrow water two furlongs long called *Trendmære Bece,* having in it one fishery. At the end of this is a pool called *West Trendmære.* There is also in that part waters whose names are *Dreigmære, Wellepool, Withibuscemære, Langemære, Keninges,* and *Musclemære.* There is also a water one mile long and up to the land, called *Deop Bece,* having in it one fishery. At the end of this water is the western boundary of the marshes and waters belonging to *Witlesmære.*

These Huntingdonshire meres were among the largest meres of the Fenland, but they were far from being the only ones.

Conditions in Lincolnshire were similar to those in the southern fens. In the north, the settlements along the western border of the fens had considerable fishing rights in the adjoining marsh. The three most important centres were at Spalding in Holland, at Bourne in Kesteven, and around Tattershall Thorpe and Coningsby in Lindsey. In Spalding,[2] there were 6 fisheries rendering 30*s.* Bourne[3] had no less than 30 fisheries rendering 72*d.* and 2500 eels. Tattershall Thorpe[4]

---

[1] "This seems to be a mistake; Well pool and Trundle Mere are in the west."—*V.C.H. Huntingdonshire,* iii, 186 (1936).

[2] D.B. i, 351 b.

[3] D.B. i, 351 b, 358 b, 364 b, 368 b, 370.

[4] D.B. i, 340 b, 341, 343, 359 b, 360.

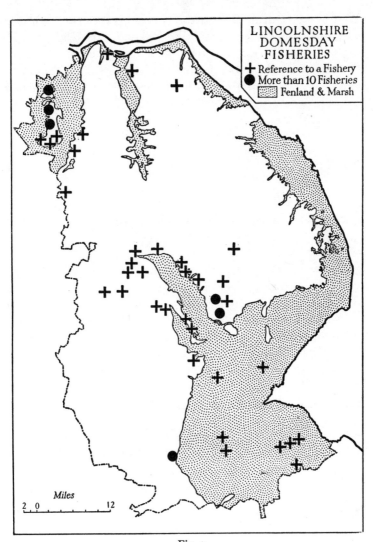

LINCOLNSHIRE
DOMESDAY
FISHERIES
+ Reference to a Fishery
● More than 10 Fisheries
░ Fenland & Marsh

Miles
2 0   12

Fig. 7

had 10½ fisheries rendering in all 20s. Coningsby[1] had 17
fisheries bringing in a total of 19s. 2d. But, in addition to
these great centres, there were a number of other fisheries
scattered among the remaining villages (see Fig. 7); in
South Kyme, for example, fishponds are mentioned;[2] and,
in Billinghay, lay the "sites of 3 fisheries".[3] Curiously
enough, the continuation of the silt belt in Norfolk Marshland
did not, according to the Domesday record, have as many
fisheries as might be expected. Isolated fisheries are entered
for some villages, but they do not rival the fishing centres of
Spalding and other places to the north. Along the eastern
edge of the Fenland, in Norfolk and Suffolk, there was also
some fishing activity. Four fisheries and a fishing boat at Ely
were connected with Richard FitzGilbert's estate at Lakenheath[4] on the margin of the peat fens. Not far away, Wilton
had six fishponds;[5] and Methwold had seven fisheries on the
demesne.[6]

Despite its many obscurities, then, the Domesday evidence
does at any rate establish the great place occupied by fisheries
in the economy of the eleventh-century Fenland, especially
in the Cambridgeshire fens. And in the following century,
about the year 1125, William of Malmesbury could write:
"Here is such a quantity of fish as to cause astonishment
in strangers, while the natives laugh at their surprise"[7]—
for the *gurgites* or weirs along the courses of the Fenland rivers
were sources of no little profit. The fish were present not only
in great plenty but also in great variety; and, as the *Liber
Eliensis* records, "in the eddy at the sluices of those waters,
there are netted innumerable eels, large water-wolves (*lupi
aquatici*), even pickerels, perch, roach, burbots, and lampreys
which we call water-snakes. It is indeed said by many men

---

[1] D.B. i, 339, 349b, 363b, 370b.   [2] D.B. i, 337b.
[3] D.B. i, 340 (*sed' piscar'*).
[4] D.B. ii, 392. There were two other fisheries also at Lakenheath.—
D.B. ii, 403.
[5] D.B. ii, 161b. Wilton is now joined to Hockwold.   [6] D.B. ii, 136.
[7] William of Malmesbury, *De Gestis Pontificum Anglorum*, ed. by
N. E. S. A. Hamilton (Rolls Series, 1870), p. 322.

that sometimes *isicii* (?) together with the royal fish, the sturgeon, are taken."[1] But despite this variety, the fact remained that eels were easily the most abundant species, and so the etymologists of the early Middle Ages readily found at hand a convenient explanation of the place-name "Ely".[2]

To repeat all the evidence concerning the importance of fisheries in the Fenland during the subsequent centuries of the Middle Ages would be tedious and pointless; there is scarcely a document that does not make some reference to fishing.[3] But there is one document that will serve to illustrate the contents of the rest and to give some idea of the continued importance of the fishery. It is the cartulary of Ramsey Abbey.[4]

In the pre-Domesday foundation charter granted by Edgar to Ramsey Abbey there was much reference to the fisherman "with his small boat and his assistants and his net"; at *Welles*, on the border of Norfolk and Cambridgeshire, there was a manor which was of profit to the abbey solely on account of its render of eels; twenty fishermen gave 60,000 eels every year for the use of the brethren.[5] This grant was confirmed

---

[1] *Liber Eliensis*, pp. 231–2. Mr C. F. Tebbutt tells me that sturgeon are still caught very occasionally in the Ouse near St Ives.

[2] See W. W. Skeat, *The Place-Names of Cambridgeshire*, pp. 51–2 (Camb. Antiq. Soc. 1901). Bede's explanation in the *Ecclesiastical History* is: "Est autem Elge...regio...in similitudinem insulae vel paludibus, ut diximus, circumdata vel aquis; unde et a copia anguillarum quae in eisdem paludibus capiuntur nomen accepit."—Lib. iv, cap. 19.

[3] It must be remembered that, as well as in fisheries of the Fenland itself, there was also considerable fishing activity along the shores of the Wash. Here, there are several indications of vigorous activity. Late in the reign of Edward III a dispute between Moulton, Holbeach and Whaplode bears witness to this. Amongst other things, it was stated that, whereas by "law and ordinance" the fishermen on the sand should take their fish to the vills and *fora* of their lordships to be sold, actually many fishermen sold their fish illegally to *extranei* on the sand.—P.R.O. Assize Roll, 529, Lincs.

[4] *Cartularium Monasterii de Ramesia*, 3 vols., ed. by W. H. Hart and P. A. Lyons (Rolls Series, 1884–86–93).

[5] Dated A.D. 974. See *Ramsey Cartulary*, ii, 55; and the *Codex Diplomaticus*, ed. by J. M. Kemble, vol. iii (1845), charter no. 581. See also charters nos. 563 and 568 for other references to fishing in charters dated A.D. 970 and 973 respectively.

many times afterwards,[1] and extents of the manor in the
twelfth and thirteenth centuries give great prominence to eel-
rents and to fishermen.[2] Many other fisher-tenants were also
mentioned in the cartulary; Alfgar of Hilgay, and Hugh the
tenant in Wiggenhall, were but two of a large number.[3] The
cartulary lists the fishers of the abbey itself as "seven fishermen and their seven assistants together with their seven little
ships".[4] Of Ramsey Mere, the place of their activity, the
chronicler of the Abbey wrote:

> In the deeps of this mere there are frequently taken, with several
> kinds of nets, as well as with baited hooks, and other fishing
> instruments, pike of extraordinary great size, called *Hakedes* by
> the country folk; and though both fishers and fowlers cease neither
> by day nor night to frequent it, yet is there always no little store of
> fish.[5]

And on the shores of the neighbouring mere of Whittlesey the
fishermen's nets spread out to dry became a familiar sight.[6]
Everywhere in the Fenland was this activity of the fisherman evident. Many were the grants of fisheries, or half-
fisheries, or quarter-fisheries; many were the divisions of
fisheries into nights, and half-nights, and even into eighths
of a night; many were the negotiations which insisted upon
the separation of the common fisheries from those held in

[1] *Ramsey Cartulary*, ii, 72, 93, 136.
[2] *Ibid.* iii, 296 for the twelfth-century extent; and ii, 318 for an
early thirteenth-century extent. See also the other references in *ibid.* i,
99; ii, 264; and iii, 164, 233. St Neots also exacted rents of a similar kind
in Wells.—W. Dugdale, *Mon. Ang.* iii, 476 (1821).
[3] *Ramsey Cartulary*, iii, 289; and ii, 279. D. C. Douglas, in *Feudal
Documents from the Abbey of Bury St Edmunds* (1932), p. cxxxii, gives an early
thirteenth-century covenant between Hugh de Northwold the abbot of
Bury and the men of Hilgay and Southery concerning eel-rents. Douglas
concludes that "the arrangements at both Southery and Wells may be
taken as examples of the survival of pre-Conquest conditions". See also
D. C. Douglas, *The Social Structure of Medieval East Anglia* (1927), p. 91.
[4] *Ramsey Cartulary*, iii, 239.
[5] *Chronicon Abbatiae Ramesiensis*, ed. by W. D. Macray (Rolls Series,
1886), p. 8.
[6] *Ramsey Cartulary*, ii, 348. For other references to these fishermen and
their messuages around Whittlesey Mere see *ibid.* i, 162; ii, 330; and iii,
157. See also p. 24 above, and p. 50 below.

severalty; and, finally, many more still were the disputes caused by all this array of complicated rights and interlocking interests.[1]

Eels, indeed, fulfilled many of the uses of currency in the region. Debts were settled by payments of eels; rentals and tithes were defined in terms of thousands of eels or in "sticks" or *stickes* of eels, every stick having twenty-five. Naturally, the time of the year when these transactions became most frequent was in Lent.[2] The eel-rents of *Welles* were to be paid "ad festum Sancti Benedicti";[3] and when, in the middle of the eleventh century, Ramsey agreed to render 4000 eels a year to the abbey of Peterborough in return for building-stone at Barnack, it was during Lent that they were to be paid.[4] Frequently, the service of presenting the lord of a manor with fish for a Lenten fast was commuted into a customary rent. There is definite evidence[5] of the commutation of the rents at *Welles* into money payments before 1130. On the Ramsey manors it was universally occurring as *fish-silver, fissilver, fissylver, phisshesilver, haringsilver, denarii ad pisces emendos, denarius ad piscem.*[6] These sums were paid at the be-

---

[1] The Ramsey cartulary is full of these things; as also are other fenland documents. At Littleport, round about the year 1300, for instance, jurors were declaring that "John Beystens drew the pools at Wellenheath by night and carried thence fish, price 6*d.*, and that he ought to be removed out of the vill".—Littleport Rolls, ed. by F. W. Maitland and W. P. Baildon in *The Court Baron* (Selden Society, 1897), p. 122. There were also other references to the stealing of eels. "Fishing by night in the fisheries of others" was a common offence. See, for instance, W. O. Ault, *Court Rolls of the Abbey of Ramsey and of the Honor of Clare* (1928), p. 117, for account of a transgressor in the abbot's separate fishery in 1305.

[2] Present-day eel-fishing shows that eels only move in the autumn, and are most readily caught in nets then. The medieval payments in Lent may have consisted of salted eels.

[3] *Ramsey Cartulary*, ii, 320.

[4] *Ibid.* ii, 79. For eel-rents at *Welles*, see p. 79 below.

[5] *Ibid.* i, 134.

[6] *Ibid. passim.* At Thorney the rent was called *fishpene*, and was paid on Ash-Wednesday or on the first Sunday in Lent, usually at the rate of a penny a virgate.—*Rotuli Hundredorum*, ii, 642, 643, 647 (1818).

For eel-rents on the Ely episcopal manor about 1250, as recorded in the

ginning of Lent, on Ash-Wednesday or on the first Sunday
in Lent.[1] The Ramsey abbots, apparently, did not fare too
badly during the Lenten fast; nor did the abbots of the other
fenland monasteries.

Reeds, Rushes and Birds. The produce of much of the fen,
particularly in the peat-lands, seems to have consisted exclusively of reeds and rushes and sedge, usually called by the
now obsolete word *lesch*,[2] which was probably a name used
to cover generally all the species of the genus *Carex*. They
constituted a valuable building material, particularly for

Old Coucher Book of Ely, see *Fenland Notes and Queries*, iii, 193 (1897).
There, the account under "Fisheries" is as follows: "Upwere with 4 weirs
and Swavesmere, which usually pay a rent of 3036 sticks of eels, but now
13*s*. 4*d*. per annum, and are held by Thomas of Thetford. Bradewere
with its appurtenances, viz., Midlestwere, Marewere, Beche, and a
mediety of Haveringmere, all Nakedwere, a mediety of Grantewere,
Belilake and Berreilode; they pay a rent of 14,500 eels on the first Sunday
in Lent, and 10*s*. per annum; they are held hereditarily by Henry the
fisherman, Thomas of Thetford and Martin of Swafham. Yrithwere with
Culdinglake, held by the Sacrist at 10*s*. per ann.; in the time of Bp. Ridel,
the rent was 3300 sticks of eels. Krechemere held hereditarily by charter
by Henry, son of Osbert de Walpole, at 5*s*. per ann. Six boats, beginning
from Haveringmere and extending to Prikewyley, of which Hugh Wade
holds the fishery of 1 boat and pays rent of 6*s*.; Henry Daly holds the
fishery of 2 boats, at 6*s*.; Moyses, the fisherman, holds the fishery of 1 boat,
at 3*s*.; Roger Fot and John Gubernator, each ditto. Total payments,
yearly, 56*s*. 4*d*., of which 18*s*. from boat fisheries; 18*s*. from Bradenserefen
are allowed with the assised rents, and 5*s*. from Crechemere 'super
scacarium'. Total of eels, 14,500."

[1] For food-rents in general see N. Neilson, *Customary Rents* (1910). Of
the fish-rents, Miss Neilson writes: "it is one of the few rents recorded in
the extents of the middle of the twelfth as well as in those of the middle
of the thirteenth century" (p. 34). At Wistow, a Huntingdonshire manor
of Ramsey, a villein's turn to pay came sometimes once in two years,
sometimes once in three (*Ramsey Cartulary*, i, 487), and once in the form
of *haringsilver* at Christmas (*ibid.* i, 299).

[2] Compare the French *laiche*, German *liesch*, and Dutch *lisch* and *lesch*,
to describe plants of the genus *Carex*. The Domesday Book does not
mention these miscellaneous items. An exception is the entry of "sixteen
pence from the rushes" for Wilburton in Cambridgeshire (see Fig. 6)—
D.B. i, 192 (*de iuncis xvi denarii*). Acres of marsh (*maresc*) are also entered
for some of the villages of Lincolnshire and Huntingdonshire.

thatching; and the sale of rushes figures in many account rolls.[1] On some manors, the cutting and binding of rushes formed part of the services which a villein might be called upon to perform; at Chatteris, a villein had to cut "eight score bundles for one work".[2] And the "works" due from each tenant are specifically defined as in the case of the more normal manor.[3] A customary rent commuting this service was frequent. On the Ely manor of Downham, a *plena terra* of fourteen acres gave 4*d.* a year for *seggesilver*, or else cut and bound sixteen cartloads each containing forty shears of great rushes.[4] On other Cambridgeshire manors, virgates paid commonly 6*d. segsilver*, half-virgates 3*d.*, cottars 2*d.* In Norfolk and Suffolk, the rate seems to have been lower.[5] All this activity was controlled by many intricate regulations. On some manors, the outside sale of thatching materials was forbidden; while, on most manors, rushes and reeds were to be cut only at "competent and reasonable times of the year", and so that the fisheries were in no way injured "by the long standing of the said rushes and reeds".[6] In all these things, as in many others, the fenman only too frequently transgressed

[1] E.g. P.R.O. Ministers Accounts (Gen. Series), 765/17 for Chatteris (? 1293–95); 877/18 for Holywell (? 1246–55)—here, the average price was five shillings per "thousand" (fourteenth century).

[2] *Ramsey Cartulary*, i, 431. See also *Rotuli Hundredorum*, ii, 601, for reference to one hundred bundles a year. In the *Ramsey Cartulary*, the phrase is "habendi, falcandi, adunandi, et asportandi roscum in marisco" (i, 206).

[3] Of some men at Broughton, in 1252, the *Ramsey Cartulary* records: "falcabit etiam in marisco de Wardeboys, cum summonitus fuerit, quadraginta garbas rosci sufficientes, per visum ballivi, praepositi et aliorum pro opere unius diei, quas non carriabit. Et falcabit, ligabit, et carriabit, pro uno opere, viginti garbas" (i, 335).

[4] British Museum, Cott. MSS. Claud. C. xi, f. 34b: "Et de seggeselver per annum quatuor denarios equaliter vel falcabit et ligabit sexdecim carectatas grossi rosci scilicet quelibet carectata de quadraginta garbis sed non cariabit. Et tunc erit quietus de predicto segselver."

[5] See N. Neilson, *Customary Rents* (1910), pp. 57–8.

[6] *Ingulph's Chronicle of the Abbey of Croyland*, ed. by H. T. Riley (1854), p. 385. The entry is from the "Continuation", and is dated 1415. See footnote 4, p. 43 below.

the law and there are many miscellaneous references to the wrongful cutting and carriage of lesch.[1]

The best view of this activity is to be seen in the records relating to the manor of Littleport. Lying on the banks of the Ouse, five miles north of Ely, Littleport parish has an area of 17,000 acres; and, as 16,000 acres were fen, sedge was an important item in the economy of the village. The court rolls of Littleport,[2] between 1285 and 1327, contain frequent reference to the *ordinacio* or *bilawe* that regulated the activity of the marsh, and to the *custodes de bilawe* appointed to make presentments of offenders.[3] So much of the fen was held in common that supervision was essential; and the overseers had a full task to deal with the many offences committed in the marsh. These offences ranged from petty larceny to breach of the "ancient custom". Examples come crowding one after another:

[The jurors say upon their oath] that John Daune is wont to break up the stacks of sedge of diverse persons and carry off handfuls.[4]

[1] Thus, in 1304, Emma le Wodeward of Ramsey was fined 12d. "because she has harboured Aylward le Turnere who was lately expelled from the manor for waste of the fen" (British Museum, Additional Charters, No. 39599). And, in 1356, the prior of Ely impleaded three men before the itinerant justices for stealing rushes and sedge to the value of £20 in the Sutton fens—Cartulary of Ely Convent (Liber M), f. 608 (Bishop's Muniment Room, Ely, G. 3).

[2] Edited by F. W. Maitland and W. P. Baildon in *The Court Baron* (Selden Society, 1897). In the first half of the thirteenth century, Bishop Hugh of Northwold granted to Littleport the right to cut lesch and rushes in Rakfen on the payment of forty shillings a year. The men of Littleport, however, far exceeded the rights thus granted to them. They produced devastation in all the common of Ely; they sold lesch to strangers; and, moreover, they wrongfully appropriated the fens of Welpmor, Brendefen, Padenhalefen, and Westfen. In the latter, they cut and sold to strangers 6000 lesch, and even bargained with labourers from Norfolk to cut and sell in the fens, receiving from them eighty shillings and thus making a clear profit of forty shillings. As a penalty, the village lost the profit of its lesch crop for one year (British Museum, Cott. MSS. Claud. C. xi, ff. 361 b-2).

[3] The Littleport Rolls, *op. cit.* p. 139: "John Manimester, John Lovering, and John Fox the elder are sworn to survey and to present from court to court trespassers in the fen, for instance by mowing and digging, and also trespassers in the warren touching the birds and beasts of the warren."

[4] *Ibid.* p. 124.

It is found by inquest that John Curteys and John Gardhaut have slandered the sedge of Hugh Beld in the fen, whereby the said Hugh has lost the sale of the said sedge.[1]

John of Elm plaintiff appears against John Fox the younger in a plea of trespass wherefore he carried off 9 hundreds of his sedge and unjustly detains them from him.[2]

It is also found that John Fox the younger delivered to John Mounfort 1,000 of sedge of worse quality than he bought of him, to his damage 18d.[3]

The rights of the lord were carefully safeguarded, and the correct times and circumstances of mowing among the commoners were enforced with vigour as these two examples show:

(1) The jurors present that John Bantelig who is not a terre-tenant mowed sedge before the feast of S. John against the general ordinance....And that John Herring keeps two men mowing in the fen where he should have but one.[4]

(2) Whereas by the custom of the vill every one who mows in the common fen for the purpose of sale between Michaelmas and Hokeday shall forfeit all that he mows to the lord, and the forfeiture of a thousand [of sedge] is by ancient custom appraised at 2s. 8d., and against this custom John Beucosin and John Fox have mowed and caused to be mown a thousand; therefore they shall forfeit 2s. 8d. to the lord. And William Akerman has mowed five hundred before the said day, namely, Hokeday; therefore he forfeits 1s. 4d. to the lord.[5]

Neither freemen nor bondmen were allowed to sell rushes outside the limits of the manor except at the will of the lord; and strangers coming into the vill were not allowed to "have or take anything in the fen save by the favour of the lord".[6]

---

[1] Littleport Rolls, *op. cit.* p. 136.   [2] *Ibid.* p. 123.
[3] *Ibid.* pp. 138–9.   [4] *Ibid.* p. 129.
[5] *Ibid.* p. 142. Take another case: "Henry Sweetgroom has mown and cut 3,000 of sedge beyond the appointed quantity; therefore the price of the said sedge, to wit, 8s. shall remain to the lord as forfeited" (pp. 145–6). See also *ibid.* p. 129 for similar offences.
[6] *Ibid.* p. 143. See also *ibid.* p. 125: "The jurors present that William Fisher sold 500 of sedge outside the commune against the ordinance. And that Peter of Weting, who is not a commoner, has mown 600 of sedge in the common without the authority of any commoner and sold them outside."

Among the reeds and rushes of the fen were birds.[1] Their variety was as remarkable as their quantity, and they provided a livelihood for many inhabitants of the region. In the twelfth century, Thomas of Ely exclaimed with wonder:

There are numberless Geese, *Fiscedulae*, Coots, Dabchicks, Water-crows, Herons, and Ducks, of which the number is indeed great. At mid-winter, or when the birds moult their quills, I have seen them caught by the hundred, and even by the three hundreds, more or less. Sometimes they are taken in nets and snares as well as by bird-lime.[2]

Unfortunately, there is no great body of material which might amplify this list of the birds of the medieval Fenland; references to fowling are not as frequent as might be expected. Incidental mention, however, indicates the part played by fowling in the economy of the region. In the middle of the thirteenth century, various religious houses were several times asked to supply the king with wild fowl for his feasts.[3] There are also references to those who trespassed "in the warren"; some of these may possibly refer to fen country.[4] The eggs of the

[1] See footnote 2, p. 8 above, and also p. 21.

[2] *Liber Eliensis*, p. 232. The Latin list is "anseres innumerae, fiscedulae, felicae, mergae, corvae aquaticae, ardeae et anetes". *Fiscedulae* is doubtful; "Querquedulae" (Teals) has been suggested as an alternative reading. *Corvae aquaticae* may refer to cormorants. The writer of the *Gesta Herwardi* has a similar reference: "For at the time when the water-fowl change their feathers and appearance, there I have often seen men bring many little birds, sometimes a hundred, occasionally two hundred and more, and very often not many less than a thousand from one single piece of water (*ex una aqua*)."—*De Gestis Herwardi*, ed. by S. H. Miller and W. D. Sweeting (1895), p. 48. This is appended to vol. iii of *Fenland Notes and Queries* (1897).

[3] In 1249, the sheriff of Cambridge was ordered on June 4th to buy in his bailiwick, for the king's use, 12 swans, 12 peacocks, 4 cranes and as many herons and bitterns as he could get (Close Rolls, 33 Henry III, m. 8). Two days later, the abbots of Peterborough, Thorney and Ramsey, and the priors of St Neots, Barnwell, Spalding and Ely were also asked for swans, herons, cranes and bitterns (Close Rolls, 33 Henry III, m. 12d). And in 1251, the abbots of Thorney, Crowland, Ramsey and Peterborough and the prior of Spalding were asked to supply the king with swans, cranes and other wild fowl against the feast of St Edward (Close Rolls, 35 Henry III, m. 23d).

[4] *Select Pleas of the Forest* (1209–1334), ed. by G. J. Turner (Selden Society, 1901), p. 131. See also Littleport Rolls, *op. cit.* pp. 124, 139.

birds were also valuable and they, too, were collected out of
the marsh. Round about 1300, the Littleport Rolls give a list
of some offenders who habitually collected eggs of the bittern
and sold them outside the fen.[1] While the Assize Rolls of the
early fourteenth century tell of a boy who went on *ligni pedes*
(pattens or stilts?) into the marsh to look for ducks' eggs
(*ova anatum*), and was drowned.[2] During the latter part of the
Middle Ages, the keeping of swans became a characteristic
fenland occupation.[3] But these are only stray references;
there is a dearth of material describing fully the regulations
and customs that governed the activity of the fowler. One
thing is certain; that if fowling was like the other activities of
the marsh, it was subject to minute regulation. For although
many of the occupations of the Fenland were individual and
peculiar to the region, they, no less than the normal activities
of upland agriculture, were subject to careful and ordered
supervision.

Salt-pans. There is frequent mention of salt-works and salt-
pans in the Domesday Book. These were either inland brine
springs or coastal pans for obtaining marine salt by evapora-
tion. One of the most characteristic districts where the latter
were to be found was along the coastal margins of the Fenland.
The silt region provided the ideal physical conditions because
the sea was continually building up a salt-marsh along the
shore; indeed, the receding water has left many former
coastal villages several miles inland. Not all the parishes of
the silt zone produced salt, as the accompanying map shows
(Fig. 8). In the Lincolnshire Fenland itself,[4] apart from the
villages of Wainfleet and Croft, all the salt-pans were in the

---

[1] Littleport Rolls, *op. cit.* p. 126.

[2] W. M. Palmer, "On the Cambridgeshire Assize Rolls", *Proc. Camb.
Antiq. Soc.* iii, 226 (1896). Here, there is also mention of men who were
sailing upon Soham Mere and got upset by a gust of wind.

[3] See H. C. Darby, *The Draining of the Fens* (1940), p. 10.

[4] Salt-pans were also recorded in some villages in north-eastern
Lincolnshire, and Fig. 8 shows three entered on the upland around the
Fens. Curiously enough, none are entered for the Axholme marshes in
the north-west.

division of Holland. There was a cluster of vills with salt-pans between the Welland and the Witham in Kirton Wapentake. Outside these limits, pans were rare; Leake (in Skirbeck Wapentake) to the north, and Spalding (in Elloe Wapentake) to the south were rather exceptional centres. The adjoining table tells its own tale.

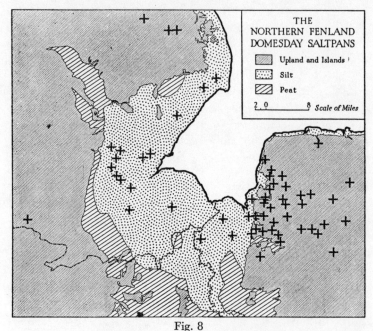

Fig. 8

The county boundaries are indicated

The salt-pans continued along the silt belt into Norfolk Marshland. Salt-pans are actually named only on three Marshland manors. But on the adjoining upland, to the east, there was a great cluster of villages responsible for the profits of salt-pans.[1] These latter may emphasise the fact that the Domesday Inquest was not a territorial survey; the salt-pans themselves must have been situated elsewhere—in

[1] H. C. Darby, "The Domesday Geography of Norfolk and Suffolk", *Geog. Journ.* lxxxv, 444 (1935).

Domesday salt-pans in Holland, Lincolnshire[1]

Bicker	1 salt-pan which is waste (340); 20 salt-pans rendering 30s. (348b); 1 salt-pan (367); 1 salt-pan rendering 16d. (368)
Cheal (in Gosberton)	1 salt-pan rendering 8d. (344b)
Donington	16 salt-pans rendering 20s. (345b); 2 salt-pans rendering 32d. (348); 9 salt-pans rendering 12s. (348)
Drayton (in Swineshead)	4 salt-pans rendering 5s. 4d. (346b); ½ salt-pan rendering 8d. (348); 1 salt-pan rendering 16d. (348); 4½ salt-pans rendering 6s. (348)
Fleet	2 salt-pans rendering 2s. (338)
Frampton	15 salt-pans rendering 20s. (348)
Gosberton	1 salt-pan rendering 4d. (344b); 2 salt-pans rendering 12d. (348b)
Kirton	2 salt-pans rendering 16d. (348)
Leake	26 salt-pans (348)
Quadring	2 salt-pans rendering 12d. (348b)
Spalding	20s. from salt-pans (351b); a plot of land with salt-pans rendering 4d. (368)
Stenning (in Swineshead)	6 salt-pans rendering 8s. (348b); 2 salt-pans rendering 2s. 8d. (363)
Surfleet	2 salt-pans rendering 12d. (369)

Norfolk Marshland and along the eastern shores of the Wash. That their numbers did not remain constant is shown by the following examples:

	1066	1086
Gaywood	30 pans	21 pans
West Walton	22	24
Wootton	20	14

Whatever the precise distribution and variation of these salt-pans, we cannot doubt that they were an important element in the economy of the silt-lands.

[1] The numbers in brackets after each entry refer to the folios of the first volume of the Domesday Book.

Later documents contain frequent reference to salt-making in these villages of the silt zone. There were many grants of salt-pans, and the "salt-rent" was an item frequently entered on the rolls.[1] Curious measures were mentioned too: thus at Terrington in Norfolk there were important salt-works paying rent to Ely in *bledes, wayes* and *gates* of salt.[2] Sometimes the pans got damaged; just before 1200, William de Roumara was granting to St Mary and the canons of Dereham the right of digging with four spades in his East Marsh belonging to Bolingbroke, for the repair of their salt-pans.[3] The activity of the salt-pan was closely bound up with the cutting of turf, for the turbary provided fuel to evaporate the brine; the Red Book of Thorney records a grant of a *salina* in *Hirneflet* with right of digging turves *extra Hassocdic ad sustenationem praedicte saline sufficientem*.[4] The custom of taking turbary sufficient for the fuel of a salt-pan was apparently a well recognised one; and it would seem that certain portions of the turbaries were specially reserved to supply associated salt-pans.[5] Nor were all the later salt-pans restricted to the

[1] The Crowland Abbey account rolls, for example, mention salt-beds at Whaplode, Gedney, and Dunton Hall. The salt was sold by a measure, apparently of 9 bushels, and most of it seems to have been used for salting meat in the abbey larder.

See (1) F. M. Page, *The Estates of Crowland Abbey* (1934), p. 117; (2) M. Wretts-Smith, "Organization of Farming at Croyland Abbey, 1257–1321", *Journ. of Econ. and Business Hist.* iv, 191 (1932).

[2] N. Neilson, *Terrier of Fleet, Lincolnshire* (1920), p. lxxx.

[3] F. M. Stenton, *Documents Illustrative of the Social and Economic History of the Danelaw* (1920), p. 381. At Tydd, in 1250, there was a certain salt-pan which returned half a load of salt annually; "it used to yield more, but it has been almost entirely destroyed by the sea (periit per mare).— *Fenland Notes and Queries*, iii, 64 (1897).

[4] Red Book of Thorney, f. 259b. The title of the grant reads: "De una acra terrae et dimidia et de una salina in Holebech cum fodione Turbarum communi marisco quas Conanus filius Elye dedit Ecclesiae Thornensio in elemosinam."—It is printed in K. Major, "Conan Son of Ellis, an Early Inhabitant of Holbeach", *Lincs. Architect. and Archaeol. Soc. Reports and Papers*, xlii, 27 (1936). Miss Major assigns "no certain date" to the document, but it is "not earlier than 1195–1200".

[5] P.R.O. Ministers Accounts (Duchy of Lanc.), 242/3885 West Fen Marsh [Lincs.], 1329–82. See p. 85 below.

Domesday salt villages.[1] In the north-east corner of the Fenland, pans were important not only in Wainfleet but also in
Wrangle and Friskney. During the late fifteenth century,
turves were being constantly carried to these places.[2]

An example of this activity is provided by a terrier of
Fleet.[3] The village of Fleet, like its neighbours, was protected
from the floods of the sea by a bank. Outside this *fossatum
maris* lay wide stretches of silt and sand overflowed in part by
the tide. A terrier of the village, dated about 1316, gives an
account of the salt-making activity[4] along the shore *extra
fossatum maris*. To the regular arable holdings of workland and
moleland within the sea-wall, there were appurtenant holdings
outside the wall called *hoga et area*, for which a rent of
salt was paid. In addition to this regular *redditus assisus*, a
bondman, whenever he boiled salt outside the vill, paid a toll
to the lord of one measure called *overgongmiddas*. If he boiled
within the vill he paid only one-half measure for every *patella*.
The lord also claimed a toll on all salt sold; from twenty
measures when sold and carried *extra portum*, he received
one penny. Moreover, all bushels of salt from Fleet itself and
from the adjoining villages of Gedney and Holbeach were
brought once a year to a "holy place" (*sanctum locum*) outside
the sea-wall, called *le mothow*; there, the bushels received the
lord's sign as evidence that they contained true measure.
Those that brought bad measure were *in misericordia*.

This example from Fleet may be taken as a type of the salt-

[1] For instance, there were no salt-pans in Domesday Holbeach, but
salt-pans "with hills and yards (where the Salt is finished)" are recorded
there in an extent of 1321.—G. W. Macdonald, *Historical Notices of the
Parish of Holbeach* (1890), pp. 49–51.
[2] P.R.O. Ministers Accounts (Duchy of Lanc.), 247/3950 [Lincs.],
1471–73.
[3] N. Neilson, *Terrier of Fleet, Lincolnshire* (1920), pp. 83–4. See also
N. Neilson, *Customary Rents* (1910), pp. 39–40.
[4] N. Neilson, *Terrier of Fleet*, pp. 83–4. *Hoga* signified a little hill;
area was probably the space around it (*op. cit.* pp. lxi–lxii). "The bank
or dike referred to in the Terrier as *fossatum maris* extended in a great
curve some miles north of Fleet Hargate, as indicated on the map, and
can still be followed for miles across flat fields which now give no hint
of nearness to the sea" (*op. cit.* p. lxi).

making activity that went on along the silt zone throughout the Middle Ages, and that continued for some time later.[1] In 1562, there was a declaration that "much salt is made in England as of sand and salt water in pits in Hollande in Lincolnshire".[2] Rock salt was not discovered in England[3] until 1670.

AGRICULTURAL ACTIVITY

The evidence relating to occupations in the Fenland, if left at this stage, may easily convey a false impression of fenland society. There is a very real danger of over-emphasising the consequences that followed from the peculiarities of the region, and of producing a distorted picture of life in the fens.[4] It has been said, for instance, that fowling "was the chief means of subsistence of the fen slodger",[5] that the people of the fens "derived a precarious subsistence from fowling and fishing"; and, again, that "they must have been an amphibious race largely employed in catching eels".[6] The features of this existence have been summarised by declaring that "the true fenlander could be called neither an agriculturalist nor a shepherd. He was a fisherman of sorts, a wild-fowler, and a gatherer of natural resources such as berries and reeds".[7] Lord Macaulay, describing the fens before the draining in the seventeenth century, dismissed both the area and its people in similar terms:

> In that dreary region, covered by vast flights of wild-fowl, a half-savage population, known by the name of Breedlings, then led an amphibious life, sometimes wading, and sometimes rowing, from one islet of firm ground to another.[8]

[1] For salt-rents at Holbeach in 1458–59, see G. W. Macdonald, *Historical Notices of the Parish of Holbeach* (1890), p. 97.
[2] See H. C. Darby, *The Draining of the Fens* (1940), p. 13 n.
[3] *Philosophical Transactions* (Royal Society, London), v, 2015 (1670).
[4] See p. 119 below.
[5] W. H. Wheeler, *The Fens of South Lincolnshire* (1896), p. 471.
[6] S. Smiles, *The Early Engineers* (1864), p. 16.
[7] J. Bygott, *Eastern England* (1923), p. 143.
[8] *History of England*, ed. by C. H. Firth, iii, 1349 (1914). For the name "breedling", see H. C. Darby, *The Draining of the Fens* (1940), p. 90.

These accounts are not wholly untrue, but they seize on what was peculiar about fen life, and describe it as characteristic. The result is the formation of hasty conclusions about the social and economic life of the Fenland.

Little enough support for this picture is given by the evidence of manorial rolls on the one hand, and by that of the monastic cartularies on the other. Even as early as the eleventh century, the Domesday entries bear out a different conclusion.[1] It is true that these entries do not give an impression of great wealth, but they certainly smack of organised agricultural activity rather than any variety of semi-nomadism. Nor is it difficult to discover one of the motive forces behind much of the industry indicated by these early records. On the islands of the peat fen many men found the fulfilment of their desires not in meditation but in work. "Laborare est orare" was their motto; and the abbots of the Fenland monasteries were not loath to turn their "attention and thoughts to the advancement of their temporal interests".[2] The marshes surrounding the monasteries sometimes offered the promise of becoming "good and fertile arable land".[3]

Considerable difficulty arises, however, when we ask at what period reclamation started, or how much reclamation took place. There is certainly no sign of any large-scale project of draining. There was, however, a continuous piecemeal encroachment upon the edges of the fens, and this was a movement that seems to have been very general. The *Historia Croylandensis* provides a story of reclamation around Crowland that is plausible enough. But so much of Ingulph's narrative has to be rejected, and so much remains under dispute, that it is impossible to be sure of many of his facts.[4] In any case,

---

[1] See pp. 120 *et seq.* below.
[2] *Ingulph, Contin.* p. 325.   [3] *Ingulph, Contin.* p. 275.
[4] The forgers of the charters showed an ignorance of early English diplomatic form and also of the history of the rights they claimed. As the Patent Rolls bear witness, the charters of Ethelbald and Edred were inspected and confirmed in 1393 and again in 1399. It was about the same time, apparently, that the *Historia Croylandensis* was compiled with the object of providing a setting for the charters and of defending the rights

we can suppose that the Crowland fabricators would not insert statements about the condition of the marsh that were untrue or not possible *at the time when they themselves wrote*; their neighbours were much too wideawake to let such discrepancies pass in a law-suit. And hence, despite its uncertainty, the Crowland Chronicle does at least tell us something very definite—namely, that by the beginning of the fourteenth century, at any rate, the marshes around Crowland had been put into a state of cultivation. Moreover, it reveals the process by which this reclamation probably took place. Further, the subsequent grants of arable land in the marsh, mentioned in the Continuations of the Chronicle, are also indicative.[1]

For what it is worth, the story that Ingulph tells is this. In the dry seasons there was, naturally, an increase in the extent of the fen pastures; and Ingulph says that, during some years of drought, towards the close of the tenth century, the marshes to the north of Crowland were put "into a state of cultivation, in four places"[2]. A century later, a mighty work was supposed to have been undertaken by Richard de Rulos in Deeping Fen:

> He excluded the river Welland by a very strong embankment, because every year it had, by its continual inundations, overflowed nearly all the meadows adjoining the banks of the said river; from which circumstance that vill had, in ancient times, received the name of Depyng, meaning "the deep meadow". Building upon the embankment numerous tenements and cottages, in a short

of the monastery in numerous lawsuits. Some writers, who distinguish between the historical portions of the history and the charters found in it, reject the latter as mere monkish invention, but, with reservation, accept the former. Three works in particular may be consulted for discussion of the Ingulph forgeries: (1) H. T. Riley, "The history and charters of Ingulph considered", *Archaeol. Journ.* xix, 32, 114 (1862); (2) W. G. Searle, *Ingulf and the Historia Croylandensis* (Camb. Antiq. Soc. 1894); (3) F. Liebermann, "Ueber ostenglische Geschichtsquellen des 12., 13., 14. Jahrhunderts, besonders den falschen Ingulf", *Gesellsch. für ältere Deutsche Gesch. Neues Archiv,* xviii, 225 (Hanover, 1893).

[1] See pp. 45–6 below. The Continuations, of course, provide valuable evidence.

[2] *Ingulph,* p. 107. See *ibid.* p. 170 for marshes let out for the purposes of cultivation in the eleventh century.

time he formed a large vill, marked out gardens, and cultivated fields; while, by shutting out the river, he found in the meadow-land which had lately been deep lakes and impassable marshes, most fertile fields and desirable land, and out of sloughs and bogs accursed made quite a pleasure garden. Having thus formed a most fertile soil, he at the same time changed the said chapel of Saint Guthlac into the parish church of his new vill.[1]

This example was supposed to have stimulated further effort.

In the following summer, the people of Hoyland at Multon, Weston, and Spalding, in imitation of those at Depyng, by a common enactment agreed to among them, divided among themselves, man by man, their marshes, which were situate above our river Asendyk; on which, some put their portions in tillage, others preserved theirs for hay, while some, again, allowed theirs, as before, to lie for pasture for their own cattle apart from the others, and found the earth to be rich and fruitful. Stimulated by this their example, I, Ingulph, the Abbot of Croyland, and L—— of Hacbeth, and some others of Cappelade, in like manner divided between ourselves our portion at Cappelade, which ran down to the same river; and, on tilling it, we found the soil equally fertile and fruitful.[2]

According to Ingulph and the continuators of his history, operations of a like nature continued down the centuries. The Second Continuation records that late in the twelfth century the men of Holland,

who are our neighbours on the northern side, greatly desire to have tenancy in common of this marsh of Croyland; for, as their own marshes, of which each vill had originally one of its own, have been dried up, they have converted the same into good and fertile arable land. Hence it is that they stand in need, beyond measure, of common pasture land for their cattle, in which they do not so greatly abound.[3]

The Second Continuation also contains references to draining in other localities.[4] Thus, in 1189, Richard I granted leave to

---

[1] *Ingulph*, p. 156.
[2] *Ingulph*, p. 193. For other references to division and the making of banks, see p. 14 above, and p. 74 below.
[3] *Ingulph, Contin.* p. 275.
[4] See p. 49 below.

the men of Holland and Kesteven "to build upon the said
marshes, and till the same and to enjoy all their easements
upon the same".[1] Confirmation of this activity is provided
by a Close Roll entry.[2]

We are on safer ground when we come to other sources.
These are not numerous, but they are scattered enough to be
representative; and they are sufficient to enable us to form an
opinion about the condition of certain fens. That improvement on a very considerable scale was profitable in the twelfth
century is shown by the statement of Nigel, bishop of Ely,
that two and a half knights' fees had been created in his
barony between 1135 and 1166 on land reclaimed from the
fen:

De purprestura marisci, quod nunquam antea lucratum
fuit:

> Reginaldus de Niuetone, dimidium militem.
> Walterus de Pampewrthe, j. militem.
> Jordanus de Sanford, j. militem.[3]

To the north, along the margins of the silt zone, it seems
likely that drainage operations were also attempted in this
century. These operations are illustrated by the career of one
Conan, "the most influential inhabitant of Holbeach in the
late twelfth and early thirteenth centuries". His career has
been unravelled by Miss Major. "Even before 1199", writes
Miss Major, "he had reclaimed sufficient land in Holbeach
to make it worth while for the monks of Crowland to litigate
about Conan's gift of half the tithes of any land he himself had
brought into cultivation. A tract known as Conan's Newland
lay towards the sea and mention is also made of drainage
carried out between Saturdaydike and Hassockdike. In this
work he was by no means alone. References are frequently
found in charters of the district to Earl's Newland, Siward's

---

[1] *Ingulph, Contin.* p. 282. The marshes were situated between the
Welland and the Witham.

[2] Close Rolls, 18 Richard II, m. 33.

[3] *Red Book of the Exchequer*, ed. by H. Hall, i, 364 (Rolls Series, 1896).

Newland, Guthlac's Newland and many others."[1] And it seems probable that these names refer to newly reclaimed land.

Further east along the silt zone, in Norfolk, before the year 1181:

There was neither any habitation, nor ground that yielded profit, within that part of Wigenhale from Busterdesdole unto the south side of the same town, except the monastery of Crabhous, with some lands belonging thereto; all being then waste and in the nature of a fen: But afterwards the inhabitants of that place, and of divers others, came; and, with draining and banking, won as much thereof, by their industry, as they could: And, that they might the more securely enjoy the same, were content to be tenants for it, unto such great men of whom they held their other lands; and upon this occasion, by a common consent amongst them, was the old Podike first raised about the year 1223.

These facts about Wiggenhall were recorded[2] in 1322. They are repeated in the Castle Acre register,[3] and in the register of Crabhouse itself. The latter[4] never lets us forget the marshy site of the nunnery; and it confirms the evidence that the nunnery contributed its share to the draining of the locality. When the house had been founded the land around was "tut savagine et de graunt partie envirun de totes pars nesteyt habitaciun de home". Afterwards, lands were described as

[1] K. Major, "Conan Son of Ellis, an Early Inhabitant of Holbeach", *Lincs. Architect. and Archaeol. Soc. Reports and Papers*, xlii, 1 (1936). Miss Major prints the relevant extracts from the Crowland cartulary. One deed mentions land "in parochia de Holbech versus mare que Conaynneulandia vocatur quam ipse Conanus inclusit primam..." (*ibid.* p. 18). Another deed concerns: "de novo incremento inter Saterdaidyk et Hassokdyk..." (*ibid.* p. 19). References to "Newland" are to be found, for example, in the Red Book of Thorney, f. 259b.

See also K. Major, "Some Early Documents Relating to Holbeach", *ibid.* xli, 39 (1934).

[2] P.R.O. Placita Coram Rege (K.B. 27), Mich. term, 15 Edw. II. See W. Dugdale, *Imbanking and Drayning*, p. 244.

[3] W. Dugdale, *Mon. Ang.* v, 69 (1825). Dugdale gives extracts from the Castle Acre register among the charters of the priory of Normansburgh in South Raynham. The greater part of the register "appears to have been written about the middle of the fourteenth century" (*ibid.* v, 46).

[4] The Crabhouse register is written partly in old French, partly in Latin and partly in English, apparently during the latter part of the fourteenth century and early fifteenth century.

newly recovered from the waste; and the register stated, too, that the drainers remained lords of their new lands in return for a rent to the king.[1]

The improvement of the fen sometimes resulted in new meadow and pasture;[2] sometimes, it produced arable land. The choice between arable and meadow[3] depended upon local circumstances, for the soils of both silt and peat areas varied considerably. One thing is certain—there was a good deal of activity. In 1196, the abbot of Ramsey leased out Staplewere Fen for twelve years, on condition that it should be returned "with any improvements which shall be made in that fen".[4] Dating from the end of the twelfth century, there is a charter in the cartulary of Thorney Abbey, granting a messuage at Yaxley "in the fen on the other side of the bank".[5] A few years later, another charter granted to Richard de Frestune a messuage in Whittlesey and also "the toft which Lord Roger sometime our Prior raised from the fen".[6] In the

[1] Mary Bateson, "The Register of Crabhouse Nunnery", *Norfolk Archaeology*, xi, 1–71 (1892). The references to recovery from the waste are:
(1) *Paragraph* 158.
"Fet a saver de les terres gysauntes en Wygenhale de Stapelwere deskes a bustardesdole, a quels eglise diversement parteynunt & de queus seniurs eus sunt tenues, kar eus sunt novelement gaynes de Wastine."
(2) *Paragraph* 183.
"Omnia ista tenementa prescripta nullum faciunt regi servicium, quae de Wastina fuerunt lucrata & qui lucrati fuerunt, elegerunt sibi dominos proprie voluntate et de eis, per servicia inter eos concessa, tenerent de Crabhus & in capite de comite Brittanie & ipse de rege."
(3) *Paragraph* 214.
"Senyurs wous devez entendre ke totes les...terre bustardesdole & Stapelwere soleyunt estre gastyne et eus ke les gaynerunt les furunt senyurs de les terres a lur volunte de tener de eus, pur certeyn rente par an, mes a Rey de ren(t)...."
See also, E. M. Beloe, "Freebridge Marshland Hundred and the Making of Lynn", *Norfolk Archaeology*, xii, 311 (1895).
[2] See pp. 79 *et seq.* below.   [3] See footnote 3, p. 50 below.
[4] *Ramsey Cartulary*, ii, 216.
[5] Red Book of Thorney, f. 422: "unum mesuagium in marisco ex altera parte ripe."—In the time of Abbot Solomon, 1172–88.
[6] *Ibid.* f. 427: "Toftum dominus Rogerus quidam Prior noster levavit de marisco."—In the time of Abbot Ralph, 1198–1216.

early part of the thirteenth century, Sawtry Abbey received
the gift of a messuage in Ely which Alan, parson of Bassing-
bourn, had "raised from the marsh at his own expense".[1]
While in the middle of the thirteenth century, Abbot Richard
of Crowland "enclosed the land which is called Aswyk from
the wide extent of the marsh; and in like manner began, with
great labour, to enclose Dovesdale, which was afterwards
completed on behalf of the convent by Abbot Thomas, his
successor".[2] Further, in the Ely cartulary's description of
the episcopal manor round about 1250, several acres of
meadowland are described as recently or newly "recovered".[3]
The Hundred Rolls, compiled in 1279, referred to several
fiefs in Sawtry and Walton enlarged by additions of from two
to fifteen acres of meadow "de nova acresca marisci"—part
of the recent acquisition from the marsh.[4] Moreover, in these
later years of the thirteenth century, a good deal of land seems
to have been reclaimed from the fen around Littleport.[5] In
1277, there is reference to "the newly enfeoffed" at Littleport, and after the description of some few small tenements

[1] British Museum, Additional Charters, No. 33072: "quod exaltavi de
marisco custis meis" (circa 1220).

[2] Ingulph, Contin. p. 325. (The entry is dated circa 1247.) In the account of "this new enclosure" on p. 326, there is mention of "the
new embankment".

[3] Fenland Notes and Queries, iii, 191 (1897). The meadowland of the
manor is entered as follows: "In Gruntefen, 17 acres. In Brasloue and
the Hay, 81¾ acres, with 20 acres recently recovered. In Blacwineserd
with the mere 22 acres. In Craswelle, Brademede, and Chinhale, 36 acres.
In Chetesfeld, 25½, also 6 acres newly recovered. In Pandenhale and
Bliynghale 44½ acres, with 7¼ acres recently recovered: also there is a
'grana' of spinney, of 6 acres: also a vineyard of 9 acres, and, within
the enclosure of this vineyard, 8 acres of pasture. Total of meadowland,
260 acres by the lesser hundred."

[4] Rotuli Hundredorum, ii, 659–63 (Record Commission, 1818).

[5] Littleport Rolls, op. cit. p. 109: "this process seems to have gone yet
further before Edward II's day, for the court rolls testify to a much more
populous manor than that which the 'extents' would lead us to expect."
Note that the Ordnance Survey Map shows Apes Hall two miles away
from the village. For these "newly enfeoffed" holdings, see the Ely
register; e.g. "Robertus Pikerel tenet quemdam hulmum pro uno
denario."—British Museum, Cott. MSS. Claud. C. xi, f. 42.

held at money rents, comes another heading, "Of the newly enfeoffed in Apesholt and elsewhere in the Marsh". This section
describes numerous tenements of three, six, twelve, twenty,
and a hundred acres held at money rents of a penny an acre
or thereabouts. It seems that a good deal of land had lately
been reclaimed from the fen. There may also be indications
of enclosure from the fens on other manors.[1] While at Over, a
certain Robert de Aula was reported to have held nine virgates
of land "ut in pratis et mariscis de vetere conquestu".[2] Early
in the next century it was recorded among the deeds of
William Clopton, who was abbot of Thorney from 1305 to
1322, that in the midst of Thorney Fen he built a house and
offices, enclosing them with ditches; and also that he enclosed
a "large part of the fen to have as arable land or meadow
with the lapse of time if good fortune would allow".[3] It was
during these years too, in 1318, that the abbot and convent
of Peterborough were granted three acres in the king's marsh
of Glatton, near Whittlesey Mere; these three acres they could
enclose and build upon, while their fishermen could spread
out their nets to dry, and save themselves "in time of tempests which often happen there".[4] While, from the end of the
same century, in 1394, there was a grant allowing the prior of
Spalding and others "to make dikes"; to lead a dike to their
lands; and to "build up and till the marsh".[5]

The names applied to the assarted land varied in different
parts of the Fenland. "Novum conquestum" was used, for

[1] British Museum, Cott. MSS. Claud. C. xi, e.g. ff. 68b (March), 74
(Wisbech).

[2] Old Coucher Book of Ely, f. 240 (Bishop's Muniment Room, Ely, G. 3).

[3] Red Book of Thorney, f. 460: "In marisco construxit quamdam
bercariam et fossatis inclusit ibidem magnam partem marisci pro terra
arabili habenda vel minuto prato ibidem processu temporis si fortuna ad
hoc se optulerit grossa."
With this may be compared a rent at *Welles* in the year 1206–7: "De
eodem [Osberto Puttok], pro quodam prato, quod habet juxta pratum
Albricti Bolle, sex denarios, quod si cultum fuerit, dabit pro qualibet
acra unum denarium" (*Ramsey Cartulary*, ii, 319).

[4] *V.C.H. Huntingdonshire*, iii, 187 (1936). The reference is from the
Charter Rolls of 11 Edward II.

[5] Close Rolls, 18 Richard II, m. 33 (August 10th, 1394).

example, in Sutton and Tydd, the territory of the village being divided into *terra de conquestu, terra ville,* and *terra nativa.* More curious designations were "innames" or "innomes",[1] while "chevacie" occurred occasionally. In Fleet, "rynt hynges" was used.[2] While, in some of the villages of Spalding Priory, the new ground was called "offoldfal". A marginal note of the Spalding cartulary, in English and much later in time, declares: "I thinke this is increase of ground frome the sea, or enclosed frome the fen & devided proportionally to the freeholders."[3] Sometimes this *offoldfal* land became *terra arabilis*[4] with appurtenant messuages and salt-pans. Consequently, the reclamation frequently necessitated new assessments of land and tenements; and there were many entries similar to one of 1324: "Et postea quod de novo agistentur quia plures terre et tenementa in dicta villa nunquam agistate fuerunt."[5]

Associated with this reclamation there seems to have grown up a definite body of assart rights and customs. But, not unnaturally, disputes were inevitable. In 1279, complaint was lodged against the abbot of Ramsey for "assarting" a certain fen which had always been common pasture.[6] In 1294, Hugh de Fenton was fined sixpence in the manor court of St Ives for ploughing up and appropriating a certain fen;[7] and in the following year one Simon the Forester was presented at the court of Ramsey because he had not given up a selion that he had appropriated from the fen.[8]

From these many references, a general impression emerges that the fenmen were continually striving to drain their lands locally, and that assarts from the fen were no uncommon feature in their lives. Sometimes, these efforts resulted in

---

[1] The term is also found in woodland areas: see A. Mawer, F. M. Stenton and J. E. B. Gover, *The Place-Names of Sussex* (1929), pp. 29–30.

[2] See N. Neilson, *Terrier of Fleet, Lincolnshire* (1920), p. lxxix.

[3] British Museum, Harleian MSS. 742, f. 166.

[4] *Ibid.* 742, ff. 111 b, 115.

[5] British Museum, Additional MSS., No. 35296, f. 258.

[6] British Museum, Additional Charters, No. 39595.

[7] British Museum, Additional Charters, No. 39597.

[8] British Museum, Additional Charters, No. 39598.

meadow or pasture;[1] with good fortune, this became arable
land, whose fields were separated from one another by ditches
and banks.[2] Silent testimony is afforded by the fact that
pre-drainage maps show numbers of straight (and therefore
probably artificial) waterways.[3] However scattered and frag-
mentary the evidence, there is enough to show that the words
of Matthew Paris, written in the thirteenth century, were not
all exaggeration:

> Concerning this marsh a wonder has happened in our time;
> for in the years past, beyond living memory, these places were
> accessible neither for man nor for beast, affording only deep mud
> with sedge and reeds, and inhabited by birds, indeed more likely
> by devils as appears from the life of St Guthlac who began to live
> there and found it a place of horror and solitude. This is now
> changed into delightful meadows and also arable ground. What
> therefore does not produce corn or hay brings forth abundant
> sedge, turf and other fuel, very useful to the inhabitants of the
> region.[4]

But one point must be emphasised. There was no extensive
project of reclamation. The time was not ripe for such an
enterprise, either from the point of view of technical equipment or from the point of view of economic conditions. And,
for that matter, it may be no exaggeration to say that, during
the Middle Ages, portions of the Fenland were more valuable
in their natural condition than if they had been converted
permanently into winter ground.[5] Common rights were no
incidental appurtenance in manorial economy.[6] They repre-
sented an important and profitable way of exploiting certain
types of terrain.

Agricultural activity was not limited to reclaimed marsh.
In the peat area, the islands themselves were cultivated to a

[1] For enclosures for meadow see p. 79 below.
[2] See pp. 48 and 50 above.
[3] References to new ditches and new drains occur in some documents.
See pp. 149, 153, and 166 below.
[4] Matthew Paris, *Chronica Maiora*, under the year 1256 (*op. cit.* iii, 570).
[5] See pp. 63 *et seq.* below.
[6] See p. 67 below.

considerable extent.[1] Many are the encomiums lavished by the monkish chroniclers upon these upland tracts; upon Ely "of fairest place";[2] upon Ramsey, "most beautiful vill"; upon Crowland[3] and Thorney, each "a very Paradise". This plenty was not confined only to necessities; the vine was cultivated and there were fruits in abundance. The twelfth-century chronicle of Ramsey opens with praise for the site of the abbey:

> In length this island extends almost two miles; but in breadth not so much, being surrounded with alders, reeds, green canes, and bulrushes, which beautify it exceedingly; and before it became inhabited, it was full of all kinds of trees (especially wild ash), the size of which may be seen from the beams and rafters in the roof of the church. But now through the space of time the woods have for the most part disappeared, and the fertility of the turf is such that the land converted to tillage bears corn plentifully; nor is it less profitable otherwise, being full of fair gardens, rich pastures, shady groves, and rich meadows; which in the spring time look most beautiful.[4]

No sooner was this wooded islet inhabited, than it drew at once inspiration and learning from the great Benedictine

---

[1] For the manor of Wilburton on the Ely upland, see F. W. Maitland, "The History of a Cambridgeshire Manor", *Eng. Hist. Rev.* ix, 417 (1894).

[2] A monk of Ely named Leo, in the time of Brithnoth the first abbot (970–81), laid out the grounds near the abbey into gardens and orchards. —*Liber Eliensis*, pp. 168–9. The Domesday Survey records, at Ely, "ibi iii arpendi vineae"—D.B. i, 192; the "arpent" being a French measure. For a vineyard at Ely in the thirteenth century, see footnote 3, p. 49 above.

[3] The Crowland Abbey court rolls (1257–1321) provide information for the island itself; and this has been summarised by Miss M. Wretts-Smith who writes (*art. cit.* p. 178): "There remains the Isle of Croyland. At its north-east corner lay the extensive manor of Aswick, which was, besides, one of the Abbey's stock farms. The chief need here was oats for provender. Aswick rarely produced less than 200 quarters and occasionally the crop rose to over 500 quarters. Bere, to feed the herdsman, and mixtil were also grown here. The other large stock farms, Monklode, Nomansland, and Brotherhouse, grew little corn except oats for the cattle, and their farm servants received grain allowances from the Granary" (i.e. from the central granary for all the Crowland manors). See also footnote 1, p. 86 below.

[4] *Chronicon Abbatiae Ramesiensis*, p. 8. Among the conjectural derivatives of the name *Ramsey* which the chronicler mentioned was *ramorum insula*— island of trees (*ibid.* p. 9).

abbey of Fleury on the Loire, and became famed abroad as
one of the English schools. To Ramsey came the great teacher
Abbo of Fleury, steeped in all the lore of the seven liberal arts.
In the prologue to his treatise *De Grammaticalibus*, he apostro-
phised the island with many a difficult word and allusion.[1]

Ramsey was not the only island to be praised. Testimony
to the amazing beauty and fertility of Thorney was given by
William of Malmesbury early in the twelfth century. He
described it as a very Paradise, in pleasure and delight
resembling Heaven itself.

The marshes there abound in trees, whose smooth height stretches
towards the stars. The plain there is as level as the sea; which
with its grass flourishing delights the eye, and which is so smooth
that there is nothing to hinder him that runs through it; neither is
there any waste place in it; for in some parts there are apple trees,
in others, vines which either spread upon poles or run along the
ground.[2]

Exaggerated though these monkish eulogies may be, they
serve to correct the picture of nomadic and lawless fenmen;
and they reveal the Fenland to be much more than a wilderness of reeds, the haunt of fowl and fish. The real fact was that
ordered control of the marshes and pastures, supplemented
by agriculture, formed the basis of life for the normal fenland
community. Thus of the seventeen thousand acres that com-
prised the manor of Littleport, sixteen thousand were nothing

---

[1] Printed in J. Mabillon, *Annales Ordinis S. Benedicti*, ĭv, 688 (1707).

[2] *De Gestis Pontificum Anglorum* (Rolls Series, 1870), pp. 326–7. The
paragraph goes on to state that the island derived its name from thorn
thickets—"Thorneiae propter condensitatem dumorum vocata." Compare this with what a monk of Peterborough wrote in the middle of the
same century: "Burgh is built in an excellent situation; for on one side it
enjoys the marsh, and excellent water; on the other side it enjoys fields,
woods, meadows and pastures in abundance. It is beautiful on all sides,
and accessible by land, save on the eastern shore whither you cannot
come save by boat. On the south side the Nene flows past the monastery;
after crossing it you may go straight on whither you will. When the
founders first saw this site, so excellent, so eminent, so pleasant, so suitable,
most fertile and most jocund, abounding in everything and most beautiful,
as it were an earthly Paradise offered them by God, they founded their
monastery here."—"Historiae Coenobii Burgensis", p. 2, in *Historiae
Anglicanae Scriptores Varii*, ed. by J. Sparke (1723).

better than unreclaimed marsh; yet the fourteenth-century court rolls of Littleport definitely indicate bread and beer to be the staples of existence. The high ground, restricted as it was, was well cultivated with cereals and pulse, with wheat and barley, oats and rye as well as with beans and peas. There is, too, a very significant entry, in the Ramsey cartulary, relating to Burwell:

Clariz et Robertus de Clervaus et Walterus de Bamevile et Radulphus de Osdene tenent unam piscaturam pro duodecim solidis.

Et quinque acras terrae arabilis ad cibum piscatoris.[1]

"Arable land for the food of the fisherman"; this last phrase is indeed illuminating, as are the frequent references[2] to the houses, the lands, and the messuages of fishermen. That there was also considerable cultivation in the villages of the south Lincolnshire silt-lands can be seen from the Crowland Abbey account rolls between 1257 and 1321. Oats, bere[3] and flax,[4] among other crops, were grown. These facts help to place the special occupations of the Fenland in their true perspective.

This agricultural activity throughout the Fenland was not carried on without much struggle. When the winter floods were serious, the embankments that had been constructed in previous years broke down before the onslaught of the swollen

---

[1] *Ramsey Cartulary*, ii, 28.

[2] E.g. *Ramsey Cartulary*, ii, 310 for a record of a fisherman "with his house and his land". See also *ibid*. ii, 330; and iii, 157.

[3] M. Wretts-Smith, *art. cit.* pp. 177–8: "South of these three were Gedney, Fenhall, and Dunton Hall. Whaplode's account seems sometimes to have merged with that of its neighbour, Gedney. These, all in the Fenlands, were oat manors, each producing over 100 quarters a year. In addition they grew bere (a small variety of barley), which was used to feed the farm servants, and large fields of mixtil. At Dunton Hall, especially, both these grains came to rival the oat crop. Mixed crops seem to have thrived on the Fens...."

[4] M. Wretts-Smith, *art. cit.* p. 191: "Flax was grown at Aswick, Fenhall, Dunton Hall, and on some of the other Holland manors, and the ground used was frequently let at high yearly rents, not only because of the value and scarcity of flax-fields, but also, presumably, because of the exhaustion of the soil by this crop. Flax-seed was sometimes bought and there are indications that the land may have been rented after sowing...."

rivers that poured down from the uplands.[1] Along the banks of the Welland in the fourteenth century "there was so much water in winter time that it covered the ground an ell and a half in depth and in a tempestuous wind two ells ".[2] In like manner, the other rivers of the Fenland "caused frequent inundations of the lands adjacent". Flood after flood is recorded, due to "snows and continued rains". That of 1467 was very bad.

Throughout the whole of this county, and in Hoyland especially, there was scarcely a house or building, but what the streams of water made their way and flowed through it. Nor must you suppose that this happened hurriedly and in a cursory manner only: but continuously, during a whole month, the waters either stood there without flowing off, or else, being agitated by strong gusts of wind, swelled and increased still more and more day after day. Nor on this occasion did the embankments offer any effectual resistance, but on the contrary, though materials had been brought from other quarters for the purpose of strengthening them, they proved of very little service for that purpose; and however diligently the work might have been attended to in the day time, as the waters swelled and rose, the spot under repair was completely laid bare during the night. Then was there grief and lamentation among all, and outcries and tumult among the Hoylanders.[3]

---

[1] E.g. *Ingulph, Contin.* pp. 350–1: "For, every year, as the waters increased to overflowing, the channel was unable to contain the increasing waters within the banks, and, consequently, by repeatedly washing away the soil, the waves overflowed the embankment. Hence, through the irruption of floods, the whole surface was inundated and covered with waters, so that the utility resulting therefrom consisted more in a supply of fish than of pasturage."

[2] Patent Rolls, 10 Edw. III, pt. ii, m. 8d. The *Ramsey Cartulary* mentions a lode, in 1342, "ab antiquo constructà et ordinata fuit, tam pro salvatione terrarum, pratorum, et pasturarum, hominum villatorum de Waltone, Sautre, et Conyngtone, contra aquas dulces ibidem descendentes" (i, 177). See also *ibid.* iii, 143, for fresh waters coming down from the upland.

[3] *Ingulph, Contin.* pp. 443–4. See also pp. 150 *et seq.* below. Of course there were droughts as well as floods in the fens. See, for example, Matthew Paris, *Chronica Maiora*, under the years 1236 (iii, 369); 1241 (iv, 177); 1252 (v, 321). In 1236, it was so dry that "paludes profundae cum stagnis siccarentur". In 1241, "paludes profundas et stagna amplissima desiccarunt". In 1252, the bad effect of the drought upon fen cattle is mentioned.

But the *Chronica Maiora* also records floods; see footnote 1, p. 58 below.

During these crises both arable and pasture land were sub-merged (except that on the higher islands), and the waters "drowned many cattle and spoiled a great quantity of corn". On the other hand, there were incursions of the waters of the sea. "But these irruptions of the sea, as they were casual (*viz.* when the north or north east winds accompanied extra-ordinary spring tides) so were they not frequent, nor did those floods so long continue upon the land, as to destroy it by drowning; the stagnation of the fresh waters producing much more damage."[1] Thus wrote Dugdale; but even so, the entries in the Patent Rolls show that salt-water floods were numerous enough and did considerable damage.[2] Many are the references to banks "broken by the rage of the sea". In the manor of Wisbech, about 1250, there were several mes-suages formerly of value but then "entirely perished by in-undation of the sea".[3] While, in the hundred years from 1250 to 1350, the Marshland district in Norfolk was flooded some twelve times. Matthew Paris in the *Chronica Maiora* gave

[1] W. Dugdale, *Imbanking and Drayning*, p. 299. The statement about "north or north east winds" needs a little expansion. "The greatest damage is done when certain factors operate in conjunction, namely flood, tide and wind. There is no withstanding a heavy flood with an incoming spring tide and a strong north-easterly wind; especially if the previous spell of weather has been one characterised by westerly winds in the Atlantic which beat up the North Sea tides."—D. A. Stevenson, "The Flooded Fens: A Tidal River and its Control", *Scot. Geog. Mag.* liii, 171-2 (1937).

[2] Occasionally, however, there are records of the reverse process: an increase of land by additions of "silt or sand" which, owing "to the seas leaving thereof, become firm ground". The "custom of the country" was that such increase "ought to belong unto him to whose firm and solid ground it first joined itself", and not to the owner of the land it ultimately adjoined. Naturally such additions provoked many disputes. In 1342, there was such a dispute between the abbots of Peterborough and Swineshead about accretions in Lincolnshire, when it was noted that the sandy soil increased "by little and little" (Patent Rolls, 16 Edw. III, pt. 1, m. 35d). The sea was constantly building up a salt-marsh, and the receding water has left villages far inland. The one-time "harbours" of Fleet and Bicker, for example, are now more than six miles from the sea. See footnote 4, p. 41 above.

Fenland Notes and Queries, iii, 124 (1897).

several references to the damage produced.[1] After the flood of 1338, a jury at Wiggenhall reviewed the disasters that had overtaken the town since Edward III had come to the throne in 1327:

On the morrow after Epiphany, in the third year of the then King, a certain bank on the west part of the said river, by means of the raging of the sea, broke; so that the tides entered and over-flowed a thousand acres of land, sowed with corn, to the great damage of the same town. And that on the west part of the said river, by reason of the like tempests, happening on the eve of S. Hillarie next before, the before-specified bank was broken and torn, so that the tides entered, bore down a house, and overflowed cc acres of land sowed with corn. And that, on the eve of S. Andrew, in the eighth year of the same King, the said bank was, by the like mishap, broken again, for the length of three furlongs, in a certain place called Burtys hithe, insomuch as the tides flowing in thereat overwhelmed a thousand acres of land sowed with corn; and that on the morrow after the Feast of S. Hillarie then last past, there was by the like means a breach made on the east part of the same river, whereby eightscore acres of land, sowed with corn, were overflowed.[2]

In Emneth, Terrington, Tilney, Walpole, West Walton and Walsoken, there had been similar inundations. Many acres and many messuages were "drowned and utterly lost for ever, by the inundation of the sea". This and many other statements record the evils wrought by the "outrageousness of the sea", by "fearful tempests", by "the violence of the tides", and by "sudden inundations and violence, as well of the sea, as of the fresh waters".[3] Nor had Marshland in Norfolk any

---

[1] See the *Chronica Maiora* under the years 1236 and 1250. The damage in 1254 was also considerable: "Mare enim, ut praedictum est, omnia latera et litora terrarum vicinarum occupaverat tempore hiemali; ita quod nec fuges poterant apparere, immo nec silvae vel pomaria virere, fronde-scere, florere, vel fructificare valuerunt. Et ut aliorum dampna unius exemplo intelligere valeamus, solus prior de Spaulingo non se poterat in omnibus terris suis mari conterminis unum saltem manipulum collegisse jactitare." For these three years, see *op. cit.* iii, 379, v, 176, and v, 461.

[2] W. Dugdale, *Imbanking and Drayning*, p. 257.

[3] See W. Dugdale, *ibid.* pp. 258 *et seq.* For the low-lying nature of the silt zone, see H. C. Darby, *The Draining of the Fens* (1940), p. 107.

monopoly of these disasters. Kesteven and Holland, to the north, were in no better plight.

Frequently, and "time out of mind", taxes were remitted in part to those townships which suffered from floods.[1] In 1336, for example, the towns of West Walton, Walsoken and Emneth petitioned for some alleviation from the "Fifteenth" which parliament had granted to the king, and they were allowed a rebate of eight out of sixty pounds.[2] Later in the century, in the *Inquisitiones Nonarum* of 1342, the amounts raised by the townships of Tydd and Newton, in Cambridgeshire, were deficient owing to inundations that had destroyed the produce of the country.[3] The same story came from Sutton in Lincolnshire early in the next century. There, in 1423, the tenants of the bishop of Ely were complaining that,

the most parte of this londe thus charged with the grete habondance of water that has falne in the said partes is suroundyd and drownde so that it may nother be tillyd ner sawne.[4]

Indeed,

the said towne of Sutton is suroundyd and specially the maner and the demene londes of the said lordschip so far forth at this tyme men may rowe in a bote in ccc acres of londe for the which the tenants er chargyd for evry acre yerely sum xxx*d*. sum iii*s*. sum ii*s*. to thare utter destruccion.

The Sutton tenants attributed this flooding to the neglect of sewers on the part of their neighbours, Whaplode, Gedney

---

[1] Close Rolls, 18 Edw. II, m. 12. See also, for example, W. Dugdale, *op. cit.* pp. 250, 258. The *Ramsey Cartulary* (ii, 200–1) contains a "Letter of the Abbot of Ramsey to the King concerning the poverty of the Abbey". It is dated 1319 and makes mention of "mariscos nostros, aquae hoc anno adeo inundaverunt".

[2] Close Rolls, 9 Edw. III, m. 18. See W. Dugdale, *op. cit.* p. 254.

[3] *Nonarum Inquisitiones* (1807), p. 203. See footnote 3, p. 63 below, for flooding by the sea at Holbeach; and footnote 3, p. 81 for sea-floods at Wisbech.

[4] P.R.O. Duchy of Lanc. Miscellanea (D.L. 41), vii/7. For the damage done in the Fenland, and in England generally, by bad weather in 1406, see J. H. Wylie, *History of England under Henry IV*, ii, 470–5 (1894), where detailed references are given.

and Holbeach; and they petitioned for some reduction of the year's rent.

Occasionally, in some localities, conditions became completely impossible, and the fenmen fought a losing battle against the waters. The *Historia Eliensis* gives an account of an island, within the precincts of the Isle of Ely,

> called Elmeneie, wherein the monks of Ely had a cell, which, by reason of those obstructions that hindered the fresh waters in their passage through this Great Level from evacuating themselves, became by the swelling of those waters almost drowned: Upon a great complaint, therefore, made by the said monks unto Alberic Picot, he gave them four acres and a half of ground in the Isle of Denney, which lay without the reach of the Fen; to the end that they might translate their house hither, and make orchards and gardens there for their use.[1]

Centuries later, the same complaint came from the men of Elm whose sewers were silted up and lands were under water, "which did so impoverish the townsmen that many of them were constrained to seek new habitations, and the rest likely to do so, except some speedy remedy were applied thereto".[2]

But records of complete failure are few. Partly by defying nature and partly by utilising its resources, the fenmen of the Middle Ages evolved an economy suited to the peculiarities of their country. The disasters they suffered but served to emphasise one point—that the most important factor in their lives was the condition of the banks and sewers. That was the basic element in the economy of the Fenland during the later Middle Ages.

---

[1] W. Dugdale, *op. cit.* p. 356. The Crabhouse register (see p. 47 above) has likewise a note of failure: "there came a flood of water, which overwhelmed the habitation, wherefore they went away and did not return again."

[2] W. Dugdale, *op. cit.* p. 317.

MEADOW, PASTURE AND TURBARY

The amount of meadow in the Fenland during Domesday times was not very great. In the Cambridgeshire folios the normal formula is "pratum x carrucis" or "pratum x bobus".[1] In Lincolnshire and Norfolk,[2] the usual phrase is "x acrae prati". The data relating to the two counties of Cambridge and Lincoln are assembled in Figs. 9–11. On these two meadow maps the most striking characteristic is the poverty of the fens compared with the abundance of the upland areas. The distribution patterns speak for themselves, and illustrate conditions in peat and silt areas alike.

But the impression left by these Domesday distributions is not that conveyed by later evidence. Most later medieval documents contain very frequent references to meadowland. This difference between the eleventh and, say, the fourteenth centuries may be due to two factors:

(1) Mention of meadow may loom proportionately larger in the subsequent terriers and rentals relating to the fens because of the relative scarcity in the Fenland of arable land and of the other ingredients of upland economy.

(2) The disparity may also be absolute because it seems that between the eleventh and the fourteenth centuries piecemeal reclamation had retrieved much meadowland from the marsh. This conjecture is strengthened by independent evidence.[3]

Probably both these elements enter into the problem. But whatever be the truth, the fact remains that meadowland constituted a most important element in the economy of the Fenland during the later Middle Ages.

The meadows themselves seem to have been of every variety, from those rarely left uncovered by water to those which remained dry during the greater part of the year; from those

[1] See H. C. Darby, "The Domesday Geography of Cambridgeshire", *Proc. Camb. Antiq. Soc.* xxxvi, 52 (1936).
[2] For a meadow map of Norfolk, see H. C. Darby, "The Domesday Geography of Norfolk and Suffolk", *Geog. Journ.* lxxxv, 444 (1935).
[3] See p. 48 above, and p. 79 and pp. 141 *et seq.* below.

in the "deep marsh" to those in the "dry marsh". Some
meadows were surrounded with water and were reached
only by boat;[1] to other meadows the cattle were driven
along paths. But whatever their condition, there can be no
doubt of their importance although there were occasional
floodings even in summer. An account roll for Wistow in the
year 1324 noted: "For the sale of hay nothing, through
floods."[2] From Somersham there comes a similar entry later
in time: "from the demesne meadow nothing accrues this
year owing to a flood of water there in the summer."[3] But
these were exceptional years, and such hazards were worth
risking. Normally, the meadows were dry in summer, and
the winter floods, provided they did not last too long, served
only to make the meadow richer for the following summer.
Some lowlands were probably more useful in their natural
state than they would have been if permanently recovered
from floods; and the possession of well-watered, well-grassed
meadows would more than compensate for the occasional loss
of the hay harvest through summer floods. In the villages of

[1] *Ramsey Cartulary*, i, 430: "Prata in marisco, scilicet Crowelode,
incipiens ad Suthfenmuthe, et durans usque Hollode, et cingitur dictum
pratum undique aquis." In 1274, there were "20 perches of meadow
in the marsh of Suttone in Estlongriche".—*Sixth Report, Commission on
Historical MSS.* (1877), p. 291. See also the Red Book of Thorney, f. 373 b
for an agreement about the boundaries of a certain meadow in the fen.

[2] British Museum, Additional Charters, No. 39894.

[3] P.R.O. Ministers Accounts (Gen. Series), 1135/10 and 11 (*temp.*
Henry VI). The sea sometimes caused flooding. In a Holbeach Extent,
of 1293, is an entry: "240 acres of land lying for pasture, every acre worth
by the year 4 pence, and not more, because inundated by a sea-storm
which happened in those parts in the 15th year of the reign, and are
yet flooded at every high tide." (P.R.O. Inquisitions Post Mortem,
21 Edw. I, No. 105.) At the same Holbeach, in 1321, there is reference
to meadow overflowed with water, and to "a certain piece of Sea
(marshland covered by the sea from time to time) for the pasture of
animals."—See G. W. Macdonald, *Historical Notices of the Parish of
Holbeach* (1890), pp. 49–50. See also footnote 3, p. 81 below for flooding
of pasture towards the sea.

For meadow and pasture "overflowed with water" at Holbeach, see
footnote 2, p. 66 below; for pasture in "divers watery places", see
p. 82 below. For flooding in general, see above, pp. 55 *et seq.*

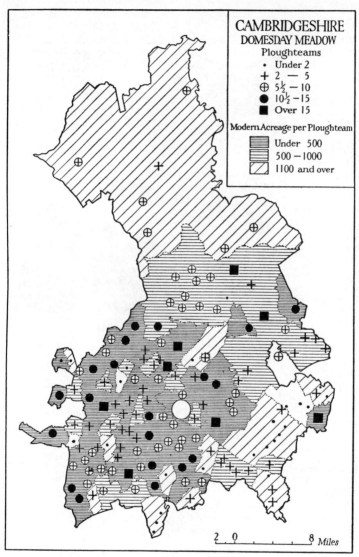

Fig. 9

From H. C. Darby, "The Domesday Geography of Cambridgeshire",
Proc. Camb. Antiq. Soc. xxxvi, 53 (1936). A dot in an empty space indicates the existence of a village for which no meadow was recorded

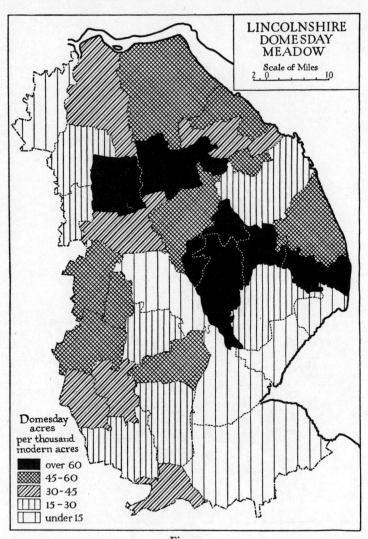

Fig. 10

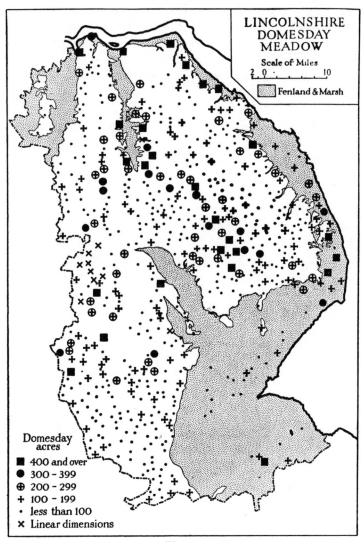

LINCOLNSHIRE
DOMESDAY
MEADOW

Scale of Miles
2 0 10

Fenland & Marsh

Domesday
acres

■ 400 and over
● 300 - 399
⊕ 200 - 299
+ 100 - 199
• less than 100
× Linear dimensions

Fig. 11

the English plain, an acre of meadow was worth more than two or more acres of the best arable land during the Middle Ages.[1] The advantages of the Fenland from this point of view can be readily seen. At Colne, Bluntisham and Earith, for example, the money rents for meadow were sometimes even twice the rents for ordinary land;[2] absolute marshland, of course, came out very low. The arable came to about 1s. per acre; the meadow, 2s.; while twenty acres of marsh were worth only 6s. 8d.

In addition to the hay crop of the meadows, there were also expanses of pasture for the feeding of animals.[3] The seasonal fluctuations in the water-level of the fens left free each year a broad zone most suitable for pasturage. During a succession of dry seasons this grazing area naturally increased considerably; and, moreover, in many portions it was kept above water for a longer time each year, or rendered more accessible, as reclamation proceeded around different centres in the fen. At least as early as the twelfth century, the grazing of animals had become one of the most important fenland occupations.[4]

[1] See F. W. Maitland, *Domesday Book and Beyond* (1897), p. 443, note: "In the thirteenth century it is common to find that the acre of meadow is deemed to be twice or three times as valuable as the best arable acre of the same village, and a much higher ratio is sometimes found."

See J. E. Thorold Rogers, *Six Centuries of Work and Wages* (1906), p. 73: "In the entire absence of all artificial grasses and winter roots, this kind of land [i.e. meadow] bore a very high rent." And see also F. G. Davenport, *The Economic Development of a Norfolk Manor*, 1086–1565 (1906), p. 31: "Acre for acre the low-lying meadows far surpassed the arable in value."

[2] P.R.O. Ministers Accounts (Bishops' Temporalities), 1136/1 (1420–25). This was not always the case, however; at Holbeach, in 1329, meadow and pasture "overflowed with water" were naturally worth less than the arable, the figures being 12d. (arable), 10d. (meadow) and 8d. (pasture) respectively.—G. W. Macdonald, *Historical Notices of the Parish of Holbeach* (1890), p. 49. See also p. 82 below.

[3] Dairy farming was an important occupation. See M. Wretts-Smith, *art. cit.* p. 191.

[4] The Lincolnshire Domesday entries contain no mention of pasture; in Cambridgeshire, however, the phrase "pastura ad pecuniam" is encountered in over one-half of the total villages in the county, and in most of the Fenland villages.—See H. C. Darby, *art. cit. Proc. Camb. Antiq. Soc.* xxxvi, 55 (1936).

Pasture rights were an integral part of manorial economy in the Fenland—much more so than corresponding rights on the upland manors around. To be deprived of pasture, by legal means or by the hand of nature, was a supreme misfortune. Bearing in mind the circumstances of medieval agriculture, we can readily appreciate that the value of a stretch of fen country did not compare so badly with that of a stretch of upland as at first might be thought. The absence of a demand for a general reclamation of the Fenland during the Middle Ages is all the more understandable. Winter floods made the pasture richer, and the damage done by summer floods was not too critical. The medieval economy of the fens was not as precarious nor as unsubstantial as easy generalisation would have us believe.

The earliest extant original charter relating to the fens of Lincolnshire is a grant about 1140 by Earl William of Lincoln to Kirkstead Abbey of the common pasture rights as he possessed in Wildmore Fen.[1] Indeed, in no part of England were common rights more important than in the Fenland, though few original twelfth-century charters remain to illustrate their working in detail. It is evident, however, that the most striking feature was the arrangement of villages in groups, governed partly by geographical position and partly by ancient administrative custom; a group of villages inter-commoned in the fen that they surrounded or adjoined. One piece of marsh thus served as common pasture for the cattle of a number of different villages (see Fig. 13). At the present day an indication of these early arrangements is preserved, as it were in a fossilised form. On the Norfolk marshes there was an extremely fertile tract of pasture known as Tilney Smeeth, upon which the cattle of seven towns intercommoned. Time and again the strong unity of the Marshland vills, in Norfolk, is brought out, and it is evident that this unity rested upon an

[1] F. M. Stenton, *Document Illustrative of the Social and Economic History of the Danelaw* (1920), p. 126.

economic foundation.[1] The modern parish map (Fig. 12) shows this area as consisting of detached portions of these villages. In one locality the partition is most minute; a space of less than 36 acres has been divided into rectangular portions among a number of villages. Formerly, the whole of this fen, like the other local fens, was held "pro indiviso", and over it the cattle wandered "horn under horn".[2] Sheep as well as cattle may have been involved too.[3] There were some instances of single vills with rights of common in the fens of two

[1] Cf. D. C. Douglas, *The Social Structure of Medieval East Anglia* (1927), pp. 196–8. "At the end of the thirteenth century the vills of Walton, Walpole, Terrington, and Walsoken seem to constitute a unity among themselves; and this unity is closely related both to the constant references to Marshland in the thirteenth century and to the 'leta integra de maresco' of the Ely extents.... The foundation of this seems to lie in the possession of a common marsh, and it is made the more secure by common payments and works to keep out the sea.... The leet of the marsh mentioned in the late thirteenth century by the Ely jurors was no new thing. It can be traced back through the twelfth century, and it appears to have been based upon an economic foundation." See also E. M. Beloe, "Freebridge Marshland Hundred and the Making of Lynn", *Norfolk Archaeology*, xii, 311 (1895).

[2] E.g. *Ramsey Cartulary*, i, 164: "...et ut pastura eis esset omnibus communis, id est, cornu sub cornu." The beasts pastured upon the fen were chiefly cattle, but sheep and swine were not unknown. Thus, in the marsh of Upwood and Raveley: "Possunt etiam esse ibi in stauro, duo tauri, et quadraginta vaccae, cum earum exitu. Sexcenti bidentes; porci viginti sex, cum duobus verris liberis; et omnes bidentes extraneorum et aliorum de villa terram non habentium, pascentes pasturam, debent jacere in falda Abbatis, et non alibi."—*Ramsey Cartulary*, i, 343. See the Littleport Rolls, *op. cit.* p. 128, for mention of ewes dying of rot.

[3] There is a record of "a shepherd keeping the sheep in the fen"— P.R.O. Mins. Accts. (Gen. Ser.) 885/32 (Wistow? 1310–12). For sheep at West Deeping, see Patent Rolls, 6 Edw. III, pt. ii, m. 34d. For the organisation of sheep farming on the estates of Crowland we are fortunate enough to have very full information which has been handled in two modern studies. See (1) F. M. Page, "Bidentes Hoylandie", *Econ. Hist.* i, 603 (1929); (2) M. Wretts-Smith, "Organization of Farming at Croyland Abbey, 1257–1321", *art. cit.* p. 181: "The title of the sheep-farm was 'Bidentes Hoylandiae', the sheep of Holland, and it seems to have moved about the fen pastures round the Isle of Croyland.... In 1160 the flock was at Monklode, on the west of the Island, in 1257 at Nomansland, at the southern corner, and in 1267 at Aswick. Between 1276 and 1299 its exact position is unknown, but in 1300 and 1303 it was at Standon...."

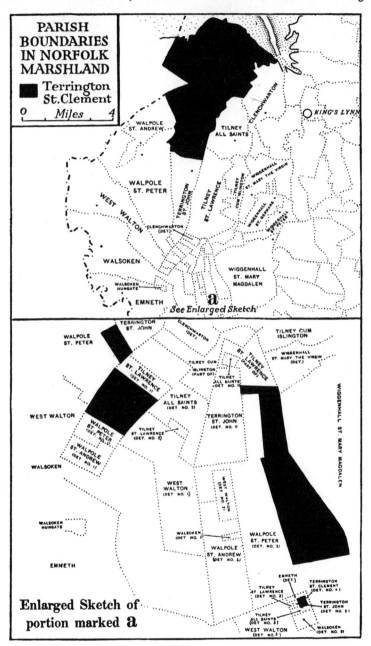

PARISH
BOUNDARIES
IN NORFOLK
MARSHLAND

Terrington
St. Clement

0   Miles   4

KING'S LYNN

WALPOLE
ST. ANDREW

TILNEY
ALL SAINTS

CLENCHWARTON

WALPOLE
ST. PETER

TERRINGTON
ST. JOHN

TILNEY
ST. LAWRENCE

TILNEY
CUM ISLINGTON

ST. MARY THE VIRGIN

WIGGENHALL
ST. GERMANS

WEST
WALTON

CLENCHWARTON
(DET.)

WALSOKEN

WIGGENHALL
ST. MARY
MAGDALEN

WALSOKEN
HUNGATE

EMNETH

a

See Enlarged Sketch

TERRINGTON
ST. JOHN

CLENCHWARTON
(DET.)

TILNEY CUM
ISLINGTON

WALPOLE
ST. PETER

TILNEY
ST. LAWRENCE
(DET. NO. 1)

TILNEY CUM
ISLINGTON
(PART OF)

ST. TILNEY
ST. LAWRENCE
(PART OF)

WIGGENHALL
ST. MARY THE VIRGIN
(DET.)

TILNEY
ALL SAINTS
(DET. NO. 3)

WEST WALTON

WALPOLE
ST. PETER
(DET. NO. 1)

TILNEY
ST. LAWRENCE
(DET. NO. 2)

TILNEY
ALL SAINTS
(DET. NO. 2)

TERRINGTON
ST. JOHN
(DET. NO. 1)

WIGGENHALL ST. MARY MAGDALEN

WALPOLE
ST. ANDREW
(DET. NO. 1)

WALSOKEN

WEST
WALTON
(DET. NO. 1)

WEST
WALTON
(DET. NO. 2)

WALSOKEN
HUNGATE

WALSOKEN
(DET. NO. 1)

WALPOLE
ST. PETER
(DET. NO. 2)

EMNETH

WALPOLE
ST. ANDREW
(DET. NO. 2)

EMNETH
(DET.)

TERRINGTON
ST. CLEMENT
(DET. NO. 4)

TILNEY
ST. LAWRENCE
(DET. NO. 3)

TERRINGTON
ST. JOHN
(DET. NO. 3)

TILNEY
ALL SAINTS
(DET. NO. 3)

WALSOKEN
(DET. NO. 2)

WEST WALTON
(DET. NO. 3)

Enlarged Sketch of
portion marked a

Fig. 12

different groups of vills. These intercommoning arrangements have been made clear by Miss N. Neilson who writes:

Such intercommoning was the custom throughout the region, and the groups everywhere were sharply defined and clearly differentiated from one another. Even when in the records of the district the waste is described as already divided and become the several of the neighbouring vills, some reference is usually made to an earlier use of the waste as common fen, preceding the partition among the vills in which it lay. The vills claimed that their right to intercommon in the fen had existed time out of mind, and the inference seems clear that the origin of such arrangements goes back to the early days of settlement. The partition and appropriation of the fen, when mentioned in the records is sometimes referred to the twelfth and succeeding centuries: sometimes the use of the fen in common by the vills continued to a much later period.[1]

The basis of the right to pasture was not the same in all cases. There were, roughly speaking, two kinds of villages— "intrinsec" and "forinsec". The intrinsic villages exercised their right by ancient custom and without payment. At best, the commoners were allowed to send any number of cattle at any time of the year into any part of the fen. Naturally, except under very special circumstances, they resisted any attempt at enclosure, sometimes with violence. But this custom of "common sans nombre" did not prevail everywhere. As time passed the idea of the rights of the lord developed to the detriment of the commoners; many villages were "forinsec", and pastured their cattle only for a definite rent and sometimes even in restricted numbers.[2] At Outwell, for instance, in the fifteenth century, the number of beasts that the commoners could turn out was defined.[3]

[1] N. Neilson, *A Terrier of Fleet, Lincolnshire* (1920), p. xlix. This is an outstanding contribution of first-rate importance to any student of the Fenland.

[2] See the Old Coucher Book of Ely, f. 227 (Bishop's Muniment Room, Ely, G. 3) for an agreement between the prior of St Neots and the bishop of Ely. "...And be it known that the Prior...if he have flocks or animals pasturing in the Bishop's fen...shall give to the Bishop..... for all such animals and flocks as do the others who have animals and flocks pasturing in the same fen."

[3] P.R.O. Chancery Proceedings, 3/66/20.—A sixteenth-century recital of an agreement made in 1446.

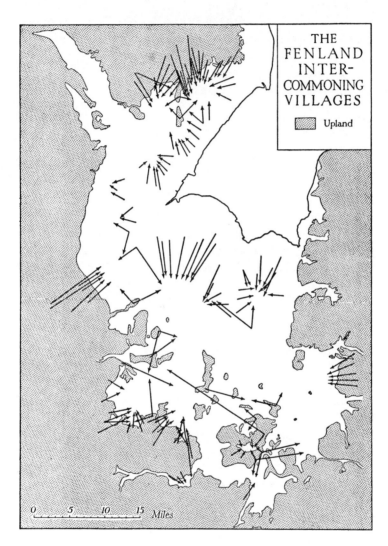

THE
FENLAND
INTER-
COMMONING
VILLAGES

Upland

0 5 10 15 Miles

Fig. 13
Redrawn from the map accompanying N. Neilson,
A Terrier of Fleet, Lincolnshire (1920)

There were also many regulations to control the actual proceedings at every juncture. In many places the fens were closed to cattle from early spring until some date in summer. Some were Lammas meadows open to common only after the lord's hay had been gathered. Thus, in the year 1189:

the abbot of Croyland, in conformity with his usual custom, put his marshlands in a proper state of defence as is usually done each year about the time of the Rogation days; and proclamation was publicly made upon the bridge of Spalding, that the men of Hoyland should prevent their cattle from entering their marsh, in order that the crop of hay might have liberty to grow.[1]

There were sometimes complaints, like the one made at Ramsey in 1384, that villages had overstocked the commons by importing cattle and sheep from less fortunate manors.[2] In Littleport, there were people who had the audacity to "pasture their sheep in autumn before the gleaners against the by-law".[3] All these routine arrangements were subject to minute regulation under the supervision of fen reeves and overseers.

One of the most frequent manorial offences was the pasturing of animals from outside vills, i.e. vills not belonging to the intercommoning group. The exclusion of the cattle of noncommoners was, indeed, an important problem, and it was solved only by means of great "drives" or "drifts", *fugaciones* as they are called in the rolls. These drives usually took place once a year, but sometimes more frequently, and they produced scenes of great activity. Thus, a bailiff and twenty-two men with twelve horses, and eight men with boats, were required for three days and three nights to drive the animals of "la Est fen" in Lincolnshire to the grange of Segdike and to impound them there. And again, a bailiff and ten men with eleven horses were required for two days and two nights to drive the animals of East Fen and North Fen to

---

[1] *Ingulph, Contin.* p. 276. The formula for the right of gathering of hay ran "ad falcandum, et levandum fenum, et asportandum, sine impedimento".—*Ramsey Cartulary*, ii, 325.
[2] British Museum, Additional Charters, No. 39625.
Littleport Rolls, *op. cit.* p. 128.

Stickney grange.[1] On these occasions, the animals were counted, and those not belonging to the rightful commoners in the fen were released only on payment of a fine; at Ramsey, in 1372, thirteen people were fined sixpence each for "having depastured with cattle and pigs in Stocking fen where they have no common".[2] Frequently, the parties concerned came to an amicable agreement about these matters.[3] A payment additional to the fine was usually enforced if the strange cattle were left in the pound by their owners for more than a day and a night. The drives were very profitable, and they were sometimes made unlawfully and at wrong times.[4]

These practices continued throughout the Middle Ages; examples from the sixteenth century show that drives still

[1] P.R.O. Mins. Accts. (Duchy of Lanc.), 242/3884 (Lincs. 1329–1403); 247/3950 (Lincs. 1469–73).
[2] British Museum, Additional Charters, No. 39618. See Littleport Rolls, *op. cit.* p. 146 for an interesting case. The jurors presented "that strangers coming from without, who hire houses from divers persons and hold nothing of the lord, common in the fen with their beasts and take other profits in the common, and such folk are called 'Undersettles'. Being asked by what warrant they use such common, they [the jurors] say that every undersettle shall mow half an acre of corn in the autumn and bind and dry it without [receiving] food [from the lord], like every 'anelepyman' and 'anelepywymman', and this is so in the terrier. And for that they show nothing why these undersettles should common their beasts save the fact that they do this service to the lord, nor is this right of common specified in the terrier, they [the jurors] are bidden to present the names of the undersettles who thus common with their beasts, and how many beasts and of what kind each of them has, in order that they may be agisted to the profit of the lord, until [other] provision be made by the council of [the lord bishop]".
[3] See Red Book of Thorney, f. 381a, for a record of the abbot of Crowland's men at Morborne being allowed to pasture their cattle in certain parts of Yaxley Fen (1216–36): "Compositio inter Abbatem Robertum Thorniensis et Abbatem Henricum Croylandensis de communa habenda pro se et hominibus suis de Moreburn in mariscis ipsius Abbatis de Thornei de Jakele et Faresheued." See also *ibid.* f. 373b, for an agreement about intercommoning in Warboys Fen.
[4] See for example P.R.O. Court Rolls (Duchy of Lanc.), 91/1252 (1462–68), for the holding of unjust drives and the making of unlawful pounds.

continued to be made, both lawfully and unlawfully. But the
span of the Middle Ages did not pass without some changes in
these matters. As early as the tenth century, if we may believe
the *Liber Eliensis*, some attempt at organised division had been
made. In the time of the first abbot, Brithnoth (970–81),
one of the monks named Leo, acting in the capacity of a
bailiff, settled the boundaries of the Isle of Ely.[1] Until this
time, says the chronicle, these limits had not been clearly
defined and had given rise to disputes. Leo called together
the neighbours concerned, and, as a result of their discussion,
the limits were settled to the satisfaction of all. They were
confirmed by King Edgar.[2] In order to make clear the
boundaries on the eastern side, he caused a ditch to be made
in the fen. This was called *Abbotesdelf*, but this name was later
changed to *Biscopesdelf*.

During the twelfth and thirteenth centuries there seems to
have been an increasing self-consciousness on the part of the

[1] *Liber Eliensis*, p. 168: "Etenim fines regionis Elge sua industria metiri
inchoavit, et tanquam munitionibus obsedit; praecavens in futurum
dolosa machinamenta, ne aut incircumcisus aut immundus quaerens
plusquam sua sunt, prave et perverse Dei servos quieti vacantes iniqua
exactione lacessando pertransiret terminos eorum, quod saepius contigisse
meminerat. Unde vocatis simul hinc et inde vicinis, utrorumque accolarum
discussa portione atque divisa, possessionum ecclesiae ad perpetuam
evidentiam, secationem fecit ipso in invio et in aquoso paludum medio,
quae vulgo usque ad hanc diem Anglice Abbotesdelf, Latine autem
Abbatis fossa sonat, ut esset tanquam firmamentum in luto aquarum, ne
quis circumpositos titulos utriusque partis temere proriperet aut con-
scenderet: sed et insulam per girum cum auctoritate regis Ædgari taxato
signavit limite, et a seculo in seculum illius statutum nequaquam valet
infringi." See pp. 14 and 44 above.

For the identification of Abbotsdelph, see Gordon Fowler, "Fenland
Waterways, Past and Present. South Level District. Part II", *Proc. Camb.
Antiq. Soc.* xxxiv, 27 (1934).

[2] *Liber Eliensis*, p. 169: "Regio autem Elge per millaria vii. in longum
extenditur, a Cotingelade viz. ad Littleport vel ad Abbotesdelf, nunc
Biscopesdelf dicitur, et iiii^or in latum a Chirchewere ad mare de
Stretham; sed terminus duorum centuriatuum, qui ad Ely ab antiquo
pertinent, amplius comprehendi noscuntur, hoc est de medietate pontis
de Tid usque ad Upwere, et de Biscopesdelf, usque ad flumen juxta
Burch quod vocatur Nen, ut in capite libri primi contexitur." See also
ibid. p. 4.

various monastic houses about their boundaries in the Fen-land.[1] How uncertain these boundaries were may be seen from the fact that, even towards the end of the thirteenth century, the boundary between the shires of Cambridge and Huntingdon ran in some of the meres just "as far as a man might reach with his barge-pole to the shore".[2] The boundary between Lincoln and Cambridge was likewise a matter of doubt.[3] In the later Middle Ages, when bounds were being more accurately established,[4] and when commons were being partitioned between their respective vills, the inevitable re-sult was much dispute. The bitterness of these disagreements serves to measure the vital position occupied by pasture rights in the economy of the Fenland.

From the northern Fenland there come a number of inter-esting examples which show how division of the fen took place. In Wildmore Fen there intercommoned the villages of the three sokes of Bolingbroke, Horncastle and Scrivelsby. During the twelfth century, contention arose between the three lord-ships "because no one of them knew what or how much pertained to his barony". A division was therefore made "between the barony of Bolingbroke and the barony of Horncastle and of Scrivelsby in the said fen, so that the men

---

[1] The twelfth-century foundation charter of Sawtry Abbey stated that, at the order of King Canute, Turkill the Dane divided the near-by fen among the neighbouring townships (between 1021 and 1039).—See (1) W. Dugdale, *Mon. Ang.* v, 522 (1825); and (2) *Ramsey Cartulary*, i, 164. See footnote 5, p. 14 above.
For reference to division in the pseudo-Ingulph, see p. 45 above, and p. 89 below.

[2] See *Ramsey Cartulary*, i, 197 *et seq.* for "Perambulatio facta de metis et bundis inter comitatus Cantebrigiae et Huntedoniae" in 1284. Another document of 1286 (*ibid.* i, 201) says: "Ita quod tota mara de Schyrmere sit in comitatu Huntedoniae, excepto tanto quo attingi possit a baculo cum uno spreto ad terram." See also Close Rolls, 14 Edward I, m. 5 d. See p. 78 below, for disputed land in Cambridgeshire or Huntingdonshire.

[3] British Museum, Harleian MSS. 742, f. 2.

[4] For dividing dikes, see *Ramsey Cartulary*, ii, 327 and 365. The latter entry mentions a dike 16 feet wide made between the marshes of Ramsey and Thorney in 1224.

of Bolingbroke might common peaceably in their part, and likewise the men of Horncastle and Scrivelsby peaceably in theirs". Eight men were appointed to make the division, one of whom was Godric of Coningsby, "the reeve of Wildmore for forty years".[1] But even after this settlement there was constant quarrelling about the pasture. Another good example of partition comes from the following century. In 1241, a division of Hauthundre fen was made "by the consent of those that had right therein"; to each village was assigned its "due proportion"; and, apparently, the fen from this time onward ceased to be held *pro indiviso*.[2] A few years later, in 1250, comes a third interesting example of division. A long document relating to common pasture in Pinchbeck, Gosberchurch and Surfleet declared that, from time out of memory, the fen had been open to all of the countryside around who wished to common in it. Afterwards "in the first habitation of the vills of Holland" (*in prima habitacione villarum hoiland*),

[1] British Museum, Additional MSS. 6118, f. 702. The eight men "tactis sacro-sanctis fecerunt purialeam in hunc modum incipientes apud Fildwerdemere distant aliquantulum de Merkne et ibidem scutum rubeum elevantes processerunt directe usque extra Newham dimittentes eam manu sinistra, et inde usque Helmerpil et Algermer et sic directe usque ad Mapull buske subtus Schirwode et quicquid erat in orientale parte pertinebat ad socam de Bullingbroke et quicquid in occidentale parte ad socam de Hornecastell et Scrivelby. Omnia ista renouata erant tempore Ranulphi Comitis Cestrie" (*ibid*. f. 706). See also P.R.O. Lincs. Assize Roll, 503. See N. Neilson, *Terrier of Fleet, Lincolnshire* (1920), p. xix.

[2] Close Rolls, 25 Henry III, m. 10d. See W. Dugdale, *Imbanking and Drayning*, p. 198: "There was a precept directed to the shireeve touching the partition of Hauthuntre fen, by the consent of those that had right therein; whereby the said King gave special command, that each town might have their due proportion thereof assigned to them: but, in the first place, that a perambulation should be made, by the oath of xii lawful and discreet knights, betwixt it and the fen, called Fenting fen.... And that so soon as the said perambulation should be thus accomplished, then to make partition of the before-mentioned fen, by the oaths of those knights, in such sort as each town might have an assignation of their particular share, to dispose and make improvement of the same, according to their own best liking."
This "Eight Hundred Fen" must have been common to eight of those villages or groups of villages (assessed at twelve carucates to the Danegeld) which were known as "hundreds" in the eleventh and twelfth centuries.

the fens were limited and separated so that the men of Pinchbeck had their fen separate to themselves as did the men of Gosberchurch and Surfleet. But the jurors pointed out that some portion of the fen had been left unenclosed; and that all the men of the said vills had continued to intercommon in this, until some thirty or twenty-four years before the date of the lawsuit.[1]

It is for the southern Fenland, however, that the material relating to these disputes is fullest. The island monasteries were constantly quarrelling with one another and with their lay neighbours about the profits and limits of their common pastures and turbaries; and their chapter-houses must have witnessed many a heated debate upon rights and wrongs "touching a marsh". The Spalding register and the Crowland chronicle, the numerous Ely documents, the cartulary of Ramsey Abbey and the Red Book of Thorney—all these contain many references to long and wearisome lawsuits. There were many disputes, for example, between the three lordships of Ely, Ramsey and Thorney in the south-western Fenland. Some time between 1133 and 1169, the bounds between some of their adjacent manors had been settled by men chosen from each lordship, with final reference to another person.[2] But early in the following century, the disputants were as violent as ever; and in their discussions the groups of intercommoning vills emerge very clearly. Thus, in 1235, in disputes between Thorney and Ely relating to Leverington, it is stated that Heyefen belonged to the manor of Wisbech and to the *villate* of Leverington, Newton, Tydd, Elm and *Welles*, and that the said vills commoned there "horn under horn with their beasts".[3] The difficulties of the time and place

---

[1] British Museum, Harleian MSS. 742, ff. 12 *et seq.*

[2] Red Book of Thorney, ff. 166 *et seq.*; 173 *et seq.* The disputed bounds lay between Thorney and the Ely manor of Wisbech on the east, and between Ramsey and the Thorney manor of Whittlesey on the west.

[3] *Ibid.* ff. 193 *et seq.* Early in the thirteenth century (1216–37) Ramsey and Thorney agreed to divide Kingsdelf Fen, and to mark the division by a ditch which was to be made half on Ramsey and half on Thorney land.—Red Book of Thorney, ff. 371–72b. See footnote 2, p. 78 below.

are well illustrated by another long dispute which began
in 1281 concerning thirty-eight hundred acres of fen to the
south. Ramsey Abbey claimed that the tenement lay in
the vill of Ramsey and so in Huntingdonshire, Thorney
claimed it as part of the vill of Whittlesey in Cambridgeshire,
and Ely likewise agreed that it lay "in many other vills
and places than in Ramsey".[1] These declarations could
only end in a compromise, and the form that the compromise might take may be illustrated from another dispute
that was going on at about the same time. The lordships of
Ramsey and Ely adjoined in the fen of Weremeremore;
the manors claiming common pasture here were the
Ramsey manors of Broughton, Bury, Raveley, Upwood,
Warboys and Wistow, and the Ely soke of Somersham
including Bluntisham, Fenton and Pidley. The record
declares that the manors intercommoned peacefully until
1270, when the *custodes* of the fen of Ely impounded the
beasts of the Ely manors in Crowlodemore. At length, agreement was reached in 1294 on a compromise whereby the
Ramsey manors were to common in Weremeremore, undis-
turbed, and the manors of the Ely soke in Crowlodemore.
The compromise was extended to include other details; the
lode or channel of Fenton was to be common to both groups,
and the abbot of Ramsey agreed to keep the lode of Needingworth shallow enough for the passage of the beasts and commoners of Ely to Holywell.[2]

To enumerate and describe all these disputes in detail
would be very tedious. For that matter, many of them must
have passed into oblivion, and anything like a complete list
would be impossible. A typical example of the sequence of

---

[1] *Ramsey Cartulary*, i, 195 *et seq.*; iii, 39. See also *Abbrevatio Placitorum*
(Record Commission, 1811), p. 223.

[2] *Ramsey Cartulary*, i, 201–8, 215 *et seq.*; ii, 320–1; iii, 57; and also
British Museum, Cott. MSS. Claud. C. xi. f. 342. The Ramsey cartulary
is full of such disputes among villages in the south-western Fenland; see
that between Ramsey and Thorney over Kingsdelf, *ibid.* i, 188; ii, 80,
364; iii, 38. See footnote 3, p. 77 above.

these disputes is provided by the affairs of the abbey of Crowland, noted below.[1]

However frequent the disputes, the fact remained that division of the intercommoning fens went on. Carried to its logical conclusion, the division could only lead to enclosure; but this was a tendency that never developed on a very large scale in the Fenland during the Middle Ages. Yet at quite an early date pieces of fen began to be enclosed with ditches and to be held in severalty by individual occupiers. As early as 1206–7, a new rental for *Welles*[2] contains some entries that are suggestive. Eel-rents for holdings are frequent: sometimes these are merely "pro clauso suo"; sometimes they are "pro quodam prato". There are also references to purprestures, and, in one instance, to the definite possibility of cultivation.[3] The phrase "de novo" repeats itself in the entries, and may or may not be significant in this connection. Here are some sample entries:[4]

De Folcardo et Simone fratre suo, pro clauso suo usque ad primam dravam, decem stikkas anguillarum.

De antiquo censu de eisdem, pro triginta acris terrae, quas habent infra primam Fendiche; et pro quodam prato, quod habent in Oxinge; et quodam prato in Hisdelfe, dimidiam marcam.

De Ailbricto Bolle, pro clauso suo, tres stikkas anguillarum de antiquo censu.

De Semanno filio Alfrici, pro clauso suo, tres stikkas anguillarum, de antiquo censu; et pro quodam prato unam stikkam de novo.

De Waltero Sole, pro quodam prato juxta pratum Semanni, unam stikkam anguillarum, de novo.

Et sciendum, quod cum praedicti homines alias purpresturas fecerint, solvent de singulis acris annuatim unum denarium.

---

[1] See Note at the end of this chapter, p. 86 below.

[2] *Ramsey Cartulary*, ii, 318–20. See also *ibid.* i, 99 for reference to rent of purprestures at *Welles*. See *ibid.* iii, 295, for "nova purpristura quinquaginta acras apud Pochedigh", between 1199 and 1216.

[3] See footnote 3, p. 50 above, for this instance.

[4] Taken from the *Ramsey Cartulary*, ii, 319–20 (1206–7).

For enclosure for pasture at Holbeach in the fifteenth century, see p. 82 below.

They speak for themselves; though it is necessary to add that *Welles* was situated upon the silt and not on the peat fen. When stressing the importance of common rights we must not forget the existence of a certain amount of enclosure on a small scale.

Examples throughout the thirteenth century confirm the impression that the practice of enclosing was frequent. Eustace, bishop of Ely from 1198 to 1215, confirmed to the prior of Ely some 280 acres of "purprestures of the fen" in Somersham, together with 1880 acres in Elm.[1] In 1230, the bishop of Ely granted out certain land in Doddington "as it is enclosed with ditches";[2] and, between 1226 and 1233, one Acelinus de Burgo received a grant of *Adelildesholm* "as Acelinus himself surrounded it with his ditch".[3] Later in the century, in 1279, the abbot of Ramsey was accused of enclosing common pasture to make a several meadow.[4] Before the end of the century, in 1294, the men of John Wake of Deeping were complaining that the prior of Spalding had enclosed tracts of the marsh of 60 or 80 acres, and had surrounded them in an unusual way with a ditch or fosse like a wall, thus keeping the commoners from their common, and so breaking the common law.[5] And in the same year, in one of the manor courts of Ramsey, there was complaint that a certain Robert Stulle had made a separate croft for himself in what had been common pasture, and for this transgression he was fined.[6] We know also, from another source, that there

---

[1] Cartulary of Ely Convent (Liber M), ff. 168–9 (Bishop's Muniment Room, Ely, G. 3).

[2] Old Coucher Book of Ely, f. 225b (Bishop's Muniment Room, Ely, G. 3).

[3] *Ramsey Cartulary*, i, 79: "Adelildesholm cum bechio et maresio sicut ipse Acelinus illud cinxit cum fossato suo." For *bechio*, see p. 84 below.

[4] British Museum, Additional Charters, No. 39595. In 1279, too, there was dispute about the appropriation of the common fen of Denton, Glatton and Holme.—*Rotuli Hundredorum*, ii, 659.

[5] British Museum, Harleian MSS. 742, ff. 13b *et seq*. See pp. 83–4 below.

[6] British Museum, Additional Charters, No. 39597.

were quite large tracts of meadow in Northee and Kingsdelf (between Whittlesey Dike and Stanground) which were enjoyed solely by the abbots of Ramsey and Thorney and certain of their tenants.[1] There are other references, too, to "nova purprestura"[2] and to the holding of fen in severalty.[3]

The practice of leasing out pieces of fen for an annual rent also became fairly general. It took place on a quite large scale at Elm;[4] and also on the Crowland manors in the early fourteenth century;[5] and at Holywell in the fifteenth century, "Haliwellefen" had its separate rental.[6] Typical of the whole practice in later times is an entry of 1456 relating to Bluntisham: "46s. 8d. for 20 acres of meadow in Chirchefen leased to divers tenants, the price per acre 2s. 4d."[7] The practice of

---

[1] *Rotuli Hundredorum*, ii, 646.

[2] There is mention in 1435–55 of "triginta acris terrae propinquioribus Trokenholt in nova purprestura".—W. Dugdale, *Mon. Ang.* ii, 610 (1819).

[3] British Museum, Additional Charters, No. 39628. See also footnote 2, p. 49 above.

One of the Ramsey references, to Warboys in 1251, runs: "Mariscus autem, dicto manerio pertinens, per has metas extenditur, videlicet...; inter quas metas dominus Abbas habet pratum separale...; in quo quidem marisco tam liberi quam villani falcant et fodiunt, praeterquam in praedicto prato separali, et in locis, quae ad falcandum roscum ballivus Abbatis ad opus domini sui annuatim elegerit."—*Ramsey Cartulary*, i, 308. At Wisbech, about 1250 also, there was a pasture towards the sea, which the Lord held in severalty, "containing about 20 acres, sometimes more, sometimes less, according as it is affected by the sea".—*Fenland Notes and Queries*, iii, 124 (1897).

[4] Cartulary of Ely Convent (Liber M), ff. 182–3, and 469 (Bishop's Muniment Room, Ely, G. 3).

[5] See M. Wretts-Smith, *art. cit.* p. 189: "Wide meadows were attached to each of the cattle farms to provide winter food and late pasturing for the herds; the surplus was let out each year for high rents. The tenants' names are not given, so their status must remain unknown; but these rents are of the greatest interest, for their high rates show not only the excellence of the meadows but the existence of married land-owners or freemen capable of paying them. The rates fluctuate, and in some cases the whole of one croft will be let for successive years at differing rents, suggesting either a change of tenants or a change in the state of the grass."

[6] P.R.O. Rentals and Surveys (Gen. Series), 8/308 (*temp.* Henry VI).

[7] P.R.O. Mins. Accts. (Bishops' Temporalities), 1136/8 (1455–57).

farming out stretches of fen became quite common during the fifteenth century, and the rent of these tracts is entered up without comment in the account rolls of the time. At Somersham, Chatteris and Holywell, leasing the meadow was a regular part of the manorial economy; and at Stanground, Yaxley and Farcet, grants were made to individuals for terms of years; while among the entries of an Holbeach Extent[1] for the years 1458–59 there are two relevant entries:

	£	s.	d.
17 acres of several pasture in divers watery places (acres per annum 6d.)	o	8	6
Also 10 acres of pasture newly enclosed lying near Snowfelde worth per annum 10s.	o	10	o

The advent of a money economy had brought many changes with it, but, important as they were, these changes did nothing to diminish the important place occupied by pastoral activity in the economic life of the Fenland.

Closely allied to pasture rights were turbary rights. Strangely enough, there is no mention of turbaries in the Domesday entries for the Fenland; but by the twelfth and thirteenth centuries the cutting and drying of turves had become one of the characteristic occupations in the region. Wood was scarce in the Fenland,[2] and turf provided a valuable substitute as fuel. It was also used by the fenmen for "the erection of their buildings, and for the repair and raising of their embankments".[3] Many of the customs and usages

[1] See G. W. Macdonald, *Historical Notices of the Parish of Holbeach* (1890), pp. 96–7.

[2] Some of the isles of the southern Fenland had woods at this time, but the Fenland as a whole was without wood. Buried trees, sometimes dug up in the peat, might have occasionally helped to provide for firing. See the woodland map in H. C. Darby, "Domesday Geography of Cambridgeshire", *Proc. Camb. Antiq. Soc.* xxxvi, 49 (1936).

[3] *Ingulph, Contin.* p. 386. In 1348, "Alan, Prior of Ely granted to Thomas Louvel the office of Constable of the castle of Wisbeach...to have [amongst other things] yearly 40,000 turves, for fire".—*Sixth Report, Commission on Historical MSS.* (1877), p. 300.

controlling the common of turbary were similar to those associated with common of pasture, and were based upon the intercommoning of neighbouring villages: indeed the two occupations were sometimes very closely connected, for the extent of the pastures and the movements of cattle were affected by activity in the turbaries. While the cutting and drying of the turves were in progress, cattle were in many cases excluded lest they should damage the stacks of turves. Digging for turf, too, was allowed only in certain parts of a fen and only at certain times of the year. As might be expected, a whole body of custom controlled the operations.[1]

The phrase defining the right of *fodicio* ran thus: "to cut, to dig, to burn, or to pare, at all times, at will, to give or to sell." In earlier times these rights may have been unrestricted; but later, as in the case of common pasture rights, restrictions appeared. Selling to outsiders was forbidden, and the commoners were allowed to take turves only for their own use. This interference naturally aroused opposition. In particular, the commoners frequently objected strongly to the custom by which the lord enclosed a section of the turf fen for the digging and drying of his own turves. One dispute between the prior of Spalding and the men of John Wake of Deeping will bring out the points involved.[2] The prior was

[1] In 1277, for instance, the jurors of Walsoken remarked: "Tota ista villata debet communare in marisco qui vocatur Wastfen cum villata de Tyrington, Walepole, Walton, et Tylneia tam fodiendo quam pascendo horn underhorne eo excepto quod nullus debet nec potest turbam dare vendere vel carriare extra predictas villas sine licentia domini episcopo et assensu et concensu aliorum percennarum predictarum villatarum."— British Museum, Cott. MSS. Claud. C. xi, f. 204b. It is also entered in the Old Coucher Book of Ely, f. 113 (Bishop's Muniment Room, Ely, G. 3).

See the Littleport Rolls, *op. cit.* p. 143: "according to the ancient custom of the said vill none shall pay more than 4d. for digging 1000 of turfs and for drying it 1½d. and 1½d. for piling it up."

[2] British Museum, Harleian MSS. 742, ff. 13b *et seq.* See Bracton's *Note-Book*, Case no. 1194, wherein a certain Robertus is described as having *dominium* in the marsh of Sykehouse and Owston, to the north of Doncaster, by which no one could dig for turves until Robertus had

accustomed, in exercising his rights of turbary, to enclose a space for the drying of his turves; around this he made some kind of hedge or ditch to keep out cattle. This practice had not gone unquestioned; but in general it had been allowed him. There was trouble ahead however. In 1294, he made complaint that the men of Deeping were removing his turves. Their reply was ready: the prior had enclosed as much as 2000 acres of the fen and had kept the tract enclosed for a number of years in an unreasonable manner. In reply, the prior asserted his long right of enclosing for turves in the common fen, and of making some protection against damage by cattle while the turves were stacked first in *musselli*, and later in great *tassi*. He claimed that his right applied everywhere in the fen, and that he should not be limited to a fixed number of acres. In 1301, he won the case but only after much discussion, and within two years the whole matter was opened up again. In the course of the dispute it was disclosed that the prior, in enclosing for turves, had left a little gap in the enclosure, and had stationed men there to let in his own cattle and to keep out the cattle of others.[1] This time the verdict went against him. That it did not always go against him the Crowland records show.[2]

The value of turbary rights made these disputes well worth while. The commoners usually measured their rights in terms of the *beschia*,[3] which was the amount of land that could be dug annually by one spade between the feast of St Philip and St James and the feast of St Peter ad Vincula (May 1st and August 1st); thus the Countess of Lincoln, in the fourteenth century, granted permission to the men of the church of first chosen his own place. Then the other commoners were allowed to choose their plots, apparently in some definite order. The proceedings were supervised by the officers of the fen, who prevented anyone from injuring the enclosure of another; if any of the disputes resulted in breaches of the peace, the fines went to the lord.

[1] British Museum, Harleian MSS. 742, f. 21 b.

[2] See below, pp. 86 *et seq.*

[3] Du Cange says: "Est autem Bescata nisi fallor tantum terre, quis ligone uno die fodere potest."—*Glossarium Mediae et Infimae Latinatis*, i, 644 (1884).

Hagnaby in Lincolnshire to carry the turves of two *bescie* to their salt-pans in Friskney or Wainfleet.[1] The custom of taking turbary sufficient for the fuel of a salt-pan was apparently well recognised.[2] In the case of the lord's own turbary, or when commercial transactions were involved, a more specifically quantitative measure was sometimes used. The lord's bailiff either leased stretches of the fen in *quarentene* of forty perches, each perch containing 20 feet, or sold the turves in *quarentene* as they lay scattered about before stacking. The profits were considerable. In the West Fen in Lincolnshire in 1296, £78 was received from 260 *quarentene* of turves sold *de remanente* at 6s. a *quarentena*; and £150. 12s. (*sic*) from 602 *quarentene* of turves sold *de exitu* at 5s. a *quarentena*; the expense of digging and drying was thus about one shilling a *quarentena*.[3] The receipts in 1304 were not as large: £57. 18s. from 193 *quarentene* of cut turves; £64. 3s. 9d. from 256¾ *quarentene* of marsh; and £9. 18s. from 11 *beschie* at farm.[4] The figures for the year of the Black Death are interesting; in 1349, 352 *quarentene* of cut turves brought in the large sum of £200. 2s.; but on the other hand no uncut turf was sold. Naturally, the returns from a turbary varied from year to year according to the state of the weather and the condition of local drainage; receipts from turbary sometimes almost disappear from the account rolls. But occasional failures did not affect the general importance of the turbary in the economy of the Fenland at a period when alternative sources of fuel were limited.

[1] P.R.O. Mins. Accts. (Duchy of Lanc.), 242/3885.—West Fen Marsh [Lincs.], 1329–82.
[2] See p. 40 above.
[3] P.R.O. Mins. Accts. (Duchy of Lanc.), 1/1—1294–96. See N. Neilson, *Terrier of Fleet, Lincolnshire* (1920), p. xiv, and pp. 175 *et seq.*
[4] P.R.O. Mins. Accts. (Duchy of Lanc.), 1/2—1303–5.

NOTE ON THE CROWLAND DISPUTES

There are rumours in the earliest Crowland records[1] of disputes in which the combatants used every act of violence against one another.[2] They "would many a time lame their cattle, oxen as well as horses, would daily impound their sheep and poultry, and frequently strike down, kill and destroy their swine and pigs".[3] We are upon surer ground in the twelfth century. In 1189, when a rumour of the death of Henry II reached the Fenland, the prior of Spalding and other lords, commoning in the marshes between Spalding and Crowland, entered into a conspiracy against the abbot of Crowland, "imagining that they could easily overcome the poor abbat of Croyland and his little house, and confiding in their own prowess and the vastness of their riches".[4] They ignored the usual proclamation of the abbot at Rogationtide

---

[1] See footnote 4, p. 43 above. For the management of the Crowland husbandry, see Miss M. Wretts-Smith, "Organization of Farming at Croyland Abbey, 1257–1321", *Journ. of Econ. and Business Hist.* iv, 168 (1932). "The Island was bounded on the north by Asendyke, on the east by the waterway called Shephee, on the south-east and south by Southee waterway, on the south-west by the River Nene and on the west by one area of the River Welland. The Welland and the Nene met at the triangular bridge of Croyland. Stone crosses were set up by the early abbots at the angles where these watercourses met....At the corners of the Island there were farms, mainly for livestock, though some of them contained enough arable land to raise small crops (pp. 169–70)....As the fen pastures were not unlimited, the size of the herds was restricted and, indeed, showed small variation. Each manor had to keep enough stock to maintain its plough-teams, and most of them carried on dairy farming. In addition, herds were kept round the Isle of Croyland, partly for profit but chiefly to supply the Abbey with beef, butter, and cheese. There were herds at Monklode, Nomansland on the south of the Island, and Aswick at the north-east in 1160, though they may not have had separate cattle farms, and these were still attached to the same pastures in 1257, when they were all three run by the overseer, Frater Henry. These herds were established at the corners of the Island, from whence they could conveniently be pastured on the fens outside and watered in the rivers and dykes" (pp. 186–7).

[2] See *Ingulph*, pp. 24–31 for a tale of conflict.

[3] *Ingulph*, p. 144.

[4] *Ingulph, Contin.* p. 276.

that the men of Holland should keep their cattle out "in order that the crop of hay might have liberty to grow". Consequently, the abbot's servants impounded the cattle found upon the fen, with the result that on May 12th the men of Holland came "to the marsh of Croyland, armed all of them, with all kinds of weapons; just as though in array for battle, and exceeding in number three thousand men". They were met by the abbot at "the embankment of the Asendyk". Fearing an attack on the monastery itself, the abbot sued for peace. The invaders pitched their tents, dug turves, cut down wood and alders, depastured upon the meadowland, and "committed other acts of violence for fifteen days, just like so many armed men in camp". In particular, "armed as they were, they proceeded through the middle of the marsh, and divided it among themselves, according to the situation of their respective vills, although located at a considerable distance around the marsh". Meanwhile, the abbot appealed to the neighbouring justices of the peace and to judges in London. After complicated negotiation and years of vexatious dispute, the case was settled in the year 1193 in favour of Crowland.[1]

But, within a short time, fresh disputes arose and "the venerable Abbot Henry" of Crowland was involved in a costly suit with the abbot of Peterborough, who had put forward a claim to the "southern marsh called Alderland". "After many conferences, discussions, delays and expenses on both sides", the abbot of Peterborough succeeded, in the year 1206, in securing rights in Alderland "to the no small detriment of the church of Croyland".[2] Likewise in the early thirteenth century, the abbot of Crowland's cattle, on the marsh of Goggisland, were impounded by Hugh Wake, lord of Deeping. This forced the abbey into yet another lawsuit, which, however, was settled at Lincoln in 1234 in favour of Crowland. About the same time, too, the abbot made an agreement with the prior of Spalding about rights of common

---

[1] *Ingulph, Contin.* p. 295.
[2] *Ingulph, Contin.* pp. 311–12.

in their respective marshes.[1] There were other successes, also; and the abbot of Peterborough was worsted[2] in 1247, and again[3] in 1260. In 1260, came another quarrel with Spalding about some common pasture lying in the fens of Baston, Crowland, Deeping, Langtoft, Pinchbeck and Spalding, to the west of the Welland; this was ended by an agreement between the rival abbots that neither would take, drive or impound the cattle of the other.[4] The times were very unsettled. Concerning the régime of Abbot Ralph (1254–81) Ingulph's Continuator wrote: "although the little bark of our house was in his times buffeted about on every side by the waves of adversity and the storms of litigation, still, it could not be made to founder."[5] Indeed, in 1278, the prior of Spalding failed to prove his claim to 100 acres of wood and 1760 acres of marsh in Moulton, Spalding and Weston; and Thomas of Moulton also failed to prove his claim to 20 acres of wood and 190 acres of marsh in Weston and 90 acres of marsh in Moulton.[6]

These differences over marsh and pasture were complicated by disputes about banks and sewers.[7] After much complica-

---

[1] *Ingulph, Contin.* pp. 319 *et seq.* "In the eighteenth year of the reign of king Henry, the before-named father Henry, abbot of Croyland, impleaded Hugh Wake, the lord of Depyng, to know by what right or title he claimed the impounding of cattle feeding in our marsh of Goggislound, which is within the boundaries of the abbey of Croyland; the same belonging both to those who have been accustomed to have common thereof, as well as to strangers who neither ought nor are wont to claim any right of common whatever in the said marsh. At last, after proposals made on both sides, and conferences held between the before-named abbot of Croyland and the said Hugh, on the morrow of Saint Luke they made a final agreement at Lincoln."
See also P.R.O. Chancery Miscellanea (C. 47), 7/5/5 (18 Edward III) which gives the tenour of the Fines of 18 and 24 Henry III. This bundle 7 also contains proceedings before Commissioners of Sewers, *temp.* Edward II–Henry VI.   [2] *Ingulph, Contin.* pp. 323 *et seq.*
[3] *V.C.H. Lincolnshire,* ii, 109 (1906).
[4] British Museum, Harleian MSS. 742, f. 10b. See also *ibid.* ff. 3b *et seq.* for some other disputes.
[5] *Ingulph, Contin.* p. 329.   [6] *V.C.H. Lincolnshire,* ii, 109 (1906).
[7] For a dispute of 1290 between Abbot Henry and Thomas Wake of Deeping, see W. Dugdale, *Imbanking and Drayning,* p. 195.

THE CROWLAND DISPUTES   89

tion, an agreement was made in 1332 between the two monasteries of Crowland and Spalding. Each was to share in some
of the spiritual advantages of the other; a monk who died
in either house was to have his absolution and requiem
celebrated in both houses.[1]

But this agreement was only with Spalding. In the same
year of 1332, Thomas Wake of Deeping prevented the bailiffs
of Crowland from holding their fair; moreover, his men
mowed rushes on the Crowland meadows at Baston, Langtoft,
Pinchbeck and Spalding and carried them away, together
with hay and turves; they stole much cattle also.[2] To the
charge of the abbot, however, Thomas Wake had a counter-
charge.[3] In the courts at Westminster, Edward III could
only inhibit both parties from injuring one another.[4] Charges
and countercharges constituted the practice of the day; and
while a case was being argued, men removed one another's
landmarks, levelled one another's trees, and set fire to one
another's turf; much of this work of destruction being done
furtively and "in the night time".[5] In 1342, Thomas Wake of
Deeping was still being troublesome.[6] And from the year 1344
came the complaint that the brethren of Crowland were
much "impoverished by men invading the manors, granges
and other places thereof against the will of the abbot and convent and keepers of the same, carrying away their goods and
driving their animals and cattle to places unknown".[7]

Under the three abbots who governed from 1378 to 1427,
Crowland was engaged upon another succession of violent
disputes "touching a marsh". In the year 1389, the commoners of Holland and Kesteven petitioned parliament for a
division between their marshes; and, accordingly, a commission was set up to see whether stone crosses or posts might

---

[1] British Museum, Additional MSS. 35296, fol. 438b.
[2] Patent Rolls, 6 Edw. III, pt. ii, m. 34d.
[3] Patent Rolls, 6 Edw. III, pt. i, m. 7d.
[4] Patent Rolls, 6 Edw. III, pt. ii, m. 23d.
[5] *Ingulph, Contin. passim.*
[6] Patent Rolls, 16 Edw. III, pt. ii, m. 34d. See p. 154 below.
[7] Patent Rolls, 18 Edw. III, pt. i, m. 26.

be placed "so that the men of both districts before-named might clearly and distinctly for the future know and recognise, by the said signs, the said metes, boundaries, and divisions".[1] Perambulation was made and the crosses erected, but the negotiations served only to breed more disputes.[2] Petitions were presented to parliament, and a long discussion followed. Abbot John of Crowland, speeding to London "with a discreet haste", and "acting with full confidence in the Lord", was enabled to triumph over his enemies.[3] But "O deceitful fortune who dost exalt us in the moment of exultation, and dost as suddenly plunge us into the abyss of sorrow!"—Abbot John died in 1392;[4] and blindness came upon his successor. Now, the men of Holland saw a chance of trespassing with impunity.[5] "With a frantic spirit and tumultuous outcries", they came armed from the vills of Moulton and Weston, in 1415, and occupied an island called "Le Purcéynt" within the bounds of the abbey. "Here, just like so many ravening dogs, they committed all sorts of excesses in their frenzy, and perpetrated many enormities in fishing, fowling, and in plundering the nets and everything else they could find; and thus continually occupying the said precinct for nearly a whole year, they would allow none of the farmers or servants of the abbat to receive any advantage whatever therefrom." The men of Spalding, too, "insultingly collected in no small multitudes with haughty and threatening

[1] *Ingulph, Contin.* p. 335. For other similar disputes and the existence of stone crosses, see footnote 5, p. 91, and p. 159 below.
[2] The men of Deeping, says Ingulph's Continuator (*ibid.* p. 338) disturbed the abbot "in his peaceable possession". They fished in "his own several piscary from Kenulphston to Brotherhouse; the nets, too, which they found there they tore to pieces". At Langtoft and Baston, "they would not permit the tenants of the abbey to dig turf and receive other advantages therefrom as they were entitled to do". Finally, they interfered with the abbot's servants who came to the market of Deeping. See p. 103 below.
[3] *Ingulph, Contin.* p. 345.
[4] *Ingulph, Contin.* p. 351. In 1393, the men of Deeping "came into the marshes with an armed force, and outrageously threw to the ground the cross called Kenulphston".
[5] *Ingulph, Contin.* pp. 366 *et seq.*

gestures", and did much damage to turf and sedge and bul-
rushes in the marsh of Goggisland. Well might the abbey
chronicler exclaim: "How long, O Lord, how long, shall the
sinners exult?" But deliverance was at hand. The conduct
of the monastery's affairs was deputed to the prior, Richard
Upton, who "manfully girded up his loins as though about to
fight with beasts". After much journeying to London, the
suit was settled to the advantage of Crowland, thanks to the
production of forged charters and documents.[1] But in 1433,
despite the award of 1415, the men of Spalding, "with great
haughtiness and abuse", were again trespassing in the marsh
of Goggisland.[2] A few years later came quarrels with the lord
of Deeping;[3] and then an expensive suit against Thomas Dacre
of Holbeach.[4] The boundaries of the marsh of Alderland, too,
disappeared and the abbot was involved in trouble with
Peterborough. In spite of the payment of large fees, this last
matter was still unsettled[5] in 1448. In 1450, there was trouble
in Baston with a lord who "went so far as to enclose the land
of the said abbot",[6] besides committing other damage. And
during this time, too, the abbey was involved in a completely
different set of disputes about banks and sewers. The monastic treasury had to meet large expenses on all sides.

[1] See footnote 4, p. 43 above.   [2] *Ingulph, Contin.* pp. 396 *et seq.*
[3] *Ingulph, Contin.* p. 398: "the cattle of all were driven away from the
marshes, and when driven as far as Depyng, were there detained; nor
were they allowed to be redeemed without a payment."
[4] *Ingulph, Contin.* pp. 404 *et seq.*: "servants of the said lord Thomas began
to take distresses in the common waste of the vill aforesaid, make attache-
ments there, and usurp many other rights, to the prejudice of the church
of Croyland."
[5] *Ingulph, Contin.* pp. 411 *et seq.*: "There is nothing so firmly fixed in the
human memory, but what it may fade away in lapse of time; hence it is
not to be wondered at that, in these days, the metes and boundaries of
our marsh of Alderlound, situate on the south-west side of the Welland,
and lying between the said marsh and the marshes of the abbat of Burgh,
and which were formerly marked out with certain crosses and signs, and
bear the names of Fyneset, Greynes, Folwardstakyng, and Southlake
(where the latter stream falls into the Welland), should have now become
decayed through lapse of time and want of repair; in consequence of
which they only afforded an obscure and confused knowledge of their
original purpose."   [6] *Ingulph, Contin.* p. 414.

Between 1470 and 1476 there was an interlude. The abbacy of John of Wisbech, who "was a truly wary man in all his doings", passed without a single lawsuit. "He enjoyed this singular and especial privilege and piece of good fortune which never fell to the lot of his predecessors. As often as any spark of litigation appeared about to be kindled, through his sagacity and the discreet moderation of his acts, he always quenched it, before it had burst into an open flame, so much so, that throughout the whole period of his pastoral duties he enjoyed perfect peace and tranquillity."[1]

Perhaps this unwarranted sense of security led the monks to elect Richard of Crowland as their next abbot. Alas, he turned out to be a scholar more interested in books than in disputes; and so, in the opinion of the abbey historian, advantage was taken of his "simple innocence and innocent simplicity". In 1484, all the powerful neighbours "arose at the same instant on all sides against this model of piety".

The men of Depyng assembled together to the number of three hundred men, and making an irruption into the marsh of Goggislound, which undoubtedly belongs to the demesne of the said monastery, seized the reeds that had been collected by the men and tenants of the monastery, and threw into the water or beat with stripes all the people they met.[2]

There were yet other disputes with the tenants of Whaplode. "These however", the scribe wrote, "are but trifling specimens of disturbances in comparison with those which... William Ramsey, abbot of Peterborough, our too near, I only wish I could say 'good', neighbour, caused with reference to the marsh of Alderlound."[3] The last instalment of the *Historia Croylandensis* is occupied with the settlement of this dispute in 1486. From that year onwards there was, apparently, but little to record. Upon all the monasteries of the fens the shadow of the Dissolution was soon to fall.[4]

[1] *Ingulph, Contin.* p. 461.   [2] *Ingulph, Contin.* p. 493.
[3] *Ingulph, Contin.* p. 494.
[4] For the remains of the abbey today, see plate 6.

CHAPTER THREE

COMMUNICATIONS

GREAT stress is frequently laid upon the inaccessibility of the Fenland during the Middle Ages.[1] Marsh is in many ways one of the most fundamental of all the physical barriers on the earth's surface. The sea can be traversed by boat; the obstructions of the land, both hill and forest, may be somehow overcome. But marsh, neither land nor water, is one of the great original barriers to movement. Of all the natural obstacles it is, writes Hilaire Belloc, "the only one wholly untraversable by unaided man".[2] And if this fact is not more generally appreciated, that is due to the comparative rarity of large stretches of marsh in Western Europe.

Despite this fact, it is probably true to say that the Fenland, during the Middle Ages, had considerable advantages over many other parts of England from the viewpoint of transport facilities. The span of years between the Conquest and the Renascence constituted a period of localism, when even the main roads of the realm were often impassable for days, sometimes for weeks, at a time. Too often, they were tracks rather than roads, tracks dangerous from the depth of their ruts, and from the quantity of mud they contained in wet seasons. In contrast to this state of affairs, the waterways of the Fenland formed commercial avenues that ran through the heart of the region, and provided outside contacts that were both varied and numerous. Not only were there waterways but, as time went on, causeways and bridges helped to redeem the inaccessible nature of fen and marsh.

FEN WATERWAYS

The rivers passing through the Fens are the Witham, the Welland, the Glen, the Nene, the Great Ouse, and the Cam, together with the smaller streams that empty over

[1] See pp. 142 et seq. below.   [2] The Road (1924), p. 14.

the borders. Upon the larger of these waterways sailed the merchant craft of medieval times, with produce from many countries. It is interesting to note the situation of certain towns in relation to the fenland streams.

River	Border Town	Estuary Town
Witham	Lincoln	Boston
Welland	Stamford	Spalding
Nene	Peterborough	Wisbech
Great Ouse	St Ives	King's Lynn
Cam	Cambridge	

Each of these ports has a full and varied history of widespread connections. The Hanse influence at Lincoln; Stourbridge Fair at Cambridge; the famous fair of St Ives—these, and other facts, stand symptomatic of relations with the wider commerce of north-western Europe. We are not concerned with these wide relations except to note their existence. This survey of the Fenland cannot take us beyond the ordinary activity to and fro between the fenland settlements themselves, which kept in touch, one with another, by the numerous streams that intersected the fens in every direction.

The streams of the southern Fenland have a complicated physical history.[1] During the early Middle Ages the waters of the Nene, the Ouse, the Cam, the Lark, the Little Ouse, and the Wissey,[2] seem to have found their way to the sea near Wisbech by complicated courses and with many meanderings. Oftentimes, the streams lost their definite channels, or broke their banks and spread "into black pools as much as two or three miles in breadth",[3] or into "deep and boggy quagmires

[1] See Gordon Fowler, "The Extinct Waterways of the Fens", *Geog. Journ.* lxxxiii, 30 (1934), for a map of the old river courses as indicated by roddons. See p. 6 above. See also Figs. 14 and 15 below.

[2] Place-name evidence, as well as the evidence of roddons, indicates that the "Wissey cannot have joined the Ouse at Hilgay, as it does now. No doubt it ran on farther westward to Wisbech or its neighbourhood and gave name to Wisbech".—E. Ekwall, *English River Names* (1928), p. 466.

[3] *Memorials of St Edmund's Abbey*, ed. by T. Arnold, i, 13 (Rolls Series, 1890).

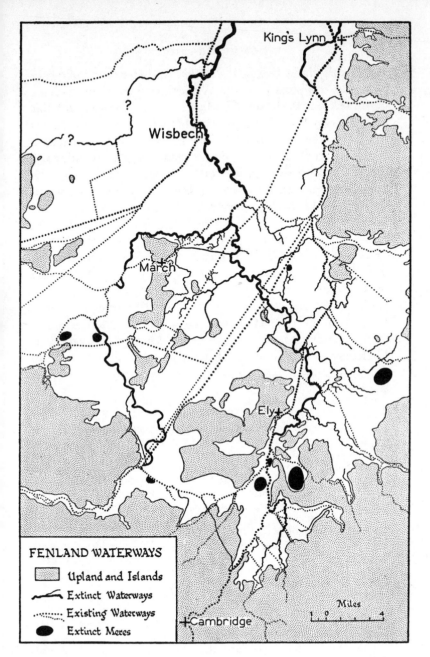

Fig. 14

Based upon (1) Gordon Fowler, "The Extinct Waterways of the Fens",
Geog. Journ. lxxxiii, 32 (1934); (2) additional information supplied
personally by Major Fowler.

The extinct waterways shown on this map are of varying date. It is
possible that a few may have been extinct by Romano-British times; on
the other hand, some were active as late as the seventeenth century.

96 COMMUNICATIONS

in breadth about two bow-shot".[1] But whatever their vag-
aries and complications, the Wisbech estuary seems to have
been the key to the drainage of the area. At Lynn, only the Nar
and the Gay, together with some other small streams, seem
to have flowed out to sea. But before the end of the thirteenth
century, certain changes had taken place which caused nearly
the whole of these fresh waters to change their courses. The
complications were far-reaching, but the cause may be stated
simply: the Wisbech estuary became choked by silt and sand
brought in and deposited by the tides. By the later decades
of the thirteenth century, part of the Nene,[2] and the western
branch of the Great Ouse, had begun to flow from Outwell
along Well Creek, and so to the sea at Lynn, by the estuary
of the Nar and the Gay.[3] To this outfall the waters of the
Little Ouse and the Wissey had, by this time, probably
been diverted also.[4] It is uncertain at what date the course
of the eastern branch of the Great Ouse was diverted at
Littleport to flow by an artificial channel towards the Lynn

[1] *Chronicon Abbatiae Ramesiensis*, ed. by W. D. Macray, p. 8 (Rolls
Series, 1886).
[2] Part of the Nene and the western branch of the Ouse joined near
Benwick; "ubi cadit Nene in Huse".—*Ramsey Cartulary*, i, 194.
[3] In the year 1293 there was mention of the damage accruing through
the alteration of the fen waters which, by this time, could not pass from
Outwell to Wisbech, whereupon King Edward I "commanded the said
commissioners, that they should forthwith go to the town of Utwelle, and
there take order, that the said fresh waters so descending that way should
have their due and antient course to the sea, as formerly...".—W. Dugdale, *Imbanking and Drayning*, p. 246, using Patent Rolls, 21 Edw. I, m. 11.
See also T. Badeslade, *The history of the ancient and present state of the
navigation of the port of King's-Lyn*...(1725), p. 18.
Sitting at Outwell, the commissioners took "into consideration what
ought to be done, for restoring these waters of Utwell (for so that great
river of Ouse, which had formerly passed that way, was then called) to
their due and ancient course".—W. Dugdale, *op. cit.* p. 300; see also p. 395.
It should be noticed that the object in this and subsequent petitions
is not to turn the eastern or Ely branch of the Ouse waters from Littleport
to Wisbech, but to preserve the southern channel of the Nene, and the
western branch of the Ouse, to Wisbech.
[4] For the changes in the course of the Little Ouse see Gordon Fowler,
"Fenland Waterways, Past and Present. South Level District. Part II",
Proc. Camb. Antiq. Soc. xxxiv, 27 (1934).

Fig. 15

This has been constructed from Fig. 14 to indicate the places
mentioned in the text

estuary.[1] But it is obvious that, as soon as the Ouse-Cam ceased to flow through Wisbech, the convenience of a more direct course from Ely to Lynn,[2] would be felt at once.

As the Wisbech outfall declined, the importance of Well Creek increased until, by the fourteenth century, it had become the great water-highway between Lynn and the Midland Counties.[3] An obstruction of "the water of the Welstreme, at the town of Welle" in the year 1301 (thus sending it to Wisbech again[4]) met with repeated opposition, later, from merchants who "were hindered from passing with their ships, boats, and other vessels, from the town of Lenne unto Yakesle, Holme, and other places lying in the counties of Huntendon

---

[1] The description of the episcopal manor of Ely about 1250, given in the Old Coucher Book of Ely (*Fenland Notes and Queries*, iii, 192), calls the course of the main river near Welney the "olde wellenhe" which suggests that it was not the only eastern channel of the Great Ouse at that time. The alteration in the river courses had apparently been made some time before that date. See (1) Old Coucher Book of Ely, f. 25 b (Bishop's Muniment Room, Ely, G. 3); and (2) British Museum, Cott. MSS. Claud. C. xi, f. 24 b.

For these changes, see Gordon Fowler, *art. cit. Proc. Camb. Antiq. Soc.* xxxiv, 20 (1934).

[2] A number of records illustrate the shipment of commodities from Cambridge and Ely down river to Lynn:

(1) About 1300 there is mention of the carriage of corn "per aquam" from Cambridge to Lynn.—*Liber Quotidianus Contrarotulatoris Garderobae* (1787), p. 130.

(2) On February 20th, 1319, safe-conduct was granted to a number of people "all of the town of Ely, men and tenants of the Bishop of Ely, going with ships laden with ale and other goods" to Lynn, Boston and elsewhere.—Patent Rolls, 12 Edw. II, pt. ii, m. 27.

(3) For the export of corn and "divers victuals" from Cambridgeshire and Huntingdonshire to the north in 1316, see Close Rolls, 10 Edw. II, m. 29 (July 30th, 1316) and Patent Rolls, 12 Edw. II, m. 23 (Sept. 28th, 1318).

[3] For the importance of the Nene in the Lynn corn trade, see N. S. B. Gras, *The Evolution of the English Corn Market* (1915), pp. 62 and 174.

In 1373, Lynn was constituted a staple port on the ground that the various streams of the counties of Warwick, Leicester, Northampton, Rutland, Bedford, Buckingham, Cambridge and Huntingdon, enabled wool and other goods to be conveyed to Lynn more easily and cheaply than to any other port.—*Rotuli Parliamentorum*, ii, 318 (n.d. Index, 1832).

[4] See T. Badeslade, *op. cit.* p. 18.

6. Crowland Abbey Church

The present parochial church is but the north aisle of the old abbey church; adjoining this, are the remains of the old nave. The upright walls are considerably off the plumb, due no doubt to the sinking of the foundations; these walls are now underpinned.

7. The island of Ely from the island of Stuntney

The two islands are separated by 1¼ miles of peat, now cultivated. In the distance stands the cathedral upon ground about 67 ft. above sea-level. The intervening ground between Ely and Stuntney ranges from sea-level to about 5 ft. above.

and Norfolk in such sort as they had formerly used to do ".[1] By 1331, jurors were prepared to swear that the course of the Nene had formerly been direct from Peterborough to Lynn, through March to Well Creek, and that there had anciently been a direct navigation from Crowland to Lynn "by which corn, wool and other commodities were carried to that haven".[2] On this occasion, juries from five counties presented that the placing of a dam in the neighbourhood of Outwell was injurious to a long-established navigation and to the safety of the fens.[3] Many "lands, meadows, pastures, and marshes" were "overflowed and drowned", and ships "were forced to go a long way about *viz.* by Old Wellenhee and Lyttleport (which in going to and fro is fifty miles and more) whereby corn, timber, wool, reed, turf, stone, and other commodities, were the dearer; and so likewise fish, herrings, and other victuals, by reason of that circuit, to the damage of the inhabitants of Norfolke cc*l.* every year".[4] The other counties were also suffering great losses, and the jurors decreed that the obstruction was to be removed. Later complaints continued to demonstrate the misfortunes of Wisbech as a seaport. Not far from Wisbech lay Walsoken, and in 1338, it was stated that "the stream of water called Wallenhee"

[1] W. Dugdale, *op. cit.* p. 301, using Patent Rolls, 17 Edw. II, pt. i, m. 6d. Boats had, in consequence of the obstruction, to turn southwards down the old course of the Ouse, by Welney, to Littleport, and thence up the main stream to Lynn. See (1) C. T. Flower, *Public Works in Medieval Law*, ii, 360 (Selden Society, 1923); (2) F. Blomefield, *History of Norfolk*, vii, 463 (1805); (3) W. Dugdale, *op. cit.* p. 301.

[2] W. Dugdale, *op. cit.* pp. 301 *et seq.*

[3] The essence of the dispute, as stated in 1329, may be summarised by saying that, about 28 years then past, Walter de Langeton, bishop of Coventry and Lichfield and treasurer to Edward I, did, "for the draining of his manor of Coldham, situate in a fenny soil, by his power and greatness, cause a dam to be made at Utwell, in the said county of Norfolk, with earth and sand, so that no navigable vessels could pass to and from Lenne, as they had wont to do"; and also that many lands were flooded. This obstruction had been continued by Edmund Peverel (son of Robert Peverel, brother of the said Walter) and Elizabeth his wife.— W. Dugdale, *op. cit.* p. 301.

[4] W. Dugdale, *op. cit.* p. 304. The dispute occupies many folios of the *Ramsey Cartulary*, iii, 121–57.

formerly running out "towards the sea, under the sea bank of Walsokne" had provided "a sufficient evacuation" for the waters of the town. But, now, since the stream had been diverted "towards Wigenhale, by Welldam; the sands were grown to that height in those chanels wherein it had formerly passed, that the waters of the said town of Walsokne could not drain any longer that way".[1] In the place of a wide estuary, a mere thread of water now trickled out to sea, leaving a wide tract of marsh between the limits of the so-called "Roman" banks.[2]

The Welland estuary was apparently suffering in the same way if not with the same consequences. An inquisition taken at Fleet, in 1395, found that

...certeine sandbancks and hills, by reason of the floweing and ebbinge of the Sea, have soe choaked and landed upp a certaine river called Spaldinge Eae, from Pegbridge unto Brotherhowse, that the water of Welland cannot have his course into the Sea, by reason whereof divers of the lands and tenements in Holland be drowned; and therefore it is requisite that the same river be repayred and made cleane by John the Prior of Spalding and the convent of the same place, which have their severall fishinges in the foresaid waters.[3]

These palliative measures might temporarily solve difficulties, but they could not alter the fact that these "stoppings" of estuaries were becoming a permanent menace in the Fenland.

However critical the effects of these changes upon the out-falls of the southern Fenland,[4] the internal waterways of the south, like those of the north,[5] continued to be thronged with traffic. From the frequent mention of boats and boat-hire it would seem that the ordinary "sewers" were the highways

[1] W. Dugdale, *op. cit.* p. 256. For other consequences of the diversion see pp. 157–8 below. [2] See footnote 4, p. 4 above.
[3] Printed in S. Wells, *Bedford Level*, ii, 6 (1830).
[4] See pp. 156–8 below.
[5] E.g. see (1) F. M. Stenton, "The Road System of Medieval England", *Econ. Hist. Rev.* vii, 20 (1936); (2) M. W. Barley, "Lincolnshire Rivers in the Middle Ages", *Lincs. Associated Architect. and Archaeol. Soc. Reports and Papers* (1938), p. 1.

from place to place.[1] We read of "ships which came through the marsh", of journeyings to and from the fenland fairs, and of the water carriage of commodities like fish, timber, metal, and stone. Indication of the convenience of water-traffic is seen in an agreement between the abbeys of Ramsey and Sawtry in 1192, by which the monks of Sawtry were to close up all the channels they had made in the marsh between Whittlesey and Ugg Mere, "except the great channel which runs from Whittlesea Mere to Sawtry, which shall remain open, for by it the monks of Sawtry bring stones and such necessaries for the building of their monastery and of their other offices".[2]

This activity was, of course, incorporated into the scheme of labour services. From the northern Fenland there comes a grant (c. 1200) of a toft, by a certain William Keal to Geoffrey the fisherman of Coningsby; in return for this, Geoffrey was to find for William a man to carry him or his men by boat as far as the fresh water of the Witham flowed (*quam longe aqua dulcis cursum suum protendit*).[3] Likewise on the manor of Wisbech, in the thirteenth century, a certain tenant "at any visit or departure of the Lord" was bound to "find a boatman as far as Somersham, Ely, Brandon, or elsewhere to the nearest manor, by fresh water, with the Lord's food".[4] And in 1277 on the manor of Wilburton, the carrying services "by land and by water", to Lynn and elsewhere, are clearly

[1] *Twelfth Report, Commission on Historical MSS., Appendix, Part viii* (1891), p. 376. For traffic on the lodes of Walton, Sawtry and Conington in 1342, see footnote 2, p. 150 below.

[2] *Ramsey Cartulary*, ii, 347. The agreement continues: "Et monachi de Saltreia habebunt unam parvam casam tantum super ipsam ladam, in qua adductores lapidum quiescere possint, cum opus fuerit, et nullam aliam casam nec domum in marisco illo facient praeter illam solam." See also i, 166 for the same agreement; and also ii, 275; iii, 223.

[3] F. M. Stenton, *Documents Illustrative of the Economic and Social History of the Danelaw* (1920), p. 358. That the Witham was navigable for fair-sized boats may be seen from an entry just one hundred years later. About the year 1300, the king and his court went from Boston to Lincoln in thirty-seven barges and boats.—*Liber Quotidianus Contrarotulatoris Garderobae* (1787), p. 60.

[4] *Fenland Notes and Queries*, iii, 129 (1897).

stated.[1] The Hundred Rolls (1283), too, note that the Bishop
of Ely had eight cottars in Horningsea who were "bound to
go on the water and carry letters from place to place when it
is necessary".[2] The tenants of the Ely and Ramsey manors,
and of other fenland manors too had to perform carriage by
water whenever grain or other supplies had to be taken to the
monks. The carriage services of some of the Ramsey tenants
show the kind of obligation involved. Here are two examples
from Chatteris:[3]

(1) Faciet etiam averagium quater per annum per aquam
usque ad Sanctum Ivonem, et Rameseiam, ad remotius, et habebit
unum panem competentem; et non computabitur pro opere, nisi
impediatur per procellam, quod non possit tempestive redire.

[1] See O. C. Pell, "On the Domesday geldable Hide", *Proc. Camb.
Antiq. Soc.* vi, 166 (1891):
"And he, [a certain Sampson] and his partners, ought to carry, yearly,
two boat loads of corn (bladi) as far as Lynn, without food, or allowance
of a work, unless they shall make delay for more than one day; and if
they shall make delay for two days, or for three days, or more, beyond the
first day, then every one of them will be quit for every other day of one
work;
"And he shall do carrying by land, and by water, short, and long; Short
to Cambridge, Willingham, Ditton, Ely, Somersham, Downham, Littleport, and such like, without food, or allowance of work, unless he shall
make delay beyond one day, as above, long as far as Lynn, Welles,
Dunnington, Benwick, Chatteris, Feltwell, Brandon, Hockwold, and the
like, without food, or allowance of work, unless he shall make delay as
above."
See also *ibid.* p. 170 for the carrying services of a certain cottar "by land,
and by water, according to the portion of his tenement".
[2] *Rotuli Hundredorum*, ii, 442. See Littleport Rolls, *op. cit.* p. 124,
for a dispute about transport: William le Meyre, boatman, refused
to carry the lord's men from outside parts whereas he could have
taken them and he contemns the lord's bailiffs. Therefore be he in
mercy (2s.) for the contempt, on the pledge of John Porteraye and John
Pexton.
[3] *Ramsey Cartulary*, i, 432. An Upwood Inquisition of 1252 gives a
glimpse of the process of the cutting, binding and carrying of rushes amid
the water of the fen: "Colliget etiam quadraginta garbas rosci in marisco,
quas, cum carecta sua, ducet ad curiam; et si profunditas marisci
ingressum carectae non permiserit, ad dictas garbas ad terram ducendas,
aysiamentum batelli Abbatis sine munere habebit."—*Ibid.* i, 346.

(2) Praeterea, excidet per annum contra Natale sex fesciculos bosci apud Hunneye, quantum unus homo potest portare singillatim, et ducet cum batello Abbatis usque ad curiam. Excidet etiam duos fesciculos ibidem virgarum vel palorum, et ducet ad curiam cum batello domini, pro uno opere, si necesse fuerit.

Commutations of carriage-services by water appear frequently as *sefare*, *sesilver*, and *seesilver*.[1]

The fourteenth-century sacrist rolls of Ely[2] show the sacrist and his fellows using the fenland waterways as their normal means of transport; whether it was to synods at Barnwell, or to buy cloth, wax, tallow, lead and other necessaries at Lynn and Boston, or merely to conduct their ordinary day-to-day business at Shippea, Quaveney, Littleport and elsewhere among the fens. The mention of boats and the payment of boat-hire (*batellagio*) are encountered again and again in their accounts. Nor does the spurious nature of Ingulph's charters impair in any way the indications provided by his Continuator under the year 1390:

> When the servants, also, of the said abbot came to the market of Depyng to purchase provisions, they beat them to the hazard of their lives, and throwing them from their boats into the water, heaped such insults and injuries upon them, that they were unable to enjoy any benefit whatever of carriage by water to the said abbey.[3]

---

[1] See N. Neilson, *Customary Rents* (1910), pp. 62–3.

[2] F. R. Chapman, *Sacrist Rolls of Ely* (1907), ii, 45, 69, 71, 94, 120, 169, 179, etc.
The treasurer's roll of 1396–97 has an entry: "Et in una batella conducta pro eisdem remigandis de Ely usque Cantebrigiam, xij*d*."— referring to the transport of two doctors of law and their clerks.—D. J. Stewart, *Architectural History of Ely Cathedral* (1868), p. 151. See also Littleport Rolls, *op. cit.* pp. 126 and 128 for disputes about the hire of a boat, etc.

[3] *Ingulph, Contin.* p. 338. Under the year 1091, in the early portion, occurs this entry: "Likewise, every person who does not hold the same freely, is bound to pay one penny, which is now called 'Rout-penny', towards the support of the men whose duty it is to carry the abbat and his people wherever he shall think fit to go by fresh water" (*Ingulph*, p. 208). Although amidst dubious surroundings, this entry is not without value, for, at any rate, it indicates conditions at the time of the forgeries. See footnote 4, p. 43 above.

There were other obstructions, also, to the free passage of ships. An example from Ramsey in the year 1434 must serve as a type of them all. Then, William Botiller placed "dammes and weres in totehil dyche" so that boats could not sail there nor the water pass as it ought.[1] This was very far from being the first complaint of its kind.

Sometimes the obstruction was due to neglect rather than to deliberate obstruction.[2] That was the case at Kyme Eau running "between Dokdyk and Brentfen, as far as the water of the Wytham"[3] in 1342. There had previously been a very convenient passage for the "ships and boats of those parts",

but in the channel thereof, mud and sedge [*paludes*] have increased to such an extent that ships cannot pass unless it be cleansed, and the banks are fallen in, so that when the water is swollen by rain, there is no adequate passage for it.

The financial solution was found in "certain specified customs on ships and boats laden with goods and merchandise passing by the said water". Frequently, in these disputes, the needs of navigation and drainage were in conflict.[4] But, in most cases, there was nothing particular or peculiar about the details of such water-traffic to ensure their survival.

To accumulate detail upon detail relating to this waterway traffic would add but little to the general point. One fact must suffice to indicate its widely spread utility. Crowland Abbey was endowed by Earl Waltheof with property at Barnack in Northamptonshire, near the edge of the fens; and from the Barnack quarries many localities derived building stone for their more prominent buildings. This famous freestone was used in the cathedrals of Peterborough, Ely and

[1] British Museum, Additional Charters, No. 39648.

[2] E.g. *Ramsey Cartulary*, i, 175: "Of the lades and trenches in Walton, Saltrey and Conington" (1342). It was presented that Monks' Lode was obstructed "through neglect of repair and by the dryness of the season". See *ibid.* ii, 325 for the injury that could be done to meadow by the lading and unlading of boats.

[3] Patent Rolls, 16 Edw. III, pt. ii, m. 16d.

[4] See *Ramsey Cartulary*, i, 174–80 for disputes in Walton, Sawtry and Conington. See also footnote 2, p. 150 below.

Lincoln, in the abbeys of Ramsey and Crowland,[1] in the churches at Boston, Spalding and Wisbech, and in many other fenland parishes as well. To places whither water transport was impossible, the difficulties of moving heavy goods which could hardly be carried on horseback must indeed have been great. They may have been laboriously drawn during summer in lightly loaded carts over rough tracks.[2] But the churches of the Fenland were more fortunate. In some of the early building accounts of Ely Cathedral, for instance, the source of the stone is mentioned thus: "1302–3, Pro petra empt. apud Bernake, 9s."[3] And a generation later, the stone for the Octagon was charged as follows:[4]

	£	s.	d.
1322–3 In diuersis petris pro nouo opere ...	29	1	8¾
In cariagio petre empt. per Simonem garcionem Vitrarii de Barnake usque aquam per terram et de aqua usque Ely	6	18	1
Item in cariagio et excisione petre empte apud Swaffham, que vocatur Pendaunt		8	9
In vadiis unius garcionis Vitrarii euntis apud Barnake per vices et existentis ibidem pro petra prouidenda ...		15	8
In hominibus conductis per vices in auxilio carectar. pro petra, calx [sic, calce?], simul et arena carianda de aqua usque Ecclesiam		7	3

Summa xxxvij*li*. xj*s*. v*d*. *ob*. *q*.

It is generally believed that the Barnack quarries were worked out towards the close of the Middle Ages,[5] but they had done

---

[1] In the *Ramsey Cartulary*, i, 192, there is an agreement that Ramsey should give 4000 eels in Lent to Peterborough in return for building stone at Barnack (1052–65). See p. 31 above.

[2] For general considerations, see J. F. Willard, "Inland Transportation in England during the Fourteenth Century", *Speculum*, i, 361 (1926).

[3] F. R. Chapman, *Sacrist Rolls of Ely* (1907), ii, 17.

[4] *Ibid*. ii, 32. See plate 1.

[5] For a discussion of the building materials of Ely Cathedral, see T. D. Atkinson, *Monastic Buildings at Ely* (1933), pp. 37 *et seq*.

good service for many centuries. And the wide distribution of their product serves as an index of the waterway traffic of the Fenland.

FEN CAUSEWAYS

Causeways constitute a link between roads and bridges. They are in fact roads over ground of such treacherous nature that they have to be built up and strengthened with stonework or timber. They thus have much in common with bridges, and, indeed, they frequently consisted of a series of bridges. Fuller's definition of them was "bridges over dirt". Through the foul and treacherous mud of the Fenland the causeways ran, making as much use as possible of the safer patches and of the islands.

The largest of the fen islands was that of Ely. The difficulty of its approach became well known in early times. Thomas of Ely, writing in the twelfth century, but referring to past times, said: "Non enim insula maris est, sed stagnorum refusionibus et paludibus inaccessa. Navigio adiri poterat sed quoniam volentibus illuc ire quondam periculosum navibus."[1] And thus surrounded "aquis magnis et paludibus", it became "velut muro forti obsita",[2] and a refuge for successive rebellions. The twelfth-century *Gesta Stephani* emphasises these points:

Est autem Eli insula delectabilis, grandis, et populosa, terra fertilis et pascuosa fœcunda, stagnis et paludibus immeabiliter undique circumcincta, nec nisi in una sui parte itineribus pervia.[3]

[1] *Liber Eliensis*, p. 4. For a discussion of this passage in the light of changes in the waterways, see Gordon Fowler, *art. cit. Proc. Camb. Antiq. Soc.* xxxiv, 23 (1934).

See also *Liber Eliensis*, p. 26, on Etheldreda's return to Ely: "Locus autem ille difficultate adeundi et arboribus hinc inde circumdatus, habens aquas collis de supercilio tenues, sed irriguas, quasi in heremo secum habitare coepit...." And p. 64: "Ipsa enim regio Elge et natura loci undique aquis et paludibus est circumdata." This latter is similar to Bede, *Historia Ecclesiastica*, iv, 19. William of Malmesbury, *De Gestis Pontificum*, p. 147, seems to repeat Thomas of Ely.

[2] *Liber Eliensis*, p. 231.

[3] *Chronicles of the Reigns of Stephen, Henry II, and Richard I*, ed. R. Howlett, iii, 62 (Rolls Series, 1886).

And in the chronicle of Richard of Devizes, Ely is said to be poisoned by its marshes—"Eliensis pagus perpetuo putidus est pro circumfusis paludibus."[1] Many later writers echo the same statement about the inaccessibility of the island.

But there were two stretches where the fen narrowed considerably—at the eastern and western ends of its southern

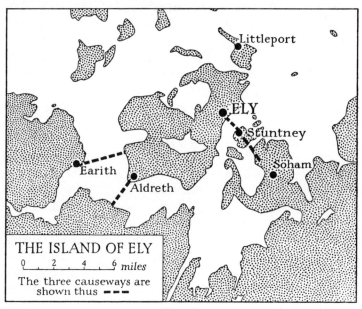

Fig. 16

shore.[2] It is possible that these two approaches were occupied during dry seasons by trackways and fords from early times. And, when causeways began to be built after the eleventh century, they were the first stretches of fen to be so crossed.

On the eastern side, near Soham, a horseshoe peninsula of Oolitic and Cretaceous rocks juts out from the upland towards Ely, the intervening fen being occupied by smaller isles

[1] *Ibid.* iii, 437.

[2] W. Dugdale, *op. cit.* p. 355, quoting the Ramsey register, writes of the Isle of Ely: "The entrances into it are these; the first at Litelport; the second at Stuntmere brigge; the third at Alderhethe brigge; and the fourth at Erith brigge."

like that of Stuntney.[1] With the coming of the twelfth century, this state of affairs was changed. Thomas of Ely concluded his account of the inaccessibility of the Isle by saying that "nunc facta via per palustre arundinetum pedibus transitur".[2] And William of Malmesbury enlarged upon the new creation: "Non enim insula tunc nisi navigio adiri poterat. Sed nostra aetas sollertior vicit naturam aggeribusque in paludem jactis, tramitem terrestrem praebuit, et insulam pedibus accessibilem fecit."[3] This was made during the time of Hervey, the first bishop of Ely (1109–31), by a certain monk named John. The *Liber Eliensis* records how: "Nam postea jussus ab ipso Episcopo, a terra de Soham coepit metiri atque arundinetum in viam sternere; alveosetiam fluminum ponticulis cinxit. Sicque ubi ille Deo dilectus in brevi proficiens opus provisum explevit, per invia paludum usque in Ely viam semitae fecit."[4] And so it remained to become a critical point in the campaigns that centred upon Ely.[5] But it was frequently in need of repair. In 1283, for example, there was a commission granted to enquire who ought to maintain the broken-down little bridges (*ponticulos*) and causeway between Soham and Stuntney.[6] The marginal heading "Custus calcet.", that occurs annually in the rolls of the Ely sacrists, shows heavy expenses incurred every year in the upkeep of the causeways of the island.[7] The words that repeat themselves are "straminando", "exaltando" and "reparando"; and the associated boats and bridges are mentioned very often.[8] The details for the year 1322–23 give an indication of the activity:[9]

---

[1] For a view across the fen from Stuntney to Ely, see plate 7.

[2] *Liber Eliensis*, p. 4.

[3] William of Malmesbury, *De Gestis Pontificum*, p. 325.

[4] H. Wharton, *Anglia Sacra*, i, 618 (1691).   [5] See p. 144 below.

[6] Patent Rolls, 12 Edw. I, m. 20d. (Dec. 11th, 1283.)

[7] The sacrist's responsibility for the care of causeways and bridges on the Stuntney road grew out of the assignment by Bishop Northwold, in the thirteenth century, of a portion of the rectory of Wentworth for the purpose. See F. R. Chapman, *Sacrist Rolls of Ely* (1907), i, 61 and 112.

[8] See F. R. Chapman, *ibid.*, *passim*, for the yearly entries.

[9] *Ibid.* ii, 27. This entry does not mention the wood (*meremium*) that was frequently bought for repairs—see *ibid.* ii, 82, etc.

	£	s.	d.
In diuersis bordis empt. pro pontibus calceti re- parandis		10	2
In leschis empt. pro calcetis de Stunteneye et Soham straminand.	4	3	7½
In stipend. diuers. operar. pro dict. calcetis exaltandis straminand. et reparand. per dietum	2	12	2½
In stipend. carpentariorum operantium super gurgites calcetorum per vices ad mensam Dni		11	4½
In vno stapulo de ferro pro magno ponte			1½
In j serrura pro eodem			2½
In vna vetere nave cum iij veteribus batellis empt. pro calcet.		3	11

Summa vjjj*li*. xi*s*. xi*d*. *ob*. [*sic*].

Entries like this continued to be made throughout the years that follow. Considerable damage was done sometimes by wind and rain and floods, and the sacrist's roll of 1339–40 gives an account of the charges incurred in building what seems to have been an entirely new bridge.[1] In any case, the "calcetum de Stuntney" seems to have gone on fulfilling its important function. As late as 1494–95, comes one entry for the carting of ballast:

In stipendio diversorum hominum conductorum ad cariandum argillam cum carectis suis a le gravelpitte usque altam pontem pro calceto de Soham in grosso, xxviii*s*.[2]

The causeway not only enabled the monks to reach easily their great grange at Stuntney, but it was an important link in the maintenance of communications with the outside world.

On the western edge of the island, there were two contacts with the mainland—at Aldreth, and across to Earith. The Aldreth Causeway, tradition has insisted, was built by William the Conqueror. The Hereward legend, as preserved

[1] F. R. Chapman, *Sacrist Rolls of Ely* (1907), ii, 91.
[2] D. J. Stewart, *Architectural History of Ely Cathedral* (1868), p. 155. See also pp. 180–5.

by the thirteenth-century *De Gestis Herwardi*[1] and in the twelfth-century *Liber Eliensis*, certainly refers to *Alrehethe* as the place of William's attack. But the topography is confused[2] and the facts may possibly be open to other interpretations.[3] Some of the Ely chronicles declare the causeway to have been laid down in the time of Bishop Hervey (1109–31): "Eo sedente strata est illa via Etheldredae quae vulgo vocatur S. Audreyes causeye."[4] But this, of course, may just imply a rebuilding. All we can say is that during the anarchy of Stephen's reign, when the Isle once more became a fortress, there was much activity around the fort of *Alherede* (or *Alrehede*).[5]

From a later decade of the same century (1177–89) comes a release by the bishop of Ely of the men of Ramsey Abbey from certain works, in return for an annual payment:

> Noverit universitas, quod nos et conventus Eliensis exegimus ab hominibus Abbatis Ramesiae in Chateris, infra libertatem Sanctae Etheldredae et nostram, et in hundredo nostro de Wicheforde manentibus, operationem quandam ab eis ex antiquo debitam, in portione quae eis competebat, in calceta de Alrehedam, sicut homines nostri, procedentes, et testificantes operationem illam deberi a praedictis hominibus, dicebant.[6]

And, between 1225–28, confirmation of this was made by Prior Richard of Ely.[7] Only a few years after this, comes a

---

[1] Printed at the end of *Fenland Notes and Queries*, vol. iii (1897).

[2] The *Liber Eliensis*, p. 229, says: "ad Alrehethe, ubi aquae insulae minus latae sunt,...tamen ad spatium quatuor stadiorum earum illic extenditur latitudo." The *De Gestis Herwardi*, p. 44, says: "minus aquis et palude praecingitur: tantum latitudo ubi quatuor stadiorum extenditur." This can hardly be right.—See *Fenland Notes and Queries*, vol. iii (1897).

[3] See (1) T. C. Lethbridge, "An Attempt to discover the Site of the Battle of Aldreth", *Proc. Camb. Antiq. Soc.* xxxi, 155 (1931); (2) *ibid.* xxxiv, 90–2 (1934).

[4] British Museum, Vesp. MSS. B. xv. f. 51; noted in D. J. Stewart, *Architectural History of Ely Cathedral* (1868), p. 159. This is a late popular etymology. Aldreth = "the landing place by the alders".

[5] See H. Wharton, *Anglia Sacra*, i, 620 *et seq.* (1691).

[6] *Ramsey Cartulary*, ii, 187–8.

[7] *Ibid.* ii, 188–9.

8. Church of Walsoken All Saints

The western tower, the nave and the chancel are pure Norman of the late period, built in the first half of the twelfth century. The lofty clerestory is late Perpendicular in style; there were also subsequent modifications.

9. Church of Terrington St Clement

It is conjectured that the original building was begun by Edmund Gonville in 1342. This was later completed and cased with Perpendicular work so as to look from the outside a perfect fifteenth-century church. The tower stands detached from the rest of the church.

reference to the contribution of some men at Chatteris towards *pontem de Alderhithe*.[1]

Some of the bad practices of the thirteenth century are shown clearly by the Hundred Rolls. The bishop of Ely, instead of keeping in repair the bridge and causeway, left it broken-down for sixteen years, and established a ferry at which he took toll of a halfpenny from every horseman and a farthing from every foot-passenger, his receipts being so large that he sometimes let the ferry at farm for as much as 20s. a year.[2] That it was left "dissoluta" at other times, too, we may infer from a reference, in 1421, to the broken and decayed state of several causeways between Ely and Soham, Ely and Littleport, and Haddenham and Willingham.[3]

The other western approach, from Earith, seems also to have provoked attention from time to time during the late Middle Ages. There are several references to the bridge of Earith in mid-thirteenth-century inquisitions concerning boundaries between Cambridge and Huntingdon.[4] In 1346,

[1] *Ramsey Cartulary*, i, 437: "Omnes praedicti dant per annum duos solidos ad Hokeday ad pontem de Alderhithe, et duos solidos pro secta hundredi, ad festum Sancti Michaelis; et nihilominus faciunt injuste."
For later compositions involving the causeway (1294 and 1339), see *ibid.* i, 217; and iii, 59. For the upkeep of a length of the causeway in 1251, see W. M. Palmer, *Proc. Camb. Antiq. Soc.* xxxvi, 88–9 (1936). Other Ely villages paid *briggebot*—see N. Neilson, *Customary Rents* (1910), p. 140.
[2] *Rotuli Hundredorum*, ii, 441: "Dicunt quod calceta et pons de Alderhethe est regalis via et fuit fracta et dissoluta jam per sexdecim annos elapsos et debet reparari per Episcopum Eliens' et per tenentes suos."
[3] Patent Rolls,8 Hen. V, pt. i, m. 32d. For a mention of the bridge in the Ely sacrist rolls of 1419–20 and 1426–27, see D. J. Stewart, *op. cit.* p. 183.
See C. H. Evelyn White, "The Aldreth Causeway, its Bridge and Surroundings", *Proc. Cambs. and Hunts. Arch. Soc.* i, 12 (1904).
[4] *Ramsey Cartulary*, i, 195, 201, 210; iii, 40. See also *V.C.H. Huntingdonshire*, ii, 153 (1932).
I am indebted to Mr C. F. Tebbutt for giving me the following reference, dated 1286, in Assize Rolls, Hunts. no. 345: "Jury present that the bridge of Ereheth and Causey of Ereheth, for want of repairs by Hugh de Balsham late Bishop of Ely, is now so old and broken that men, horses and footmen who were accustomed to cross, and also carts, cannot now go; and therefore they order the Sheriff to repair the bridge and causey at the cost of the executors of the said Bishop." The Assize Rolls are in the Norris Library at St Ives.

the country folk around complained to parliament that the bridge, which had been used from ancient times, was in complete decay. A commission was issued to William Moyne and others to make an enquiry and to compel those liable to carry out the necessary repairs.[1] Subsequently, at any rate, the causeway over Haddenham Fen was looked after by hermits. The Church indeed regarded the work of maintenance as an act of piety, and indulgences were granted in 1397 to Richard de Grymston, a poor hermit, and in 1401 to Henry Bourne, for the repair of Earith Causeway.[2] In 1455, a carpenter was paid for repairing the roadway of the Great Bridge of Earith which probably indicates that it was of timber.[3] And before the close of the century, in 1491, there is record of the "profession" of J. Thomson,[4] hermit of Earith Causeway.

Later evidence indicates that the causeways of Earith and Aldreth were maintained by the bishops of Ely "by right of sundry great manors belonging to the see".[5] During the long vacancy of the see, however, in Elizabeth's reign they were repaired by the Crown; and, later, when the bishop surrendered several of the manors of the see to the Crown, the Crown grantee became liable. But when the question of liability was raised[6] about the year 1638, the Aldreth Bridge over the Ouse had been down for about 25 years, and on the spot there was being maintained a very unsatisfactory ferry.

---

[1] Patent Rolls, Sept. 16th, 1346, 20 Edw. III, m. 1d.
[2] A. Gibbons, *Ely Episcopal Records* (1891), p. 401. The profits from the manor of Earith sprang from its fishery and ferry (i.e. the road to Cambridge, via Over).—*Rotuli Hundredorum*, ii, 606.
[3] P.R.O. Mins. Accts. (Bishops' Temporalities), 1136/7 (1454–56).
[4] A. Gibbons, *op. cit.* p. 414.
[5] *V.C.H. Huntingdonshire*, ii, 154 (1932).
[6] S.P. Dom. Chas. I, ccccvi, 44 (1638?). "About 25 years ago the high bridge over the Ouse fell down, and no new bridge having been built, a ferry is kept, in the right of the said Earl [of Arundel], who exacts ferriage, to the great loss of his Majesty's subjects, some six or seven having lost their lives there, and the great market at Audry for fat cattle being thereby quite decayed, to the particular damage of the bishop of Ely, and the impoverishment of the tenants of the bishop, and the dean and chapter, and all others."

Earith Bridge seems to have been still in existence in 1637.[1]

The monk of Peterborough, who wrote about 1150, ascribed three causeways to the Isle of Ely, presumably those of Earith, Stuntney and Aldreth, and he also referred to other places, where the monks of Ramsey, Thorney, Crowland and many others lived, "to which there is no access but by water, except to Ramsey where, on one side, a causeway has been built with much labour".[2] The Ramsey chronicle, compiled probably before the end of the twelfth century, enlarges upon this road:

Attamen ne adjacentem materiam omnino intactam praetergrediamur, locum illum a parte occidentali (nam alias palustria loco humanis gressibus haud pervia longius praetenduntur) a tellure solidiori duobus fere balistae jactibus interjacentes luteae salebrae dirimunt. Qui locus olim segni tantummodo amne naves serena advectas aura placido jocundi marginis excipiens gremio, nunc, gravi labore et sumptu, lignorum arenae pariter et lapidum congerie lutosa obstructa abysso, via publica vel calle solido in eadem parte pedibus aditur.[3]

And the cartulary of the Abbey makes frequent reference to carts, carters, and cart-horses, and to loads of hay,[4] some of which presumably reached the island over the causeway.

Despite its situation on a peninsula of gravel, Crowland, wrote William of Malmesbury, early in the twelfth century, was accessible only by water:

Croland est una insularum jacentium in illo tractu orientalium stagnorum, quae a meditullio terrae orientia, et per centum et eo

---

[1] S. Wells, *Bedford Level*, ii, 271 (1830).

[2] "Historiae Coenobii Burgensis", p. 2, in *Historiae Anglicanae Scriptores Varii*, ed. by J. Sparke (1723). Hugo added: "Ely is an island in the same district, seven miles long and as many broad, containing twenty-two vills: it is surrounded on all sides by marsh and water, but is distinguished by the possession of three bridges."

[3] *Chronicon Abbatiae Ramesiensis*, ed. W. D. Macray (Rolls Series, 1886), p. 7.

[4] *Ramsey Cartulary, passim.*

amplius milia fluentia, in mare cum multis et magnis fluminibus
impetu suo praecipitantur.... Quamvis enim locus, nisi per aquam,
nusquam adiri possit, tamen ante portam monasterii publicus, ut
ita dicam, praeternavigantium trames habetur.[1]

By the end of the Middle Ages it was being said that "all the
carts that go to Crowland are shod with silver",[2] for indeed
they had not wheels but keels. Thorney likewise was remote:
"insula inclusorum vel solitoriorum. Non enim venitur illuc
nisi navigio ex una parte, ita palude conclusa est."[3] And so
it remained. About the time of the drainage, it was still "a
place inaccessible in winter-time".[4] But there were many
districts still more inaccessible; diverse petty isles or, as the
Ramsey Cartulary put it, "remotas partes".[5] For some
months of the year, at any rate, they could be reached only by
boat.[6]

In the northern Fenland, the construction and maintenance
of roads and causeways and bridges had long been a source
of strife. Their repair, like that of banks and sewers, was
usually associated with the size of a holding or tenement; and,
in their case, too, liability was frequently divided among a

---

[1] *De Gestis Pontificum*, p. 321. It is interesting to note that Ingulph
has a comment on the weather of 1085: "the winter came on with more
severity than usual; on which, all the waters around us were frozen
with hard ice, and the entire passage for vessels was for some days cut off;
but still, the ice was not so strong or so thick as to suffice for the support
of vehicles or waggons for the carriage of any necessaries to the monastery,
though it was so hard and thick that all navigation was entirely put an
end to." The danger of famine was relieved by a miraculous supply of
food!—*Ingulph, op. cit.* p. 191. Neither the story itself nor its dubious
setting alter the geographical possibilities as they appeared to later eyes.
See footnote 4, p. 43 above.

[2] T. Fuller, *Worthies of England* (1662), p. 152. Crowland is "in a
Morasse and Fenny ground, so that an horse can hardly come to it.
But, whether this place since the draining of the Fenns, hath acquired
more firmnesse than formerly, is to me unknown."

[3] Thomas Sprott, *Chronica*, ed. T. Hearne (1719), p. 172.

[4] S.P. Dom, Chas. I, ccccix, 170 (Jan. 21st, 1638–39).

[5] *Ramsey Cartulary*, i, 458.

[6] *Ibid.* i, 430.

number of people.[1] Sometimes, the causeways were maintained by religious houses who had land granted to them for this purpose. Too frequently, the conditions of maintenance were not clear, while the difficulties of maintenance were always great. In 1263, Northdyke Causeway was reported to be in such a bad state that, every year, several people were drowned whilst travelling upon it. On one occasion "it happened that two men carrying a corpse from Stickeney to Cibecey, to be buried in the church yard there, drowned it on North dyke causey".[2] And all this took place despite the fact that the abbey of Revesby had 120 acres of land worth £6 a year with which to repair the causeway for ever. This particular causeway was one of a chain—Long Causeway, Hilldyke Causeway and Northdyke Causeway, and from them another causeway branched off towards Wainfleet. In 1359, various complaints were made to the king that "a certain causey called Hildyke, which is the king's highway from Boston towards the river Humber, and divers banks in the town of Sibceye", were "so ruinous and broken that the men of those parts suffered much damage"; and an enquiry was instituted into those responsible for the repair.[3] Later in the century, in 1383, the "common road called Hill Dyke" was still liable to flooding.[4]

---

[1] For example, in the Michaelmas term, 1375, the jurors of Elloe present that "a bridge in Gedney called Normanbrygge is broken and ought to be repaired by that township: that the king's road there called Chalunarlake ought to be repaired by the said township: that the king's road in Fleet close by called Spittillake ought to be repaired by the township of Fleet: and that the king's road in Holbeach and Whaplode called Satirdaydyke and Goldynges ought to be repaired by the said townships."—C. T. Flower, *Public Works in Medieval Law* (1915), i, 274, using P.R.O. Ancient Indictments (K.B. 9), File 59, m. 44.

For another example, see Littleport Rolls, *op. cit.* p. 132, where, in 1320, the jurors declared that "Thomas Thame the chaplain has not repaired his portion on the road, to wit, 4 perches, to the nuisance of all that pass thereby".

For rates levied to build a certain causeway around Wisbech, in 1340, see pp. 160–61 below.   [2] W. Dugdale, *op. cit.* p. 219.

[3] Patent Rolls, 32 Edw. III, pt. ii, m. 16d. See W. Dugdale, *op. cit.* p. 157.   [4] See C. T. Flower, *op. cit.* i, 280.

To the south of Boston, another causeway started near Skirbeck, and continued probably to Sutterton where it swerved to the right towards Bicker and Donnington to avoid the estuary of Bicker Haven.[1] At Donnington, this causeway joined the Holland Causeway which came from Spalding to Donington through Gosberton, and extended to Bridge End, where the Convent of St Saviour stood. It was an important line, and there was much mention of it. One occasion was in 1295, when,

upon an inquisition taken at Gosberchirche, within this province of Holland, on Friday in Whitson week, before Adam de Croke-dayk and William Inge; it was found, that all the landholders within Donynton, in this province, ought, according to the proportion of what they held, to repair and maintain the causey of Holand, with little bridges; and likewise ditches on each side thereof, from the said town of Donyngton to the new ditch. And that the Prior of S. Saviour's ought to repair and maintain the same, in manner as aforesaid, from the said ditch to the town of S. Saviour's; in regard that the said Prior had lands in that town worth xx.l a year for the repair thereof. And it was then presented by the said jurors, that there were very many defects at that time in the same causey, for default of its repair by the said Prior and inhabitants of Donington; and most of all for want of bridges, which had been carried away on each side of that new ditch.[2]

The St Saviour section contained no less than thirty bridges, each 10 feet broad and 8 feet high; and it was wide enough for two carts to meet and pass. In the Trinity term of 1331, thirteen of the bridges were presented to be out of repair.[3] This was far from being the second time that complaint had been made, nor could the prior of St Saviour escape his obligations.

Another very interesting set of disputes comes from the country still farther south—between Spalding and Crowland.

[1] It is interesting to note that, in 1295, the river of Bicker "was not then so deep as it had used to be...." (W. Dugdale, *op. cit.* p. 225.)

[2] W. Dugdale, *op. cit.* p. 224.

[3] See (1) P.R.O. Placita Coram Rege (K.B. 27), Mich. term, 5 Edw. III, m. 58; (2) Close Rolls, 7 Edw. III, pt. i, m. 24. See also (3) C. T. Flower, *op. cit.* i, 308; (4) W. Dugdale, *op. cit.* p. 234.

In a petition to parliament, in 1337, the men of Holland and Kesteven stated that the ways between Crowland and Spalding were in a very dangerous condition and that this could be remedied if the abbot would make a causeway on his soil between Crowland and one of his manors called Brotherhouse —on the understanding, of course, that he and his successors should take tolls for its construction and maintenance.[1] Negotiations with the abbot followed, but he pointed out that

...between the great bridge at Croyland and le Brotherhous, where the dangerous part of the way is, there are three leagues (*leuce*) of marshy land along the bank of the Weland, on which it would be difficult to make a causey, inasmuch as, the land lying deep in a morass, the causey would have to be by the sand bank and, since the bank is liable to be flooded in winter, the land whereon it would be made is at such times greatly loosened, as well by the passing of sailors and boatmen as by the forces of the wind, and falls away to such an extent that any causey on it would be destroyed, unless deep and high and well protected; that for the convenience of the people of those parts there would also have to be several bridges over the river Weland both at Croyland and across the causey, which must be built at great cost to be high enough for laden ships and boats to pass under them, and strong enough for carts to pass over them.[2]

Nor could the prospect of double tolls "in time of flood and wind" raise any enthusiasm, and the matter seems to have passed into the limbo of forgotten projects. But the complaints continued. One complaint of 1350 stated that the king's road from Spalding to Brotherhouse, wide enough for horses, carts and cattle, ought to be repaired; and that bridges ought to be made over the trenches therein between Brotherhouse and Crowland by the abbot and township of Crowland, "so that the passage of travellers might not be injured". But the ingenuous abbot was equal to the emergency, and replied that there was no king's road from Brother-

[1] Patent Rolls, 10 Edw. III, pt. ii, m. 8. See W. Dugdale, *op. cit.* pp. 212–13.
[2] Patent Rolls, 11 Edw. III, pt. i, m. 8d.

house to Crowland except by the river Welland for persons travelling by ships or boats.[1]

The construction and repair of causeways were intimately bound up with the drainage of the country and with the navigation upon its waters. Quarrels, in which all these different interests were mixed up in various ways, became inevitable. The details are overwhelmingly abundant, but enough has been said to illustrate the part played by causeways in the life of the Fenland. Despite their many deficiencies and their frequent lack of repair, these causeways often did provide, both for merchants and for pilgrims, a dry, as well as a safe, crossing over many a difficult stretch of country.

[1] P.R.O. Placita Coram Rege (K.B. 27), Hil. term, 24 Edw. III, m. 34. See (1) C. T. Flower, *op. cit.* i, 310; (2) W. Dugdale, *op. cit.* p. 214. Brotherhouse is about 5 miles south of Spalding.

But the monks of Crowland were not oblivious to the advantages of causeways. The dubious Ingulph under the year 1048 describes the origin of Deeping Causeway: "Egelric, a monk of Burgh, was at this time made bishop of Durham, through the influence of earl Godwin. After he had obtained this bishopric, and had collected infinite sums of money, he caused a solid highway for travellers to be made through the middle of most dense forests and the extremely deep marshes of Depyng as far as Spalding, constructed of timber and sand—a most costly work, and one of the greatest utility. This road up to this day bears, and as long as it shall last, will continue to bear, the name of 'Elricherode' derived from Egelric, its maker. For this work all the Gervii, and the people of Mid Anglia, and all the Saxons lavished blessings upon him; while the people of the diocese of Durham greatly censured him."—*Ingulph*, pp. 129–30.

CHAPTER FOUR

THE CHANGING PROSPERITY OF
THE FENLAND

A GRAPHIC picture has often been drawn of the social consequences of the economy of the Fenland.[1] It is a picture of a people "composed of scattered units whose daily life was such that individual action rather than organised effort was customary".[2] This individualism fostered a peculiar exclusiveness which made the fenmen a race apart. "Each family became virtually an economic unit capable of supporting itself."[2] And these qualities, in turn, developed peculiar political sympathies and social tendencies. One writer has declared:

Famine could never be known for the land literally overflowed with food, and as a consequence the people degenerated into a thriftless race, whose only strong passion was a love of freedom.[3]

As a result of which another writer has noted, "they have always been distinguished for their sturdy independence and hatred of foreigners".[4] "Half-savage", was Macaulay's epithet.[5]

But the picture of a roving and lawless existence, drawn by these and other writers, contains many elements of paradox. It is true that there were certain physical circumstances which invited or provoked certain human responses. The argument may sound attractive—the fens, water, fishing, boats and, if one is rash enough, semi-nomadism and freedom, differentiation and aloofness, and, finally, even rebellion. The spirit of the marshland is the spirit of freedom, we are told. But how full of illusions is this argument. These hasty deductions

[1] See, for example, E. Semple, *Influences of Geographic Environment* (1911), p. 372; H. Belloc, *Hills and the Sea* (1930), p. 62; M. R. Lambert and R. Walker, *Boston, Tattershall and Croyland* (1930), p. 7.

[2] J. Bygott, *Eastern England* (1923), pp. 142-4.

[3] S. B. J. Skertchly, *The Geology of the Fenland* (1877), p. 17.

[4] C. Marlowe, *Legends of the Fenland People* (1926), p. xi. See also W. Camden, *Britannia* (1637 edition), p. 491.

[5] See p. 42 above.

find little support in historical record. The fenlanders are described as individualistic but, as we have repeatedly seen, it is clear that they were far from lacking in co-operative enterprise.[1] The complicated division of fisheries, even to one-eighth of a night; the minute regulations controlling the utilisation of turbaries and other resources of the marsh; the remarkable development of common pasture rights, and the intercommoning of neighbouring villages; the detailed and divided responsibilities for the maintenance of banks and sewers—as examples of communal effort, these compare with anything in the rest of medieval England. The marsh men are called lazy; but their unceasing struggle against the floods of both land and sea, and the difficulties they encountered in their early efforts at reclamation, are not unworthy of an epic story in the vein of Schiller:

> And many a bitter day they toiled to clear
> The woodland with its wide entangled roots.[2]

In the Fenland, however, the obstacle was not wood but marsh with its treacherous surface and complicated watercourses.

DOMESDAY STATISTICS

Even as early as the eleventh century the Domesday entries bear out an impression of steady and well-ordered industry, and point to a varied and general activity carried on within the framework of the manorial system. The settlements of Whittlesey and West Walton, very normal communities within the peat and silt areas respectively, will serve to indicate this activity. The entries relating to Whittlesey[3] were two:

(1) Manor. In *Witesie* the Church of Ely holds 2 hides. There is land for 4 ploughs and a half. In demesne there is one hide, and there is one plough and a half. There are 8 villeins and 4 cottars with 3 ploughs. There are 3 serfs; meadow for one plough; pasture for the cattle of the village; 2 shillings from a weir. It is worth 4 pounds; when received 3 pounds; T.R.E. 100 shillings. This manor lies, and always lay, in the demesne farm of the Church of Ely.

---

[1] See chapter ii above.   [2] *Wilhelm Tell*, ii, ii, 1241–42.
[3] D.B. i, 191b and 192b. Whittlesey was situated on an "island" of gravel and clay, surrounded by peat fen.

(2) The Abbot of Thorney holds 4 hides in *Witesie*. There is land for 6 ploughs. In demesne there are two hides, and there are two ploughs; and 16 villeins with 8 acres each, and six cottars with 4 ploughs. There is one serf; meadow for six ploughs; pasture for the cattle of the village; 4 shillings from a weir, and besides this, 20 shillings from fish. In all, it is worth 6 pounds; when received 20 shillings. T.R.E. 7 pounds. The manor lay and lies in the demesne of the Church of Thorney, but the Abbot of Ely has the soke.

West Walton, on the silt lands, had four entries:[1]

(1) *Waltuna* was held by Toche a freeman T.R.E. Now St Peter holds (it as) 4 ploughlands; then as now 9 villeins. Then 63 bordars, now 66. Then 14 serfs, now 8, and 100 acres of meadow. Then 6 ploughs on the demesne; afterwards none, now 5; then as now 6 ploughs belonging to the men. Then 1½ saltpans, now 7. Then 14 rounceys, now 8. Then 36 mares, now none. Then 24 animals, now 23. Then 100 swine, now 114. Then 700 sheep, now 800. To this manor belong 6 sokemen, 1 ploughland and 10 acres (of land), and 30 acres of meadow; then as now 17 bordars, and 3½ ploughs and 7 saltpans. The whole is worth 17 pounds and 10 shillings. The whole is 4 leagues in length and 2 furlongs in breadth, whosoever may hold there, and pays 2 shillings in a geld of 20 shillings. This is of the fee of F(r)ederic.

(2) *Waltuna* was held by St Etheldreda T.R.E. for 4 ploughlands. Then as now (there are) 20 villeins (and) 40 bordars. Then 17 serfs, now 13, 100 acres of meadow, 1 fishery. Then as now 5 ploughs on the demesne and 3 ploughs belonging to the men. Then 22 saltpans, now 24. Then as now 6 rounceys. Then 18 animals, now 16. Then 22 swine, now 23. Then as now 1300 sheep. To this manor belong 47 acres of land in *Esingatuna* (Islington) which now as then are held by 2 villeins. And 7 sokemen with one ploughland, and 11 bordars and 3 serfs. Then as now 2 ploughs. Now as then it is worth 15 pounds.

(3) In *Waltuna* Bunde a freemen held 1 ploughland T.R.E. Now Odar holds it. And (there are) 4 villeins and 8 bordars and 4 acres of meadow. Then as now (there was) 1 plough on the demesne, and 1 plough belonging to the men, and 1 freeman with 8 acres of land, and it is worth 20 shillings.

(4) In *Waltuna* 3 freemen (had) 91 acres which Bordin holds. Then as now (there were) 9 bordars and 12 acres of meadow. Then (there were) 1½ ploughs, now 1. It is worth 9 shillings and

[1] D.B. i, 160–160b, 213, 226 and 274b.

4 pence. And in this (his predecessor had nothing) but the commendation. Half a church (holds) 15 acres, and is worth 2 shillings.

These are representative villages, and the facts speak for themselves. But, on the other hand, ordered utilisation must not be taken to imply great wealth. The sparse distribution of Domesday villages (Fig. 3) suggests that the Fenland was an area of comparative poverty in the eleventh century. This suggestion is supported by an analysis of the Domesday statistics relating to the fenland counties. Two sets of data throw considerable light on the relative prosperity of Fenland and upland in 1086. On the accompanying maps of Cambridgeshire, averages have been plotted out per thousand acres for a number of units.[1] The greater number of these units are the old hundreds of the county, but, along the margins of the Fenland, the hundreds have been abandoned, and new groupings have been made in order to give a closer picture of reality, undistorted by fictitious averages.

Fig. 17 shows the distribution of the recorded population. But the survey was not intended to be a census of population. There may have been many people who, for one reason or another, were not enumerated; and, on the other hand, it may be possible that some people were recorded more than once in different connections. Yet we can assume that, as far as the agricultural population was concerned, these figures do provide a clue to the relative importance of the different units. Nor need these ratios involve us in a discussion about the actual population.

Fig. 18, showing the distribution of plough-teams, must reflect even more clearly the variation in agricultural activity, and in their general implications the two distributions confirm one another. The striking feature of both is the great difference between the upland and the Fenland. Here is no vague generalisation about the comparative values of fen and upland, but definite statistical evidence. Significantly enough,

[1] See H. C. Darby, "The Domesday Geography of Cambridgeshire", *Proc. Camb. Antiq. Soc.* xxxvi, 35 (1936).

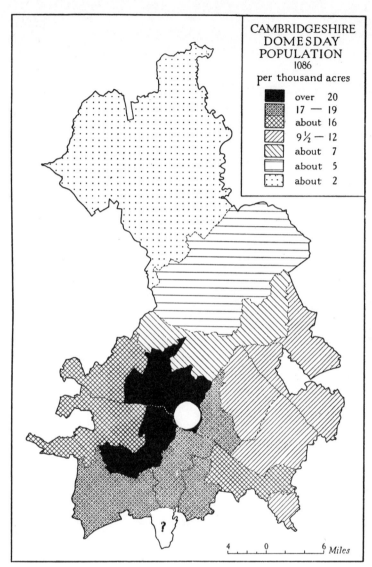

Fig. 17

From H. C. Darby, "The Domesday Geography of Cambridgeshire",
Proc. Camb. Antiq. Soc. xxxvi, 41 (1936).
The position of Cambridge town is marked by a white circle, and its
figures are excluded from these ratios, so as not to complicate the rural
distributions. The area queried in the south of the county was not
recorded in the Cambridgeshire folios. It belonged to Essex, and so was
included in the Little Domesday Book.

the ratios are even more divergent in the case of plough-teams than in the case of recorded population; the other occupations of the fens did something to bridge the gap. It is important to remember that for the southern Fenland the arable land of the island of Ely substantially raised the figures. Very roughly speaking, the ratios between the upland, the southern Fenland around Ely, and the northern fens, are as follows:

	Upland	Southern Fens	Northern Fens
Recorded population	About 15	About 5	About 2
Plough-teams	About 5	Just over 1	About $\frac{1}{4}$

These conclusions are generally confirmed by the variation in the "values" of manors in different parts of the county; but the different methods of recording these values do not lend themselves to plotting so easily in this way.

The corresponding figures for Norfolk are also indicative of the disparity between upland and Fenland.[1] The figures for Lincolnshire are particularly revealing. Figs. 19 and 20 show, respectively, the distribution of recorded population and of plough-teams. Here, again, the outstanding fact is the great difference between the upland and the Fenland. Very roughly speaking, the Lincolnshire ratios are as follows:

	Upland	Fenland
Recorded population	About 16	From 2 to 8
Plough-teams	About 4	From $\frac{1}{2}$ to 2

Of the three wapentakes of the silt zone, Elloe comes out the worst. Its population ratio was less than one-half that of Skirbeck and Kirton, while its plough-team ratio fell nearly to one-quarter. This was due to the large stretch of unoccupied waterlogged country in the extreme south of the county.[2]

Direct comparison of these two sets of figures, from Cambridgeshire and from Lincolnshire, raises difficulties, but one thing is clear: the peat area of Cambridgeshire compared much worse with the upland of the county than did the

[1] See H. C. Darby "The Domesday Geography of Norfolk and Suffolk", *Geog. Journ.* lxxxv, 432 (1935).

[2] See p. 137 below for the same effect upon the later figures.

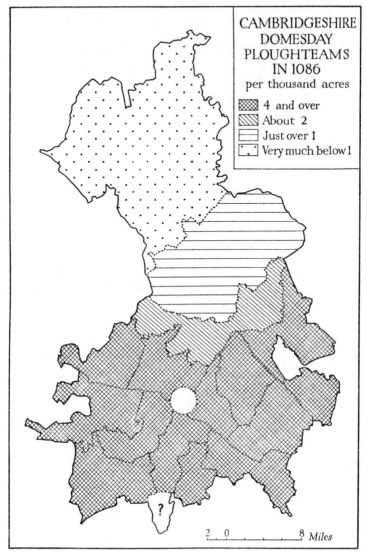

CAMBRIDGESHIRE
DOMESDAY
PLOUGHTEAMS
IN 1086
per thousand acres

4 and over
About 2
Just over 1
Very much below 1

2 0   8 *Miles*

Fig. 18

The position of Cambridge town is marked by a white circle, and its figures are excluded from these ratios, so as not to complicate the rural distributions. The area queried in the south of the county was not recorded in the Cambridgeshire folios. It belonged to Essex, and so was included in the Little Domesday Book.

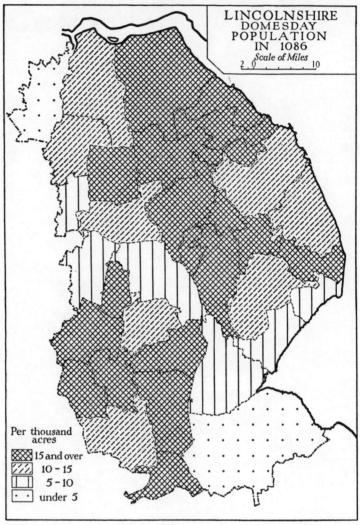

Fig. 19

The figures for Lincoln, Stamford and Torksey are excluded from these ratios, so as not to complicate the rural distributions. The two wapentakes "under 5" are Axholme in the north, and Elloe in the south.

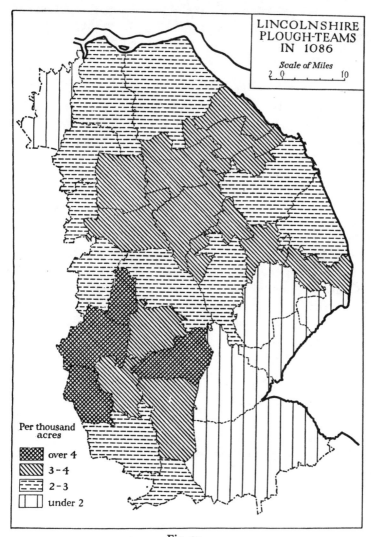

Fig. 20

The figures for Lincoln, Stamford and Torksey are excluded from these ratios, so as not to complicate the rural distributions.

Lincolnshire silt area with its upland. As the figures stand, the silt zone was evidently many times more prosperous than the peat areas. That much is evident from the village map alone (Fig. 3), but the fact is mentioned here again because it is relevant to an argument later in this chapter.[1]

FOURTEENTH-CENTURY STATISTICS

Some 250 years after the Domesday Survey, a series of medieval taxes, frequently exacted "to the uttermost far-thing", enable the wealth of Fenland and upland to be compared with a moderate degree of accuracy. An index to conditions in the southern Fenland is provided by the Lay Subsidy of 1327 for Cambridgeshire.[2] This tax was a twentieth of personal income imposed on movables, cattle, crops, stock-in-trade, etc. The totals for the Cambridgeshire villages show that it is difficult to distinguish the villages of the Fenland from those of the upland, either by their numbers of con-tributors or by the amounts of their assessments. Both groups of villages show the same variations from small sums to fairly large amounts. Fairly normal and ordered activity seems to have been going on in the fens. When, however, account is taken of the size of each hundred compared with its assess-ment, another fact is revealed. A comparison of the average amounts for each hundred shows that the Fenland was not, acre for acre, as productive as the upland (see Fig. 21).

With the exception of some hundreds in the east part of the county, all the upland area works out at over 20s. per thou-sand acres. Many districts come out at well above this figure. In contrast to this state of affairs, the corresponding figure for the hundred of Ely is as low as 9s. 2d., while that for the two

[1] See pp. 141–2 below.

[2] P.R.O. Lay Subsidy Roll 81/6. Printed by J. J. Muskett in *The East Anglian*, vols. x–xii *passim* (1903–8).

See also W. M. Palmer, *Cambridgeshire Subsidy Rolls*, 1250–1695 (1912)—reprinted from *The East Anglian*, vols. vii–xiii (1898–1909), *passim*. For other taxes upon the upland only, see J. B. Pearson, "The Assessments of Cambridgeshire 1291–1889", *Proc. Camb. Antiq. Soc.* viii, 283 (1895); and J. B. Pearson, "On the Cambridgeshire Subsidies", *Proc. Camb. Antiq. Soc.* ix, 120 (1899).

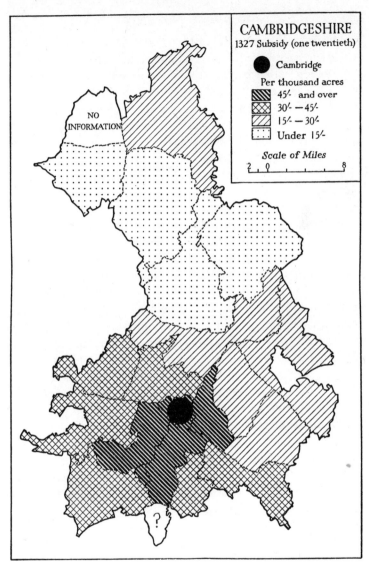

CAMBRIDGESHIRE
1327 Subsidy (one twentieth)

● Cambridge

Per thousand acres

45/- and over
30/- — 45/-
15/- — 30/-
Under 15/-

Scale of Miles

NO INFORMATION

?

Fig. 21

The figures for the town of Cambridge are excluded from these ratios so as not to complicate the rural distributions. The area queried in the south of the county formed part of Essex at this time.

It is interesting to compare these distributions with those of the 1640–41 Subsidy.—See H. C. Darby, *The Draining of the Fens* (1940), Fig. 5.

hundreds of Witchford is only 5s. 10d. The Ely Hundred, it must be remembered, included the upland villages of the isle itself which raised its average, but the Witchford Hundreds covered a large extent of peat fen in the north-west of the county. These comparative figures show that although, acre for acre, the fen country was not as wealthy as that of the upland, yet the fenland villages themselves seem to have been communities quite as prosperous as their upland neighbours. Lightness of settlement did not necessarily mean poverty of existence. This generalisation gives at once the meaning and limitation of the phrase "prosperity of the fens". Further, the map shows that conditions in the most northerly fenland hundred, that of Wisbech, were individual. Here the tax per thousand acres works out as high as 24s. 2d.; this is actually higher than the corresponding figures for the upland hundreds of Radfield (20s. 2d.), Staploe (17s. 2d.)[1] and Cheveley (22s. 10d.). How is this apparent anomaly to be explained? The soil map (Fig. 2) provides a ready answer. In the north of the county, peat fen is replaced by silt fen, and this more wealthy terrain was naturally reflected in the returns. Stated thus, these conclusions may seem obvious, but it is necessary to state them thus to obtain a true idea of the economic status of the fen country in medieval England.[2] The alternative has so often led the way into easy generalisation and error.

What was true for the silt lands of Cambridgeshire was even more true for the silt area of the Fenland in general. During the later Middle Ages, this silt zone, between sea and peat fen, seems to have been among the most prosperous parts

---

[1] This contained Soham Mere; without the two parishes of Soham and Wicken, the figure would be just over 20s.

[2] The figures for the Norwich Valuation of 1254 and like valuations, contained in *The Valuation of Norwich* by W. E. Lunt (1926), yield similar conclusions when worked out in this manner. The returns for the Diocese of Ely are contained in the *Liber Memorandorum Ecclesie de Bernewelle*, ed. by J. W. Clark (1907), pp. 191-9. The entries for the northern deanery of Wisbech are surprisingly large; Leverington in particular stands out. The entries for the deanery of Ely itself are not as large, but they compare on equal terms with the rest of the diocese from the point of view of the average assessment per parish.

of England. The massive parish churches of the area were famous—and still are famous. Their building was no sudden effort, quickly spent, but continued for centuries. The twelfth- to fifteenth-century spires and towers that point to heaven marked everywhere the prosperity of the land. Clustering in Norfolk are the Norman of Tilney, and its grander form at Walsoken (plate 8), the Early English at Walton, the Perpendicular at Walpole, and the church with minster-like proportions of many periods at Terrington (plate 9). To the north, beyond the Welland, are the magnificent Perpendicular churches of Swineshead, Donington, Quadring, Gosberton and Pinchbeck. Between them come other fine churches, Sutton, Gedney, and Holbeach, and there are yet other churches recording the same tale of wealth and prosperity during the late Middle Ages—a prosperity which was based upon fertile acres of corn and rich herds of cattle and flocks of sheep.[1] Further, in the silt zone, as in the peat area, statistical evidence is not wanting for both the counties concerned—Norfolk and Lincoln.

In the county of Norfolk the assessments of a "Tenth and a Fifteenth"[2] in the year 1334 show that, apart from Yarmouth (£100), Norwich (£94. 12s.) and Lynn (£50+£18 for South Lynn), the places with the highest assessments lay in the western portion of Freebridge Hundred, thus:

Terrington	... ...	£40
Wiggenhall	... ...	£37
Walpole	... ...	£35
Tilney...	... ...	£30
Walsoken	... ...	£26. 8s.
West Walton ...	...	£23

They are followed by Swaffham, £20; Snettisham, £19;

[1] See *The Fen and Marshland Churches*, by J. Davies, etc., 3 vols. (n.d.). See also A. F. Sutton, "Churches visited from Wisbech", *Lincs. Architect. and Archaeol. Soc. Reports and Papers*, xxvii, 245 (1904).

[2] W. Hudson, "The Assessment of the Townships of the County of Norfolk, 1334", *Norfolk Archaeology*, xii, 243 (1895). The Indenture, which prefaces the lists, describes the tax as a "*Tenth* from the Cities, Boroughs, and Demesnes of the King, and a *Fifteenth* from the Commonalty of the County".

Heacham, £16. 10s.; Thetford, £16; Sedgeford £15. 10s.; and
Gayton and North Walsham, each with £15. All the other
townships in the county were assessed at a figure below £15.
The adjoining map (Fig. 22) shows the distribution of those
townships with an assessment of over £10. Their concentra-
tion in Freebridge Hundred is noticeable. Freebridge Hundred likewise heads the list of hundreds showing the average
assessment per township. Its average is £11. 17s. 3d.; and it is
followed by Smithdon with only £8. 4s. 4d. and Clacklose
with £7. 4s. 2d. Indeed, if Freebridge Hundred, excluding
Lynn, is divided into its Marshland and upland portions, the
figures become even more striking.

	1334 Assessment	Parishes	Average per parish
	£ s. d.		
Freebridge Marshland	205 0 0	7	About £29
Freebridge Upland	173 5 0	25	About £7

Further analysis of the figures reveals another point; not only
were the townships of Marshland more wealthy than those of
the rest of the county, but the Marshland terrain itself was
also considerably richer than the greater part of the rest of
the county. This is seen for example when, excluding Lynn,
a comparison is made between the Marshland and the upland
portions of Freebridge Hundred:

	1334 Assessment	Acreage	Tax per 1000 acres
	£ s. d.		s.
Freebridge Marshland	205 7 0	57,280	72
Freebridge Upland	173 5 0	75,770	46
Lynn (and South Lynn)	68 0 0	6,393	—
Totals	446 12 0	139,443	—

Seventy-two shillings, as against forty-six, per thousand acres

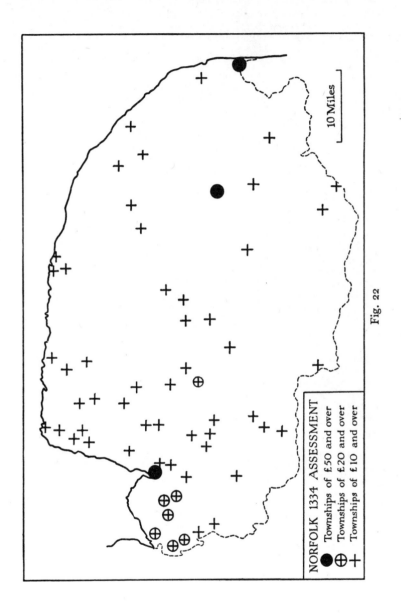

NORFOLK 1334 ASSESSMENT

●   Townships of £50 and over
⊕   Townships of £20 and over
+   Townships of £10 and over

10 Miles

Fig. 22

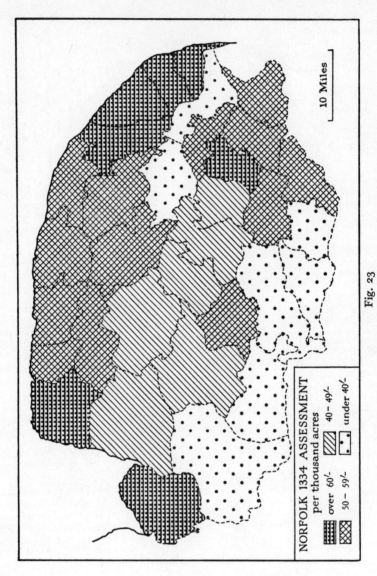

NORFOLK 1334 ASSESSMENT
per thousand acres

over 60/-　　40 — 49/-

50 — 59/-　　under 40/-

10 Miles

Fig. 23

The figures for Yarmouth, Norwich and Lynn are excluded from these ratios
so as not to complicate the rural distributions.

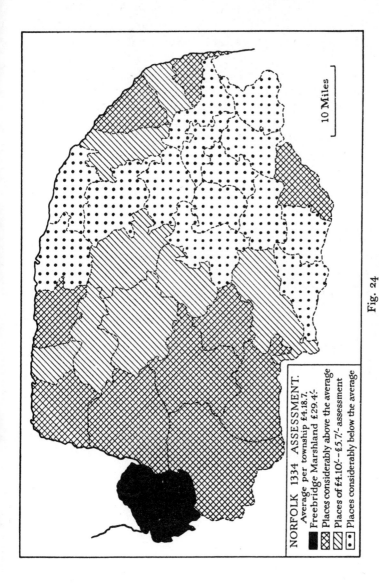

NORFOLK 1334 ASSESSMENT.
Average per township £4.18.7.
Freebridge Marshland £29.4/-.
■ Places considerably above the average
▨ Places of £4.10/- – £5.7/- assessment
▧ Places considerably below the average

10 Miles

Fig. 24

The figures for Yarmouth, Norwich and Lynn are excluded from these ratios
so as not to complicate the rural distributions.

indicates considerable superiority. The corresponding figures for the other hundreds of the county exceeded this figure only in three cases—East Flegg with 82*s.*, Smithdon with 80*s.* and West Flegg with 77*s.* Tunstead came near with 71*s.*; the next highest figure is well down in the sixties. And it is only fair to remember that Norfolk as a whole was regarded as one of the richest counties of the realm.[1] The accompanying maps (Figs. 22, 23 and 24) tell their own tale about the distribution of wealth and fertility within the county itself.[2] Regarded from all points of view, Norfolk Marshland was an exceptionally wealthy area.[3]

The Lincolnshire Fenland might be expected to resemble that of Norfolk in many ways, and this expectation can be tested by the Lay Subsidy[4] of 1332. An analysis of some

[1] See, for instance, J. E. Thorold Rogers, *Six Centuries of Work and Wages* (8th edition, 1906), pp. 115, 130. He stated the cause as "the inclusion of the opulent city of Norwich within the assessment". Examination of the figures, however, does not show this to be so. See W. Hudson, *art. cit.* (1895), pp. 247–8.

[2] Commentary upon these facts is provided by the taxation of the county in the fifteenth century. Then, owing to a check in the general prosperity of England, the assessment was reduced for the relief of lands "greatly impoverished, or else to the said tax over greatly charged". The deduction for the whole county was about one-sixth. "Only seven of the hundreds received just that deduction. Most of them receive from one-fifth to one-seventh. Holt stands at one extreme with a reduction of nearly one-fourth, while at the other is East Flegg, with no more than one-eleventh; and Taverham, Walsham, and Diss are scarcely more liberally dealt with."—W. Hudson, *art. cit.* (1895), p. 259. The reduction for Freebridge Hundred as a whole was just over one-seventh, but a separation of Marshland entries from the others shows how small a reduction was allowed in the fenland villages. Walsoken and Terrington were only allowed less than one-twentieth; Tilney one-fifteenth; Wiggenhall one-twelfth; Emneth and West Walton about one-eighth each. Walpole's allowance, however, was surprisingly large—nearly one-quarter.

[3] These conclusions, like those for Cambridgeshire, are borne out generally by ecclesiastical taxation. See W. Hudson, "The Norwich Taxation of 1254, so far as it related to the Diocese of Norwich", *Norfolk Archaeology*, xvii, 46 (1910).

[4] P.R.O. Lay Subsidy Roll (E. 179) 135/14, 15 and 16. Grant of a fifteenth (from the countryside) and a tenth (from cities and boroughs). I am indebted to the late Canon C. W. Foster of Timberland for allowing me to make use of his transcript of this MS.

sample figures from each district, set out in the following table (p. 138), summarises the situation. The silt-land villages of Holland were all large judging by their average tax per parish; and this is confirmed when the number of contributors in each village is considered. The villages of the upland wapentakes have rarely more than 40 contributors, usually not more than 30, and frequently not more than 20. The villages of the three wapentakes of the silt lands, on the other hand, have rarely less than 40; indeed, their average per village works out at about 100 contributors. There were, in Lincolnshire, in 1332, twenty-three places[1] with over 100 payers of the subsidy, fifteen in Holland, one in Kesteven, and seven in Lindsey, together with Lincoln having 432, and Stamford having 183 payers. The amounts paid follow a like distribution. After Lincoln, the most was paid by Boston (over £60). Pinchbeck and Spalding each paid over £40, while nine other places in Holland paid over £20, and fifteen paid over £10. Every parish in Kirton, every parish in Elloe, except Crowland and Tydd, and every parish in Skirbeck, except Butterwick and Toft, paid over £10. In Kesteven, only six places, and in Lindsey only four, paid over £10. It is evident that the fenland villages of Lincolnshire like those of Norfolk were large, scattered, and prosperous communities. There was, however, more variety in the fertility acre per acre (see Fig. 25); the average for Elloe fell so low because of the expanse of ill-drained silt land lying to the north of the Nene and behind the inhabited margins near the coast of the Wash;[2] Skirbeck, in the north-east corner, easily outstripped the rest of Holland in fertility, although its villages were not so large as those of Elloe wapentake.

---

[1] For the list that follows, see *V.C.H. Lincolnshire*, ii, 314 (1906): Barton-upon-Humber (126); Belton (102); Bennington (119); Boston (131); East Deeping (119); Frampton (102); Freiston (121); Gosberton (126); Ingoldmells (123); Kirton (151); Leek (*sic*) (164); Leverton (140); Mablethorpe (112); Moulton (181); Mumby (106); Pinchbeck (223); Quadring (105); Skidbrook (137); Sutterton (160); Sutton (170); Spalding (149); Theddlethorpe (139); Whaplode (164).

[2] See p. 124 above for the same effect upon the Domesday figures.

Representative Wapentakes from the Lincolnshire Lay Subsidy of 1332

Wapentake	Assessment £	s.	d.	Parishes	Acreage	Tax per parish £	s.	d.	Tax per 1000 acres s.
Holland:									
Elloe	251	17	3	11	148,560	22	17	11	34
Kirton	206	19	3¾	12	71,660	17	14	11	57
Skirbeck	158	15	2½	9	36,100	17	12	10	91
Kesteven:									
Aveland	145	12	0¾	36	53,220	4	0	11	55
Loveden	82	12	9	21	47,340	3	18	8	35
Flaxwell	75	11	6½	18	37,420	4	4	0	41
Lindsey:									
Wraggoe	74	3	10¼	26	58,900	2	17	1	27
Aslacoe	53	0	11¼	19	46,240	2	15	10	23
Bolingbroke	45	10	1¼	18	56,980	2	10	7	16

(See pp. 137 and 140 for comments)

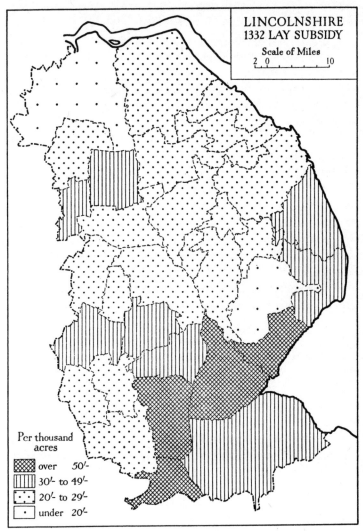

Fig. 25

This map records only the distribution of the "fifteenth" so as
not to complicate rural distributions—see footnote 4, p. 136.

The Kesteven figures show that, to the west of the Fenland, there was an area fertile enough in its terrain, exceeding Elloe in this respect, and even approaching Kirton but still below Skirbeck. But the villages of this district were more numerous and very much smaller in size—only one-fourth the size of the fenland villages. To the north, in Lindsey, the villages were not only smaller still, but their terrain was also less fertile. The Wolds appear to have been a region very thickly studded with small and rather poor communities. The high averages for the wapentakes of Candleshoe and Calcewath may, possibly, be associated with the coastal marsh that played a prominent part in the economy of some of their villages. On the other hand, the averages for the villages that lay in Horncastle and Bolingbroke fall so low because the southern portion of these two sokes included the watery waste associated with Wildmore Fen, West Fen and East Fen. These points, and others with them,[1] are brought out by the map (Fig. 25).

In this survey of the three counties, Cambridgeshire, Norfolk, and Lincolnshire, comparison between Fenland and upland has been instructive enough because the figures for the upland have acted as a "control" to test the abnormality of the fenland villages. This abnormality was not as great as might be expected, and along the silt belt at any rate the fenland villages emerge triumphant from the comparison. There were economic differences, it is true, but these differences did not succeed in making out of the fen settlements anything other than flourishing communities. In discussing the medieval economy of the Fenland, it is as well to remember that the conditions prevailing in the area were as much the product of an epoch as of a locality. Any idea that lack of respect for law and order and a tendency to violence in dispute were peculiar to the area is soon dispelled by a general examination of, say, the Patent or the Assize Rolls.

[1] See Table on p. 138 for details of certain representative wapentakes.

TWO HUNDRED AND FIFTY YEARS' CHANGE

Comparison of the Domesday statistics with those of the early fourteenth century brings out a remarkable change in the circumstances of the Fenland. The data for Lincolnshire are particularly clear. In 1086, the prosperity of the upland was many times that of the Fenland. By 1332, the situation was reversed, and the greater part of the Fenland seems to have been many times as prosperous as that of the upland.[1] The Fenland is seen to have gained relatively very considerably indeed. This relative gain can hardly be explained in terms of deterioration in the upland;[2] it must therefore have been due to actual improvement in the fen—an improvement that is measured clearly enough in the contrast between these two sets of data. One point must be mentioned—the greater part of this Lincolnshire Fenland was silt; and the prominence of the silt area of Norfolk Marshland is no less outstanding.

On the peat lands of Cambridgeshire, the change is not so striking. The fen hundreds of Ely and of North and South Witchford, it is true, were not so poor, relative to the upland, as they had been in 1086; yet, even so, they were still only one quarter to a half as wealthy per unit area. To this generalisation about the Cambridgeshire fens there was one exception. The silt-land hundred of Wisbech, so very poor in 1086, was, by 1327, slightly more wealthy than some of the upland hundreds. This is not as great as the change on the Lincolnshire silts but, even so, it is striking enough. Taken together, the indications are clear. The stray pieces of miscellaneous information about assarts and purprestures, exemplified in the second chapter of this book, are but scattered glimpses. For these stray assarts and local "raisings from the fen" came to constitute, within the span of 250 years, a great revolution in

[1] The Poll Tax Returns of 1377 confirm the superiority of the Fenland over the upland in Lincolnshire.—See R. A. Pelham, "Fourteenth-Century England", in *An Historical Geography of England before* A.D. 1800, ed. by H. C. Darby (1936), p. 232.

[2] There may have been some absolute increase in the population of the upland.—*V.C.H. Lincolnshire*, ii, 314 (1906).

economic geography.[1] This change in prosperity, while not leaving the peat lands untouched, reached its most dramatic expression, understandably enough, upon the fertile silt lands.

THE SOCIAL CONSEQUENCES OF FEN ECONOMY

In discussions about the peculiarities of fenmen great emphasis is usually laid upon the inaccessible nature of their land. It is true that in English history much of the significance of the marsh, like that of the mountain, lay in its inaccessible character; but the inaccessibility of these two types of physical features was of a very different quality. In mountainous regions, the military and strategic difficulties of approach but served to emphasise the social exclusiveness bred of the land. But the fens were different. Partly owing to their location in the centre of the English plain, and partly owing to the existence of an arterial system of waterways, these two ideas, strategic and social, can be separated. During medieval times, the fens, although always inaccessible from a strategic point of view, were never prevented from sharing in the civilisation of the rest of the English plain. Pictures have been drawn of the fenmen as people accustomed from infancy to complete isolation, keeping alive the customs and superstitions of their forefathers, and preserving intact the folklore of generations. There are, indeed, many old traditions and customs in this land, but these cannot be looked upon as the peculiar products of a marsh society. They are survivals of localisms prevalent in an age of localism; they are common to the whole of the English plain; and, it would be difficult to show that they are more common in the Fenland than in any other district. We cannot, therefore, look upon the Fenland as being in any sense the repository of old ways and customs; the inaccessibility of the marsh has been of an order quite different from that of the mountain. Nor can we regard the fenmen of the past as having been in any way possessed by an inherent hostility to their fellow-countrymen.

[1] See, for example, pp. 61 *et seq.* above for the increase in pasture and meadow.

There were many local rebellions both of political and of economic origin in medieval England; but it is significant that the people of the fens never took part in any of these. This is a point that is sometimes not realised. Their country certainly became a centre of resistance to authority, but to interpret that fact as the expression of any spirit of freedom fundamental in marshland peoples is quite unwarranted. The opposition to central authority that took place in the fens did not consist of resistance on the part of the fenlanders themselves, but was essentially external and baronial in origin. On each occasion a group of nobles seized and utilised the strategic opportunities offered by the marsh. That was a very different order of cause and effect. The role of the Fenland in English history has been passive rather than active. It was repeatedly a region of refuge, rather than a breeding ground of freedom and discontent. It presented possibilities of defence that were utilised during phases of national upheaval— a very different thing from dictating a political creed to its people. Stated thus, the problem of fenland rebellion is not a social one with an economic background, but a military one with a topographical background.

A general formula can be devised to cover the story of the rebellions. In each of them there may be discerned three phases.

(1) A group of people seized the island of Ely, with or without the consent of its abbot or bishop, and fortified it. Thus entrenched, a small band of defenders, secure in their food supply, and possessed of the local lore of streamlet and safe ground, could harass any would-be invaders in such a manner as to do damage out of all proportion to their number. Even if the marsh could be negotiated by devious paths and winding channels, these were methods that might easily be countered for a time. No great body of invaders dare venture over sodden trails or along precarious watercourses.

A period of lawlessness and amphibious guerilla warfare followed. More and more people flocked to Ely from all over the country. They found resources enough to keep them for

some time. The Hereward legend put into the mouth of a
supporter these words:

In our isle men are not troubling themselves; the ploughman
has not taken his hand from the plough, nor has the hunter cast
aside his arrow, nor does the fowler desist from taking birds.
And yet something more. If you wish to hear what I have known
and seen, I will reveal all to you. The isle is within itself plentifully
endowed; it is supplied with various kinds of herbage and, for its
richer soil, surpasses the rest of England. Most delightful for its
charming fields and pastures, it is also remarkable for its beasts of
chase and is in no ordinary way fertile in flocks and herds. Its
woods and vineyards are not worthy of equal praise, but it is
beset by great meres and fens as though by a strong wall.[1]

Thus, comparatively safe from attack, the castellans were
within striking distance of much booty, and the settlements
along the borders of the surrounding upland were raided and
pillaged. Other islands like Ramsey were also plundered and
occupied. On occasions, even places as far away as Norwich
and Bury St Edmunds suffered.

(2) Ultimately, the royal army arrived to invest and block-
ade the region; and the encounters that ensued were most
intense around the two southerly approaches to the Isle,
at Aldreth and Soham respectively.[2] This state of affairs
continued for months, or even years, for the besiegers failed
time after time to effect an entrance into the Isle. The
result was great devastation of the surrounding countryside.
The twelfth-century rebellion of Geoffrey de Mandeville, for
instance, resulted in much wasting of the countryside around.
The writer of the *Historia Eliensis* is loud in complaint:

For the space of twenty or even thirty miles neither ox nor
plough was to be seen; barely could the smallest bushel of grain
be bought for two hundred pence. The people, by hundreds and
thousands, were perishing for want of bread, and their corpses lay

---

[1] *Liber Eliensis*, ed. by D. J. Stewart (1848), p. 231. See *Gesta Stephani*,
ed. by R. Howlett (Rolls Series, 1886), p. 62, for a similar description
with reference to the rebellion of 1142.
[2] For these approaches see above, pp. 107 *et seq.*

unburied in the fields, a prey to beasts and to fowls of the air. Not for ages past had there been such tribulation....[1]

The other chronicles repeat the same story, and it has been suggested that the awful description of the anarchy of Stephen's reign, recorded in the Anglo-Saxon Chronicle under the year 1137, and written by a monk of Peterborough, may have gained some of its vividness from a personal experience of the Ely rebels.[2]

In any district, damage of this kind would have been a serious matter, but in the Fenland it must have been critical; for it meant that the whole network of sewers and channels was disturbed, and the drainage arrangements must have suffered enormously. At last, usually through the treachery of some one within the Isle, the forces of the king gained an entrance into Ely and its defenders could do nothing more than flee.

(3) The rebellion over, there followed a period of nervousness and hesitation on the part of the royal authorities. The island was kept semi-fortified lest it should be seized again. Nor did the Palatine nature of its jurisdiction serve to mitigate these fears. The Patent Rolls for the latter part of the thirteenth century, for example, are full of these fears. On July 26th, 1272, for example, a warning was issued,

To the bishop of Ely, the prior of Ely, and all abbots and other priors and tenants within the isle of Ely. Whereas the isle of Ely is held to be one of the stronger refuges (*fortius receptaculum*) of the realm, and as such should be properly guarded, that none may enter therein by whose entry any spark of disturbance against the king or them may arise; mandate to them on the fealty homage and affection wherein they are bound to the king to cause

---

[1] H. Wharton, *Anglia Sacra* (1691), p. 623. It was the same at Ramsey. See *Chronicon Abbatiae Ramesiensis*, ed. by W. D. Macray (Rolls Series, 1886), pp. 327 *et seq.*

[2] J. H. Round, *Geoffrey de Maundeville* (1892), p. 220. For indications of the anarchy of 1265 in the Cambridge Assize Rolls, see E. F. Jacob, *Studies in the Period of Baronial Reform and Rebellion*, 1258–1267 (1925), pp. 222 ff.

the island to be kept prudently by night and day, that danger may not arise to the king or them by the entry of any therein.[1]

Within a few decades of rebellion, however, affairs resumed a more normal course, until the memory of these scenes of violence passed into tradition.

This cycle of events was repeated four times: when Hereward defied the Normans in the eleventh century; in 1139 and 1142, during the turmoil of Stephen's reign; when the barons held out against King John in 1216; and, in 1265, during the reign of Henry III. After these occasions, the tradition of Ely as a camp of refuge continued for a long time. But from that tradition we cannot construct a generalisation about fenland society. The fenmen, like the other inhabitants of the English plain, were men trying to work out a satisfactory economic basis for their life. In fairness it must be said that their task was not a simple one. Moreover, they had their fair share of the weaknesses and of the strength of ordinary folk, but it is not easy to see how they were endowed with any qualities of desperate wildness extracted by some mystical influence from reeds and rushes.

[1] Patent Rolls, 56 Henry III, m. 8.

CHAPTER FIVE

THE CARE OF BANKS AND CHANNELS

IT is overwhelmingly evident that the determining factor in the economy of the Fenland during the later Middle Ages was the condition of sewers and drains. The word *fossatum* (often *fossata*, occasionally *fossatus*) is not always easy to translate. Sometimes it implied a minor boundary ditch; sometimes it stood for one of the great dykes of the Fenland.[1] At any rate, it is a word that is found very frequently in the records of the time; not unnaturally, for the fenmen were very much alive to the importance of their sewers.[2] It was upon the strength of their sewer-banks that the extent, to say nothing of the existence, of the "summer grounds" of the region depended. Indeed, it is safe to say that almost every stream and bank in the Fenland had, in one way or another, someone who was held responsible for it— persons holding "lands, tenements, common of fishing, or pasture, who might have safeguard, defence or benefit by the making or repair"[3] of associated banks and sewers. Maintenance of these was, in many cases, but an incident of land tenure.[4] Not only individuals, but townships and ecclesiastical authorities shared in the burden of responsibilities. The Prior and Convent of Ely, for instance, leased pieces of fen for an annual rent on condition that the lessees "made

[1] C. T. Flower, *Public Works in Medieval Law*, i, xxvii (1923).

[2] "Sewer" was the technical name given to any watercourse or artificial channel whose primary purpose was land drainage. It still survives in the Norfolk Court of Sewers, and in several existing Commissions of Sewers.

[3] Patent Rolls, 47 Edw. III, m. 8d (1263). See W. Dugdale, *Imbanking and Drayning* (1772), p. 311.

[4] For services at Fleet, in 1316, see N. Neilson, *A Terrier of Fleet, Lincolnshire* (1920), p. lxviii. Included in the week-work "were *vallatio*, the making of one-half perch's length of wall, three feet thick and five feet high, and *fodicio*, the digging of one perch's length of ditch, three feet deep and five feet wide".

the ditches and performed the *essewycia* (sewer service?) belonging to the said land".[1] And there is more than one
reference to trench-digging as one of the customary villein
services.[2]

It is clear that a number of practices, established "time out
of memory", and "according to ancient custom", had grown
up to regulate the management of the fenland streams. The
business of the sewer courts was, indeed, the maintenance of
what was variously called the *consuetudo marisci*, the *consuetudo
patrie*, or the *forma et custuma marisci*. It is clear, too, that these
ancient arrangements were based upon the common consent
of certain localities. In north Wainfleet, it was the custom,
at any rate in the thirteenth century, to view the marsh
ditches yearly on the feast of St Andrew, and to present de-
faults to the court of the earl of Lincoln, who could impose a
fine of sixteen pence.[3] Again, in the next century, in 1375, it
was declared, that Bourne Eau ought to be cleaned every
fourth year from Pinchbeck to the sea "according to ancient
custom and to the ordinances of the justices of sewers".[4] And
in the same year, too, it was reported that the River Bicker,
near Swineshead, had to be kept open all the year, and that
the sewers between Holland and Kesteven ought to be kept
open from the middle of March until Martinmas by the
townships of Donington and Quadring.[5] These hints, and
many like them in the presentments of the time, bear witness
to a whole body of local right and custom that had been

[1] Cartulary of Ely Convent (Liber M), ff. 333 and 367 (Bishop's
Muniment Room, Ely, G. 3).
[2] British Museum, Additional Charters, No. 34808, for four people at
Upwood in 1339 amerced because they did not go to the "ditching" at
Ramsey when summoned. See also P.R.O. Mins. Accts. (Gen. Ser.),
1135/8 (*temp.* Edw. III), for sums spent in ditching at Somersham valued
in terms of customary "works" at $\frac{1}{2}d.$ for each work.
[3] W. Dugdale, *op. cit.* p. 155 (dated 1289). For an excellent discussion,
with examples, of sewer construction in medieval England, see C. T.
Flower, *Public Works in Medieval Law*, 2 vols. (Selden Society, 1915 and
1923).
[4] P.R.O. Placita Coram Rege (K.B. 27), Hil., 50 Edw. III, m. 21 d.
[5] P.R.O. Ancient Indictments (K.B. 9), File 59, m. 65.

evolved through the ages to meet the exigencies of fen life. It is, however, one thing to know that detailed arrangements existed for keeping the Fenland in good order, but quite another to assume that they were in constant operation.

COMPLAINTS AND DISPUTES

Misunderstandings and abuses in connection with the sewers were very frequent. The majority of cases indicate nothing more than failure to clean the channels, and the consequent accumulation of an obstruction. Presentment after presentment declared that certain "clowes"[1] had been stopped; that certain channels should be repaired, or cleansed, or made wider, or straightened; that certain banks ought to be restored and made higher; and that certain sluices must be constructed.[2] Particulars about these matters were repeatedly noted in the monastic cartularies,[3] for the fenland monasteries were continually entering agreements about the duties of sewer construction and maintenance. When Ramsey and Thorney Abbeys agreed to divide Kingsdelf Fen, the boundary ditch was to be made half on Ramsey and half on Thorney ground.[4] And there is frequent reference[5] to "new ditch" and "new lode" in documents describing fen boun-

---

[1] A "clow" was a sluice or floodgate. For variants see the *Oxford English Dictionary*.

[2] For the proceedings of the Commissioners of Sewers at Boston in 1316, and at Donington in 1325, see W. Dugdale, *op. cit.* pp. 199–203.

[3] The *Ramsey Cartulary*, for instance, is full of these. E.g. vol. i, pp. 174, 463, 476 *et seq.*; vol. ii, pp. 2, 17, 23, 28 *et seq.*

[4] Red Book of Thorney. Cambridge University Library, Additional MSS. 3021, ff. 371–72b (1216–37). See footnote 3, p. 77 above. For this division, see also *Ramsey Cartulary*, i, 188; ii, 80, 364; iii, 38. See also British Museum, Additional Charters, No. 34360: at Ramsey in the early fourteenth century the jurors said that the men of Benwick by making a ditch appropriated to themselves a portion of Ramsey common near "Packelode", to the extent of five acres.

At Upwood, in 1307, the court ordered that the whole village should rectify the watercourse at "Systowebroke" which had left its proper course and was causing much damage.—British Museum, Additional Charters, No. 34799.　　　　　[5] E.g. see p. 166 below.

daries. But the practice of building new ditches was not
always popular; and, frequently, they had to be filled in because they were a nuisance or because they were unjust.[1]
A multiplicity of these small dikes interfered with the passage
of the village flocks to the common pastures, and there are
presentments of ditches "per quos homines qui habent com-
munam pasturam perturbantur".[2] Again, in an agreement,
of 1294, between the bishop of Ely and the abbot of Ramsey
concerning the common fens of Somersham and Holywell
there was special provision that "the lode which leads from
Needingworth to the great bank shall not be so deep but
that the cattle of the bishop, and his men, and the other
commoners, may cross it to their pasture towards Holywell
without damage".[3]

These were local problems. But there were others, con-

---

[1] *Ramsey Cartulary*, i, 166. See also *ibid*. ii, 347: "Unde placitum fuit
inter eos in curia domini Regis; scilicet quod omnes ladae, quas monachi
de Saltreia fecerant in illo marisco, obstupabuntur, excepta illa magna
lada, quae vadit de Witelsmare versus Saltreiam, quae remanebit aperta."

[2] British Museum, Additional Charters, No. 34354. This concerned
new trenches made by the vill of Conington to the disturbance of the
men of Upwood, Great Raveley and Wood Walton (1342–43). In Warboys,
in 1306, there was a presentment of a new ditch made in the fen "ad magnum dampnum communarum"—*ibid*. No. 34895. The various points that
arose and the complicated interests involved in these disputes are illustrated in a discussion of the lodes of Walton, Sawtry and Conington in
1342 (*Ramsey Cartulary*, i, 175): "Querulam diversorum hominum
comitatus Huntedoniae accepimus, continentem, quod diversae ladae et
trencheae in villis de Waltone, Sautre, et Conyngtone in eodem comitatu,
tam pro salvatione partium illarum et terrarum, pratorum, et pasturarum
hominum inibi morantium contra aquas dulces ibidem descendentes,
quam pro navibus et batellis quorumcunque hominum blada, turbas et
alias res ad diversa loca, tam infra comitatum praedictum quam extra,
ducere et cariare volentium per easdem ladas et trencheas navigantibus,
ab antiquo ordinatae et constructae per quosdam villarum praedictarum,
in tantum sunt artatae et obstructae, quod naves seu batelli aliqui per
easdem navigare, seu hujusmodi aquae dulces ad mare descendere non
poterunt per easdem, ut deberent; quodque diversae ladae et trencheae
per aliquos de villis praedictis in communa pasturae quamplurimum
hominum ejusdem comitatus jam de novo factae sunt et constructae, in
ipsorum hominum partium earundem damnum non modicum et
gravamen."   [3] *Ramsey Cartulary*, i, 216.

nected with the main drainage channels themselves. About these latter, complaints become monotonous and their detail becomes multitudinous. Nor is the topography of these entries easy to identify among the many subsequent changes in the fenland channels. Even without changes it would be difficult, for the original pattern of streams and drains was complicated enough. Very frequent verbs, relating to these disputes, that occur in the presentments and inquisitions of the time, are "obstruitur" and "obstupatur", "inundantur" and "submerguntur". Thus, in 1285, the lands of the bishop of Ely's men at *Welle*, Elm, Wisbech, Leverington, Newton, and Tyd were flooded by water "flowing towards the Welle-strem", the floods being caused by the neglect of those whose duty it was to repair the dykes "according to the custom of the fen".[1] In neglecting their duty these villagers of northern Cambridgeshire were but yielding to the spirit of the time and place. Typical enough of the whole of the Fenland was a Lincolnshire presentment, in the Easter Term of 1349, stating that Spalding marsh had been flooded several times owing to neglect:

Iuratores diversorum hundredorum comitatus predicti alias scilicet termino Pasche anno regni domini Edwardi nuper regis Anglie avi domini regis nunc vicesimo tercio coram ipso avo apud Lincoln' presentaverunt quod villata de Baston' debet et tenetur reparare fossatum vocatum Edyk' de Catebrigge usque Estkote ex parte australi ripe vocate le Brunne Hee et non faciunt ad grave dampnum tocius populi: per quod mariscus de Spaldyng' inundatur per plures vices.[2]

In 1383, the argument was still going on.[2] The damage caused by these floods was considerable. In 1375, a jury of Skirbeck wapentake was complaining that, owing to a default of the abbot of Kirkstead, the marsh of West Fen and East Fen was flooded every year to the extent of £2000 damage.[3]

[1] Patent Rolls, 13 Edw. I, m. 24d.
[2] P.R.O. Placita Coram Rege (K.B. 27), Trin. term, 6 & 7 Richard II, m. 3. See C. T. Flower, *op. cit.* i, 240 and 245.
[3] P.R.O. Ancient Indictments (K.B. 9), File 59, m. 8. In 1396, the marshes of East Fen and West Fen, and various lands, meadows and pastures in Leake, Wrangle, Friskney and Wainfleet were submerged

Too frequently, the disputes dragged on for a long time. In many cases the responsibility for maintenance could not be conclusively fixed; thus, in 1359, the sea-dykes and marsh-dykes of Surfleet, Gosberton and Quadring were much too weak and far too low, but it was not known who should repair them.[1] Later in the century, in the winter of 1375, the town of Spalding was in danger of being submerged by the flow of the sea and by the descent of the fresh waters, because, since the Black Death (1349), the lands of the township had been so divided and alienated that the keepers of the ditches knew not by whom they ought to be repaired.[2] And in consequence of this, the whole township and the holders of land therein were held responsible for their repair.[3] Unfortunately, the terms of these agreements were frequently made capable of more than one interpretation by the insertion of dubious clauses. Phrases like "unless the said inundations and over-flows shall be excessive and more heavy than usual"[4] really begged the question. It all amounts to saying that the net-

owing to the defect of a weir in Wainfleet, which prevented the water from flowing freely to sea.—P.R.O. Placita Coram Rege (K.B. 27), Easter term, 19 Richard II, m. 27d. See C. T. Flower, op. cit. i, 286.

[1] P.R.O. Placita Coram Rege (K.B. 27), Mich. term, 35 Edw. III, 17.

[2] For a discussion of the effects of the Black Death see (1) C. T. Flower, op. cit. i, xxviii; (2) H. G. Richardson, "The Early History of Commissions of Sewers", Eng. Hist. Rev. xxxiv, 385 (1919).

It is obvious that the network of fenland channels must have been very sensitive to any dislocation in organisation. Even though the Black Death did not produce great consequences generally, the neglect of watercourses for but a few months might produce considerable damage in some localities.

[3] P.R.O. Ancient Indictments (K.B. 9), File 59, m. 51d. The relevant extract runs: "Item dicunt quod villata de Pynchebek est in periculo submercionis per fluxum maris et per inundacionem aquarum recencium tempore yemali versus mariscum ob defectum quod terre villate predicte post primam pestilenciam sic diversimodo ceparantur et diversis hominibus in Pynchebek alienantur ut custodes fossatorum villate predicte non possint habere noticiam per quos fossata predicta in pluribus locis deberent de iure reparari: propter quod fossata predicta predicte ville indigent et debent de novo agistari et reparari per totam villatam de Pynchebek et per omnes homines habentes terras in predicta villa."—See C. T. Flower, op. cit. i, 271.

[4] Ingulph, Contin. p. 396.

work of the fenland drainage channels was so intricate that responsibility was difficult to divide; that formal agreements were, too often, capable of evasion or misinterpretation; and that much of the actual work of repair was executed unwillingly and in an inferior manner.[1]

Sometimes it was alleged, and apparently not without reason, that damage was deliberately committed. Individuals were repeatedly presented for obstructing drains for their private benefit and to the common danger. And, indeed, it frequently happened that measures taken to drain one spot merely had the effect of flooding another region, or of interfering with neighbouring mills and fisheries, or of impeding navigation. In 1375, the jurors of Aveland wapentake presented that Walter Newson of Wainfleet and seventy-seven other people (who were named), on Thursday, May 11th, 1374, came and stopped up certain sewers, called le Delflet and Stangermal, which drained the several lands of the prior of Kyme, thus causing much damage; the jurors also declared that when the servants of the prior opened and flooded the ditch and the sewers on July 20th, the said Walter came with others and again stopped them up.[2]

The making of new trenches likewise produced much disturbance and complaint;[3] and interference with fishing rights, too, was always a source of discord. Typical presentments

---

[1] Writing of a new embankment, in 1433, Ingulph's Continuator adds: "The same shall be made in a workmanlike manner, and built of sufficient height, without any breach therein, or any oozing therefrom."—*Ingulph, Contin.* p. 396.

[2] P.R.O. Ancient Indictments (K.B. 9), File 59, m. 38. (See C. T. Flower, *op. cit.* i, 285.) One hundred years later, in 1481, comes a note in the *Ramsey Cartulary* (ii, 167–8) recording the wilful destruction of Knar Ditch and the consequent flooding of the fen around Thorney.

[3] Presentment was made in 1382 that Walter Gouke, William Cooke and others constructed twelve trenches, 30 feet wide and of a great depth on the bank of the Witham, whereby the water of the said stream flooded all the marshes from Witham bank to Wainfleet to the damage of the duke of Lancaster, lord of the said marshes, and to the annihilation of his agistments and profits thereof, and to the harm of the whole adjacent country.—P.R.O. Ancient Indictments (K.B. 9), File 63, m. 10. See C. T. Flower, *op. cit.* i, 280–2.

were those by juries in Spalding[1] that Thomas Halmere and
Simon Malle of Spalding and John Hare of Weston, in the
years 1394–96, narrowed the common sewer in Weston, called
Westonmere, with nets and other engines for fishing, to the
damage of the said townships. Another presentment stated that
John, one time servant of Thomas de Cloune of Pinchbeck
and now of John Bradhon, smith of Spalding, on March 12th,
1395–96, cut a dyke called Lathegrenedyke in Pinchbeck to set
nets there and take fish, whereby the "new water" entered
the said town and flooded a field called Penycostfeld to the
damage of the townsfolk.[1] A third presentment was that Guy
Bullok of Holbeach, on February 1st, 1396, narrowed the
common river of Holbeach at Holbeach weir to the damage
of the whole community.[1] Feeling ran very high at times. In
1329, the abbot of Crowland was complaining how

Walter prior of Spaldyng...and others, cut in pieces the beams
placed to strengthen the dykes constructed to prevent the abbey
from being submerged and washed away, overthrew the sand-
dikes, filled up the trenches so that the land in cultivation is more
flooded to the great injury of the abbey....[2]

And a few years later, on June 8th, 1342, complaint was made
by Thomas Wake of Deeping,

that Henry Abbot of Croyland...and others broke a dyke raised
in his marsh at Depyng, county Lincoln, to protect the same
against the flow of fresh water there, whereby the marsh was
inundated; his turves dug therein were destroyed, and he lost
his profit of the marsh for a great while; and they fished in his free
fishery there and took and carried away fish.[3]

Disputes of this kind were, indeed, very frequent incidents[4]
in the history of every fenland monastery.

[1] P.R.O. Ancient Indictments (K.B. 9), File 62, m. 20. (See C. T.
Flower, op. cit. i, 273–5.)
[2] Patent Rolls, 3 Edw. III, pt. i, m. 3d.
[3] Patent Rolls, 16 Edw. III, pt. ii, m. 34d. For similar disputes, see
ibid. 11 Edw. I, m. 22d; and 10 Edw. II, pt. i, m. 29d.
[4] The Ramsey Cartulary, for instance, contains very many references to
the activities of the fenland vills in maintaining dikes and protecting them
against disturbers. Only a few of these have been noted above.

THE COMMISSION OF SEWERS

Many of these disputes measure the failure of the traditional and minutely detailed arrangements to keep the fens in good order. Left to itself, the "ancient custom" was not proving sufficient to deal with the intricacies of the situation. Consequently, before the end of the thirteenth century, the central authority of the realm had been called in to organise and supplement the local arrangements.[1] Thus, in 1258, a commission was issued to Henry de Bathe for the parts of Holland in Lincolnshire. This appears to be the first Commission of Sewers entered upon the Patent Rolls. It recited that

whereas the king has learned that a recent inundation of the sea and marsh in the parts of Holland has caused great cost and danger and at another time he has commanded the sheriff of Lincoln to distrain all persons having lands and tenements in those parts who ought to repair and keep up the dikes, bridges and walls of the sea and marsh there, the king has appointed him [Henry de Bathonia] to provide and ordain with the said sheriff, for making the said repairs and distraint; and therefore he commands him at his next passing through those parts to attend to this.[2]

"This", writes H. G. Richardson, "may be regarded as beginning the regular series of commissions of sewers".[3] In 1266, another commission was issued "to enquire by jury of the parts of Holland" the names of those responsible for repairs; "and to distrain all who have lands in the wapentake of Elloe in Hoyland to make walls, dykes, gutters, bridges and

[1] For an excellent account, see two papers by H. G. Richardson:
(a) "Note on the Constitution and Records of Commissions of Sewers", *Report of Royal Commission on Public Records*, vol. ii (part ii), p. 98 (1914).
(b) "The Early History of Commissions of Sewers", *Eng. Hist. Rev.* xxxiv, 385 (1919).
[2] Patent Rolls, 42 Henry III, m. 14 d.
[3] H. G. Richardson, *Eng. Hist. Rev.* xxxiv, 389 (1919). H. G. Richardson says in another paper (*art. cit.* 1914, p. 98) that this year of 1258 "may be taken as the date when the Commission of Sewers assumed distinct form", since the commission issued in the previous year to Henry de Bathe about Romney Marsh was one of Oyer and Terminer.—See *Cal. Patent Rolls, Henry III*, 1247–58, p. 592.

sewers."[1] The sheriff of Lincoln was to be of aid, and was to provide juries. Other commissions followed,[2] and a stiffening of the machinery of administration is everywhere evident towards the end of the thirteenth century. The juries summoned by these commissioners presented, over and over again, a dreary tale of obligations neglected.

In an unravelling of the full history of the sewer courts, many complications in their working will become apparent, and many uncertainties must remain about their relation to other judicial units of the realm.[3] But one fact is clear. From 1300 onwards the sewer courts became increasingly frequent, until, at length, the practice of granting commissions hardened into a regular system. Sometimes they were granted for a specific purpose; more often they were established to oversee the ordinary business of repairs and to arrange for the necessary "works". Not that the new system had anything original besides organisation to contribute to a solution of fenland disorder, and even that organisation was not too good. The new system simply took over the ancient customs and practices and attempted to enforce them. Thus, a writ of 1295 in Holland and Kesteven inquired about liability for the maintenance of sewers and banks in times past, and the resulting inquest merely accepted the ancient customary regulations.[4]

The loss of the Wisbech outfall by the late thirteenth century[5] may have intensified the need for some outside vigour in the southern Fenland. Water, if left to itself, will naturally

---

[1] *Cal. Patent Rolls, Henry III*, 1258–66, p. 657.

[2] See W. Dugdale, *op. cit.* pp. 220 *et seq.*

[3] See S. and B. Webb, *English Local Government: Statutory Authorities for Special Purposes* (1922), p. 19.

[4] P.R.O. Assize Roll, 504, m. 30. See p. 148 above for the phrase "according to ancient custom and to the ordinances of the justices of sewers" (1375). From the year 1438 comes the following phrase: "as well by the said custom as by the judgement and assignation of certain justices of sewers."—W. Dugdale, *op. cit.* p. 319.

[5] See p. 96 above. Attention has often been drawn to the possibility of pronounced wetness and storminess in W. Europe between 1000 and 1250. The consequences of this for an area like the Fenland are obvious— but, of course, this factor cannot be assessed without detailed evidence.

choose a channel with the most effective slope to the sea. Consequently, the abandonment of the outfall at Wisbech in favour of the longer passage to the sea at Lynn is a sufficient indication of the extent to which tidal deposits had raised the bed of the original estuary. And the consequences of this change in direction were far greater than may have appeared at the time. The slope in the surface of the fens was so slight that, during floods, an adverse effect must have been felt very soon after the alteration. Moreover, all the minor watercourses, whether natural streams or artificial sewers of obscure origin, were adapted for the Wisbech outfall and, in some cases, they had to reverse the direction of their flow in order to meet the new circumstances. It is therefore not difficult to see that the addition of anything up to 50 miles in the passage of water from the uplands to the sea should have increased the danger of inundation. On the contrary, it is surprising that there is not more evidence of distress in the southern parts of the Fenland. The diversion of the main rivers from their natural outfall to the smaller and less convenient estuary of the Nar and the Gay at Lynn must have been a powerful factor working against efficient drainage.

In the years that followed, there was much mention of the silting up of the Wisbech channel and its associated sewers. The men of Norfolk Marshland suffered as much from the water which passed by Lynn as from that which could not pass by Wisbech. In 1362, the inhabitants of some Marshland towns sent up "a doleful petition" to Edward II showing that,

Whereas the river (going to Lenne) had used to run betwixt certain banks, distant asunder twelve perches, at which time all people had sufficient passage with their boats to and fro, the fresh waters free course to the sea; the banks on one side of the river were at that time so low, by reason of the before specified floods, that the said river was then a full mile in breadth.[1]

Later petitions show that the evil still continued, and "that all the towns in those parts were frequently overflowed"

[1] W. Dugdale, *op. cit.* pp. 260-1.

owing to the wearing away of the river-banks.[1] It thus
appears that at Lynn, as might be expected, the river formed
a much larger channel than before it received the waters of
the Great Ouse. Up to a certain point, the increasing size of
the Lynn river was of great benefit to the town, which rose
rapidly in importance. But, as the river was allowed to
hollow out for itself a wide estuary in which the stream lost
much of its force, the haven began to silt up. Parallel with
the complaint about excessive breadth come others. As early
as 1350, "the Mayor, Aldermen, and Constables of Lenne
were commanded to view the ditches compassing that town;
which, by reason of its situation upon an arm of the sea, were,
through the ebbing and flowing of the tides, filled up with
mud and other filth, to the great damage of the town".[2]

It would appear, then, that the diversion of the main
waters from their natural outfall at Wisbech to the smaller
and less convenient estuary at Lynn was a disturbing influence of considerable importance. Indeed, it might not be
too much to say that just when the effects of the loss of the
Wisbech outfall were beginning to be felt, some outside influence may have been necessary to deal with the situation.

The proceedings of the early commissioners of sewers, collected from various sources by Dugdale, provide a picture of
the means they employed to keep the waterways open.[3] They

---

[1] W. Dugdale, *op. cit.* p. 260; see also Patent Rolls, 2 Ric. II, pt. ii,
m. 10d.

[2] W. Dugdale, *op. cit.* p. 291, using Patent Rolls, 44 Edw. III, pt. i,
m. 15d.

[3] See, for example, W. Dugdale, *op. cit.* pp. 299–354, for the northern
Cambridgeshire Commissions. Around Wisbech, Elm, Upwell, and
Outwell, there were long stretches of bank designed to protect the low-
lying fields of these townships from the enormous force of water con-
centrated there. The tide flowing up Wisbech River must have penetrated
far up towards Peterborough, and the Lynn River itself must have been
tidal for many miles above Salter's Lode, both on the Ely Channel and
along Well Creek. Hence the particular care directed to the very tangled
network of banks and watercourses between Salter's Lode and Guyhirne.
Salt and fresh water floods were a continual menace.

form a tale of woe—of obstructions in channels, and of inundations of marsh, and of many signs of neglect and decay.
In 1352, for example, the inhabitants of the fens of Kesteven
and Holland made petition "to the King and his Council in
Parliament",

> shewing that, whereas the ancient boundary, called Midfen dike,
> and other metes, which go through the said fens, from the river
> of Weland to the stream of Withum, which had wont to be the
> old limits betwixt these two provinces (as by certain crosses of
> stone, then continuing, was very evident) were at that time, by
> reason of floods and other impediments, so obscured, that no
> certain knowledge could be thereof; insomuch as great contro-
> versies and debates were occasioned betwixt the inhabitants in
> those parts, upon execution of the King's writs and otherwise....[1]

And, accordingly, the king assigned men to view the said
boundaries and to take steps "for the scouring and cleansing"
of the dikes. It was a common occurrence.

The general practice of the commissioners was to hold
inquisitions, from time to time, about the drainage works
affecting a group of townships which were considered to form
a distinct system. In 1339, for example, it is recorded how,

> the King being informed that the banks, ditches, and sewers
> about Wysebeche, Elme and Welle were broken, and out of
> repair, issued a commission unto Mr John de Hildesley Chancellor
> of his Exchequer, Richard de Bayeaux, John de Walton, John de
> Stoken, and Will. Neuport, to enquire thereof; and through whose
> default they became so ruinous; and who were landholders there-
> abouts, or had safeguard by the said banks; and to distrain them
> for their repair, according to the proportion of their lands.[2]

The duty of the commissioners was fourfold: to enquire, to
survey, to reform, and to compel by distraint or, in default of
distraint, by amercement. They were, in fact, the conser-
vators of the fens. The principle upon which their assessments
rested was that every landholder should, "according to the
proportion of his tenure, repair, maintain and new make" the

---

[1] W. Dugdale, *op. cit.* p. 203, using Patent Rolls, 25 Edw. III, pt. i,
m. 23d. For the erection of stone crosses, see footnote 5, p. 91 above.
[2] W. Dugdale, *op. cit.* p. 306.

banks and sewers "as often as any defect might happen to be therein";[1] and not only "according to the proportion of his tenure" but also according to the benefit he received, or, as the documents put it, "according to the quantity thereof and the commodity he had thereby". The same principle was applied to the sea-banks. In 1348, it was declared[2] that the inhabitants of West Walton "did yearly repair, for every acre of land lying in the said town, six feet and two inches of the said sea-banks; and likewise for every acre, one foot of the said bank Pokediche"; while at Walsoken every acre re-paired four feet of sea-bank and one foot of Pokedike.

The "ancient custom", although providing the basis for computation, could not be followed rigidly, but had to be tempered by newer expediency. Later inquests extended their assessments to include any improvements in the fen that were not covered by the customary regulations.[3] The reasons given for these new ratings were that many lands had never before been assessed, and that some lands, once assessed for the re-pair of some *perticate* of the walls, were now *distracte* and in the hands of *extranei*. Benefit derived from fishing or from rights of common pasture came also to be included in the basis of assessment.

In some localities, the obligation to repair was commuted for a payment—*acreshot*, or acre silver; but sometimes the service was actually rendered and this, most probably, was the *menework* mentioned in some documents.[4] In addition to these traditional dues of maintenance, there were occasional "agist-ments", or assessments for public purposes in times of stress. In 1340, for instance, every acre of land in Elm, in *Welle*, and on the south side of Wisbech, was agisted at twopence "and more if need required"[5] for stopping up a certain injurious

---

[1] W. Dugdale, *op. cit.* p. 320; from a session of sewers dated 1438. See Appendix, pp. 175 *et seq.* below.

[2] W. Dugdale, *op. cit.* pp. 258–9.

[3] See (1) p. 51 above; (2) N. Neilson, *A Terrier of Fleet* (1920), p. lvii.

[4] E.g. W. Dugdale, *op. cit.* p. 251 (1329); and p. 293 (1410).

[5] W. Dugdale, *op. cit.* p. 307.

10. Opening paragraph of a report of a Commission of Sewers at Wisbech in 1438

P.R.O. Chancery Miscellanea (c. 47), 7/5

A. T. Ball

11. Morton's Leam, looking North from the Dog and Doublet Sluice

stream and for the building of a certain causeway. A year later, every acre of land from a certain "New Diche" to Needham Ditch in Elm was agisted at one penny, and other lands at a half penny, "for the repair of the said New Diche".[1] Comparable with these impositions may have been the occasion for that undated list, in the Ramsey Cartulary, of contributions varying from 6s. 8d. to 40s. levied for the clearing out of *Welle* (*in exstupatione de Welle*).[2] In 1380, there is another record in the Patent Rolls of certain men appointed to examine the Isle of Ely and "to make agistments for the safeguard of those parts by the number of acres or perches, to be now surveyed as often as need should require, and to constitute trusty and diligent dike-reeves for the same purpose".[3]

How these arrangements worked can be seen from the fourteenth-century Bailiff's Compotus Rolls of Wisbech Barton.[4] They have an entry entitled *Custus Fossatorum* which gives an account of the amounts spent on ditching and diking, and the manner in which these expenses were defrayed.[5] Scouring out old ditches cost anything up to 2½d. per perch; new ditches cost from 2d. to 3d. per perch to make; the regular wage of labourers on this kind of work was 4d. per day—quite a high figure. Towards these expenses, 700 acres contributed a levy of ¼d. or ½d. per acre annually; and, occasionally, a further levy was made to deal with specific pieces of work. Early in the next century, there is the following entry on one roll for the year 1408–9: "To the scouring of 400 perches of ditch round various of the lord's fields as it was ordained by inquisition on the day of the leet, 66s. 8d." Similar entries relate to other areas: at Holywell, in 1430, "le Rawte Dyche"

[1] W. Dugdale, *op. cit.* p. 309. [2] *Ramsey Cartulary*, i, 74.
[3] Patent Rolls, 3 Rich. II, pt. i, m. 35d.
[4] Bishop's Muniment Room, Ely, D. 8. The arrangements within Wisbech itself are interesting. Certain sewers and dikes were maintained by certain groups of tenants within the vill, especially those with land in the "infields". Tenants in the old market repaired a sea-wall, tenants in Townhende repaired a bank called Eebrynck, tenants in Fenhende repaired Newdike, etc. See W. Dugdale, *op. cit.* p. 320.
[5] See H. C. Darby and P. M. Ramsden, "The Middle Level of the Fens and its Reclamation", *V.C.H. Huntingdonshire*, iii, 255 (1936).

and "the water-course in Needingworth" were ordered to be put in order within a week, and the "Fendyche" and the "Marshdyche" were to be repaired before the feast of the Nativity of St John.[1] Similar to this, was the order issued three years later at Ramsey that "Pybakeres Dyche" should be repaired before Michaelmas under penalty of a fine of 12*d.* for each defaulter.[2]

The dike-reeves, *prepositi fossatorum*, or *custodes fossatorum*, were officers who are mentioned frequently in later documents. They were responsible for the general maintenance of established custom. That the details of this custom were complicated enough can be seen from scattered notices in presentments and inquisitions of various dates. In Wisbech Hundred no one was permitted to pasture any animals, with the exception of sheep, on the banks themselves. Swine were particularly dangerous to the banks, and the dike-reeves claimed a penny for every pig found unringed near the *fossata saluacionum*.[3] Various methods were adopted to protect the crests of banks from injury by animals, because the "chasing and rechasing" of cattle was always a menace. Further, great care was taken to regulate the methods by which men dug earth to repair their portions of the dikes lest they committed further damage. Along some banks, willows were planted for their better preservation; and if, perchance, these trees were destroyed by cattle, they had to be replaced by the owner of the cattle. It would be possible to enumerate very many more of these details of administration. Every possible misdemeanour seems to have been prepared for, and every contingency guarded against—at any rate on paper. In Norfolk Marshland, the fines collected by the dike-reeves for breach of the ancient custom were known as the penalty of *bylaw*, *biscot*, *triscot* and *wopeny*.[4] "Bylaw" was levied for

[1] British Museum, Additional Charters, No. 39480.
[2] British Museum, Additional Charters, No. 39647.
[3] See N. Neilson, *A Terrier of Fleet, Lincolnshire* (1920), pp. xlviii and 174 (dated 1193).
[4] W. Dugdale, *op. cit.* pp. 271 and 292 *et seq.* For *byscot* see N. Neilson, *Customary Rents* (1910), p. 106.

neglect of the first summons to repair; "biscot", double in amount, was the penalty for failure to respond to the second summons; "triscot", three times the "bylaw", followed upon the third failure; "wopeny" was a penny taken by a person distraining for each distress. There may have been further punishment. William Harrison mentions a traditional and cruel practice of placing an offender in a sea-wall and building him in.[1] I have found no reference to this punishment in the Fenland.

THE FIFTEENTH CENTURY

During the following century, the interference of the central administration in the affairs of the Fenland was regularised by statute. The activity of the *ad hoc* commissions was defined more particularly by an Act of 1427 which merely continued the existing machinery, and which does not seem to have inaugurated any new policy.[2] Its preamble declared that:

Our sovereign lord the King, by the advice and assent aforesaid, considering the great damage and losses, which now late be happened by the great inundations of waters in divers parts of the realm, and that much greater damage is very like to ensue, if remedy be not speedily provided, hath ordained and granted, (1) that during ten years next ensuing several commissions of sewers shall be made to divers persons by the chancellor of *England* for the time being, to be sent into all parts of the realm where shall be needful, according to the form that followeth....

The statutory form of the commission, thus prescribed, authorised the commissioners to summon juries, to assess liability, and to make ordinances for the convenient administration of the marsh. They were

to enquire by the oath as well of knights, as other good and lawful men of the said county, as well within liberties as without, by whom the truth of the matter may be best known, by whose default such damages have there happened, and who doth hold lands and tenements or hath any common of pasture or fishing in those parts, or else in any wise have, or may have, the defence,

---

[1] W. Harrison, "The Description of Britaine" in R. Holinshed, *Chronicles of England, Scotlande, and Irelande* (1577), i, 108.
[2] 6 Henry VI, cap. v.

profit, and safeguard, as well in peril nigh, as from the same far off, by the said walls, ditches, gutters, sewers, bridges, causeys, and wears, and also hurt or commodity by the same trenches, and there to distrain all them for the quantity of their lands and tenements, either by the number of acres, or by their plow lands, for the rate of the portion of their tenure, or for the quantity of their common of pasture or fishing, together with the bailiffs of liberties, and other places of the counties and places aforesaid, to repair the said walls, ditches, gutters, sewers, bridges, causeys, and wears, in the places necessary, and the same or other, as often and where shall be needful to make of new, and to cleanse the said trenches in places necessary, and if need be to stop them up.

Thus, the authority of the commissioners to tax was based on the presentment of a jury. Provided they observed the law of England, "doing therein as to justice pertaineth", their acts were not examinable by any court of law. This procedure remained the basis of subsequent commissions until the General Sewers Act[1] of 1531.

But, on the other hand, this form of commission and this machinery are already apparent in the preceding century. Beyond making *de jure* what had been *de facto*, the purpose of the statute is obscure.[2] Dugdale sought an explanation[3] of the statute in the direction given to the commissioners

to make and ordain necessary and convenient statutes and ordinances for the defence and safety of the said sea banks and marshes, and the parts adjoining, according to the laws and customs of *Romney* marsh, and to hear and determine according to the laws and custom of our realm of *England*, and the custom of *Romney* marsh, all and singular the premises, as well at our suit, as the suit of any other that will complain before you in this behalf.

Yet, apart from this, there is no other indication that the object of the statute was to establish the custom of Romney Marsh[4] as a model. The Romney custom had already been

---

[1] See H. C. Darby, *The Draining of the Fens* (1940), pp. 3 *et seq.*

[2] For a discussion, see H. G. Richardson, *Eng. Hist. Rev.* xxxiv, 391 (1919).   [3] W. Dugdale, *op. cit.* p. 34.

[4] The ancient customs of Romney Marsh, established in 1250, provided for the repair of sea-banks at the charge of the landholders within the marsh, according to the quantity of land held by each. The tax was fixed by twenty-four men elected by the commonalty; and they, in turn, appointed a marsh bailiff to assess and levy the tax.

applied to areas in the Fenland before 1427. In 1395, it had been applied in the area north of the Witham;[1] in 1399 to the banks and sewers between Boston and Friskney;[2] in 1416, in Holland and Kesteven generally.[3] And, in the years succeeding 1427, the laws of Romney Marsh did become, as Dugdale said, "the rule and standard"[4] for the other marshes of the realm,[5] although absolute conformity was not possible.

The statute of 1427 granted the right to summon commissions for ten years; two years later[6] the commissioners were allowed to "execute their own ordinance". But, in 1439, "many towns and lands in great quantity be drowned and destroyed, to the great hindrance of the said realm", and provisions were made to extend the period of the grant for another ten years.[7]

The truth of this generalisation about flooding may be seen, for example, from the complaints of a jury in 1439; through neglect of sewers by a variety of landholders, "the whole fen, called Wisebeche fen, belonging to the Bishop of Ely, was drowned; so that the said Bishop and his tenants of Wisebeche hundred could not receive any benefit in the same".[8] The numerous presentments for neglect, at another session of sewers at Wisbech in the preceding year, speak for themselves.[9] The repetition visible in successive ordinances of the commissioners is, in itself, an indication of the insufficiency of their efforts. But still their work had a great palliative effect. "Great losses were like to have come if remedy had not been lately provided"; and, in 1444, the right of summoning commissions was extended to the fifteen

[1] Patent Rolls, 18 Richard II, pt. ii, m. 14d.
[2] Patent Rolls, 1 Henry IV, pt. iv, m. 32d.
[3] Patent Rolls, 3 Henry V, pt. i, m. 17d.
[4] W. Dugdale, *op. cit.* p. 16.
[5] See, for example, the references in the commission of sewers at Wisbech in 1438 (pp. 176 *et seq.* below). See also the reference to the Romney customs in the Statute of Sewers, 1531.—H. C. Darby, *The Draining of the Fens* (1940), p. 5.　　　　[6] 8 Henry VI, cap. iii.
[7] 18 Henry VI, cap. x.　　　　[8] W. Dugdale, *op. cit.* p. 328.
[9] See Appendix, pp. 175 *et seq.* below.

years "next ensuing".[1] In 1472, this was continued for another term of fifteen years.[2] Finally, in 1487, the term was extended for another twenty-five years.[3] Thus, during the fifteenth century, the practice of regulating fen economy by commissions had settled down into a steady system.[4]

The actual proceedings of the commissioners at this time are best illustrated by a transcript[5] of an inquisition taken in 1438. By this, known as Haltoft's Commission, the rivers around Wisbech and Guyhirne were scoured and their banks repaired. The word "repair" is indeed the clue to the whole of the activity produced by this system of commissions. For though they had large powers, the attention of the commissioners was limited mainly to the maintenance and improvement of existing channels. "To mend rather than to make" was their motto. A constant refrain in all their proceedings was the clause "as anciently they had used to do".[6] "Newdike", "Newdrayne", and "New-leame", are frequent in documents describing fen boundaries;[7] and new ditches were frequently made,[8] of course, as the circumstances of time and place demanded, but these were rarely of more than local importance, a further contribution to the maintenance of the *status quo*. As far as record survives, the fourteenth and fifteenth centuries were marked not by visionary projects for a general drainage, but by the diligent and humdrum labours

---

[1] 23 Henry VI, cap. ix.   [2] 12 Edw. IV, cap. vi.

[3] 4 Henry VI, cap. i.

[4] For the Statute of Sewers, 1531, see H. C. Darby, *The Draining of the Fens* (1940), pp. 3 *et seq.*

[5] See p. 175 below; see also plate 10. Gilbert Haltoft, one of the Barons of the Exchequer, resided near *Welle* in the Isle of Ely.

[6] See p. 148 above; see also footnote 4, p. 156.

[7] See (1) W. Dugdale, *op. cit.* p. 372; (2) pp. 149 and 153 above.

[8] See W. Dugdale, *op. cit.* p. 371 for a controversy in 1615 about the making of new drains. The practice of earlier times was examined, and it was concluded "that the commissioners had no power to raise new banks, drains, or sluices, where there had been none before". As Dugdale goes on to show, the situation was controversial; some new banks had certainly been made—witness their names. See also p. 101 above; and H. C. Darby, *The Draining of the Fens* (1940), p. 31.

of successive generations of commissioners battling against the difficulties of drains and outfalls.

To this generalisation there were certain exceptions. Hondius, who published Mercator's *Atlas* in 1636, referred to a drainage scheme ascribed to John of Gaunt at the latter end of the fourteenth century.[1] If this ever existed, no other mention of it has survived; but it should be noted that John of Gaunt resided at Bolingbroke Castle on the border of the Fenland, and that, as Duke of Lancaster, he held considerable fenland estates. At any rate, nothing was done in the matter. No trace likewise has remained of another design[2] which Hondius ascribed to Margaret Countess of Richmond, the mother of Henry VII. Again, this may have been an error on the part of the Netherlander.

These hypothetical projects do not exhaust the achievement of the late Middle Ages in the way of original drainage-works. In 1223, for example, the inhabitants of Marshland in Norfolk had erected the bank called Old Podyke to defend their land against the descent of upland waters. Its story was the one common to most fen banks—a succession of breaches caused by nature or by evildoers, and successive drownings of the neighbouring country. In 1422, the Commissioners judged it incapable of being repaired on account of the weakness of the ground upon which it stood;[3] and, accordingly, the New Podyke was made, extending westward from Salter's Lode.

But towering above all effort was the work of Bishop Morton shortly before the end of the fifteenth century. He seems to have been the first person not only to project but also to carry into effect a large design for draining.[4] At con-

[1] H. Hondius and G. Mercator, *Atlas, or A Geographicke Description* (1636), p. 66. [2] *Ibid.*
[3] See W. Dugdale, *op. cit.* pp. 263 *et seq.*
[4] S. B. J. Skertchly, *Geology of the Fenland* (1877), p. 73, comments on this: "It is singular that no contemporary records remain respecting the construction of this work. Thus Dugdale, whose splendid compilation of the records of ancient drainage stands without a rival, has no notice of *any* work executed between the years 1468 and 1528. Gough and Camden

siderable expense a straight cut was made from Stanground
near Peterborough to Guyhirne on the assumption that the
upland waters would seek the greater gradient of the direct
route in preference to their circuitous course. This cut yet
bears the name of Morton's Leam[1]; it was 12 miles long, 40
feet broad and 4 feet deep, and by means of it, and its associated dams, the River Nene was conveyed in direct line to
Wisbech.[2] At Guyhirne, the bishop built a tower so that he
might see his workmen afar off in the level. This brick tower
was often referred to in later Inquisitions and Drainage Acts;
and it was still standing in 1810 when the Barrier Banks Act
was passed.[3] The significance of Morton's work lay in the fact
that he adopted on a large scale the practice of straight cuts
and artificial rivers. This practice became an example for all
subsequent drainage work in the Fenland. His work suffered
the common fate of most fen drains; just before the general
reclamation of the seventeenth century, the water in the New
Leam or Morton's Leam was flowing from Guyhirne by Elm
and Outwell to the Ouse, instead of taking its course directly
through Wisbech to the sea.[4] But that the scheme can be
criticised is beside the argument. Coming at the close of the
century and at the close of the Middle Ages, it pointed forward to a new regime. But there was yet to be a century of
experiment before any "designe" for a general draining
emerged.

were equally silent, and though Armstrong dates the work as executed in
the year 1490 he gives no authority to prove it." Skertchly adds, giving
reasons, that the Leam was made "pretty much along the site of an old
water-course".   [1] See plate 11.

[2] W. Dugdale, *op. cit.* pp. 372–3.

[3] *Fenland Notes and Queries*, v, 72–3 (1903).

[4] MS. Volume on Draining, f. 187 (Bishop's Muniment Room, Ely,
A. 8). This dates from the early seventeenth century, but contains
transcripts of older documents.

William Camden, in the *Britannia*, referred to Morton's scheme, "Which
fell out quite contrary: For it standeth now in no great steed, and the
neighbour inhabitants complaine that the course of *Nen* into the sea by
Clowscrosse, is by this meanes altogether hindered and stopped." (1637
edition, p. 495.)

SOURCES & BIBLIOGRAPHY

A. UNPUBLISHED

1. At the Public Record Office

Ancient Indictments.
Chancery Proceedings.
Coram Rege Rolls.
Duchy of Lancaster, Court Rolls.
Duchy of Lancaster, Miscellaneous Rolls.
Ministers Accounts, Bishops' Temporalities.
Ministers Accounts, Duchy of Lancaster.
Ministers Accounts, General Series.
Rentals and Surveys, General Series.

2. At the British Museum

Additional Charters.
Additional MSS.
Cott. MSS. Vesp. xv.
Ely Register, Cott. MSS. Claud. C. xi.
Spalding Cartulary. Parts i, ii, iii, Additional MSS. 35296. Parts iv, v, Harleian MSS. 742.

3. Other Manuscripts

Cartulary of Ely Convent (Liber M), Bishop's Muniment Room, Ely, G. 3.
Old Coucher Book of Ely, Bishop's Muniment Room, Ely, G. 3.
Red Book of Thorney, Cambridge University Library (Additional MSS. 3021–2).
Seventeenth-century MS. Volume on Draining, Bishop's Muniment Room, Ely, A. 8.

B. PUBLISHED

(Arranged alphabetically)

Abbreviatio Placitorum (Record Commission, 1811).
Anglo-Saxon Chronicle. The best edition is that of J. Earle and C. Plummer, 2 vols. (1892–99). The Rolls Series volume, with a translation, was edited by B. Thorpe. 2 vols. (1861).
ARMSTRONG, T. The history of the ancient and present state of the navigation of the port of King's Lyn, and of Cambridge...and... of the...Bedford Level. Also the history of the ancient and present state of draining in that Level...(1725, reprinted in 1766).

ARNOLD, T. Memorials of St Edmund's Abbey (Rolls Series, 3 vols. 1890–96).

ATKINSON, T. D. An Architectural History of the Benedictine Monastery of Saint Etheldreda at Ely. 2 vols. (1933).

AULT, W. O. Court Rolls of the Abbey of Ramsey and of the Honor of Clare (1928).

BARLEY, M. W. "Lincolnshire Rivers in the Middle Ages." *Lincs. Associated Architect. and Archaeol. Soc. Reports and Papers* (1938), 1.

BATESON, MARY. "The register of Crabhouse Nunnery." *Norfolk Archaeology*, xi, 1–71 (1892).

BEDDOE, M. A. S. Mem. Anthropological Society (1869).

BEDE. Historiae Ecclesiasticae gentis Anglorum libri quinque. Ed. by Charles Plummer. 2 vols. (1896).

BELLOC, H. The Road (1924).

— Hills and the Sea (1930).

BELOE, E. M. "Freebridge Marshland Hundred and the Making of Lynn." *Norfolk Archaeology*, xii, 311 (1895).

BENTHAM, J. History and Antiquities of the Conventual and Cathedral Church of Ely. 2 vols. (1771). 2nd edition in one vol. (1812), with Supplement, by William Stevenson (1817).

BIRCH, W. DE GRAY. Memorials of St Guthlac of Crowland (1881).

— Cartularium Saxonicum. 3 vols. (1885–93).

BLOMEFIELD, F. An Essay towards a Topographical History of the County of Norfolk. 5 vols. (1739–75). Another edition, 11 vols. (1805–10).

BRACTON, HENRY DE. Notebook. Ed. by F. W. Maitland (Rolls Series, 3 vols. 1887).

BYGOTT, J. Eastern England (1923).

CAMDEN, W. Britannia (1637).

CHAPMAN, F. R. The Sacrist Rolls of Ely. 2 vols. (1907).

CLARK, J. G. D. "Recent Researches on the Post-glacial Deposits of the English Fenland." *Irish Naturalists' Journal*, v, 144 (1934).

CLARK, J. W. (ed.). Liber Memorandorum Ecclesie de Bernewelle (1907).

CLIFFORD, M. H. See Godwin, H.

Close Rolls, Calendars.

Commission on Historical Manuscripts: Sixth Report (1877); Twelfth Report, Appendix, pt. viii (1891).

DARBY, H. C. "The Fenland Frontier in Anglo-Saxon England." *Antiquity*, vii, 185 (1934).

— "The Domesday Geography of Norfolk and Suffolk." *Geog. Journ.* lxxxv, 432 (1935).

— (ed.). An Historical Geography of England before A.D. 1800 (1936).

— "The Domesday Geography of Cambridgeshire." *Proc. Camb. Antiq. Soc.* xxxvi, 35 (1936).

— (ed.). The Cambridge Region (1938).

— The Draining of the Fens (1940).

DARBY, H. C. and RAMSDEN, P. M. "The Middle Level of the Fens and its Reclamation." *Victoria County History of Huntingdonshire*, iii, 249 (1936).

DAVENPORT, F. G. The Economic Development of a Norfolk Manor, 1086–1565 (1906).

DAVIES, J. etc. The Fen and Marshland Churches. 3 vols. (n.d.).

Domesday Book (Record Commission) seu Liber Censualis Wilhelmi Primi regis Angliae. Vols. i–ii, ed. by Abraham Farley (1783); vols. iii–iv, ed. by Henry Ellis (1816).

DOUGLAS, D. C. Social Structure of Medieval East Anglia (1927).

— Feudal Documents from the Abbey of Bury St Edmunds (1932).

DRAYTON, M. Polyolbion, or a Chorographical Description of Great Britain, digested into a Poem (1622).

DU CANGE, C. D. Glossarium Mediae et Infimae Latinatis. Ed. by G. A. L. Henschel. 7 vols. (1840–50).

DUGDALE, W. History of Imbanking and Drayning (1662). 2nd edition ed. by C. N. Cole (1772).

— Monasticon Anglicanum. 3 vols. (1655–73). Two additional volumes by John Stevens (1722–23). New edition in 6 vols. (1817–30; reprinted in 1846).

EKWALL, E. English River Names (1928).

— "The Scandinavian Element", being chapter iv of the Introduction to the Survey of English Place-Names. Ed. by A. Mawer and F. M. Stenton (1929).

Fenland Notes and Queries. 9 vols. (1891–1904).

Fenland Survey Exhibition Catalogue (Heffer, Cambridge, 1934).

FLOWER, C. T. Public Works in Medieval Law. 2 vols. (Selden Society, 1915 and 1923).

FOWLER, G. "The Old River Beds in the Fenlands." Geog. Journ. lxxxix, 210 (1932).

— "Fenland Waterways, Past and Present. South Level District. Parts I and II." Proc. Camb. Antiq. Soc. xxxiii, 108 (1933); and ibid. xxxiv, 17 (1934).

— "The Extinct Waterways of the Fenland." Geog. Journ. lxxxiii, 30 (1934).

Fox, C. The Archaeology of the Cambridge Region (1923).

FULLER, T. Worthies of England (1662).

GIBBONS, A. Ely Episcopal Records (1891).

GODWIN, H. "The Origin of Roddons." Geog. Journ. xci, 241 (1938).

GODWIN, H. and CLIFFORD, M. H. "Studies of the Post-Glacial History of British Vegetation." Phil. Trans. Roy. Soc. London (Series B), ccxxix, 323 (1938).

GOODWIN, C. W. The Anglo-Saxon version of the life of St Guthlac, originally written by Felix of Crowland, with a translation (1848).

GRAS, N. S. B. The Evolution of the English Corn Market (1915).

HALL, H. Red Book of the Exchequer (Rolls Series, 3 vols. 1896).

HAMILTON, N. E. S. A. (ed.). William of Malmesbury, De Gestis Pontificum Anglorum (Rolls Series, 1870).

— Inquisitio Comitatus Cantabrigiensis (1876).

HART, W. H. and LYONS, P. A. Cartularium Monasterii de Rameseia (Rolls Series, 1884–93).

HEARNE, T. Thomas Sprott's *Chronica* (1719).

HOLINSHED, R. Chronicles of England, Scotlande, and Irelande (1577).

HONDIUS, H. and MERCATOR, G. Atlas, or A Geographicke Description (1636).

HOWLETT, R. Chronicles of the Reigns of Stephen, Henry II, and Richard (Rolls Series. 4 vols. 1884–89).

HUDSON, W. "The Assessment of the Townships of the County of Norfolk, 1334." *Norfolk Archaeology*, xii, 243 (1895).

— "The Norwich Taxation of 1254, so far as it related to the Diocese of Norwich." *Norfolk Archaeology*, xvii, 46 (1910).

JACOB, E. F. Studies in the Period of Baronial Reform and Rebellion, 1258–67 (1925).

KEMBLE, J. M. Codex diplomaticus aevi Saxonici. 6 vols. (1839–48).

KENNY, E. J. A. "A Roman Bridge in the Fens." *Geog. Journ.* lxxxii, 434 (1933).

LAMBERT, M. R. and WALKER, R. Boston, Tattershall and Croyland (1930).

LETHBRIDGE, T. C. "An Attempt to discover the Site of the Battle of Aldreth." *Proc. Camb. Antiq. Soc.* xxxi, 155 (1931); and *ibid.* xxxiv, 90 (1934).

Liber Quotidianus Contrarotulatoris Garderobae (1787).

LIEBERMANN, F. "Über ostenglische Geschichtsquellen des 12., 13., 14. Jahrhunderts, besonders den falschen Ingulf." *Gesellsch. fur ältere Deutsche Gesch. Neues Archiv*, xviii, 225 (Hanover, 1893).

LONGFIELD, T. E. The Subsidence of London (Ordnance Survey Professional Paper, 1933).

LUARD, H. R. Matthew Paris, Chronica Maiora (Rolls Series, 7 vols. 1872–83).

— Flores Historiarum (Rolls Series, 3 vols. 1890).

LUNT, W. E. The Valuation of Norwich (1926).

MABILLON, J. Annales Ordinis S. Benedicti, iv, 688 (1707).

MACAULAY, LORD. History of England. Ed. C. H. Firth (1914).

MACDONALD, G. W. Historical Notices of the Parish of Holbeach (1890).

MACRAY, W. D. Chronicon Abbatiae Ramesiensis (Rolls Series, 1886).

MAITLAND, F. W. "The History of a Cambridgeshire Manor." *Eng. Hist. Rev.* ix, 417 (1894).

— Domesday Book and Beyond (1897).

MAITLAND, F. W. and BAILDON, W. P. The Court Baron, together with select pleas from the Bishop of Ely's court of Littleport (Selden Society, 1891).

MAJOR, K. "Some Early Documents Relating to Holbeach." *Lincs. Associated Architect. and Archaeol. Soc. Reports and Papers*, xli, 39 (1934).

— "Conan Son of Ellis, an Early Inhabitant of Holbeach." *Lincs. Associated Architect. and Archaeol. Soc. Reports and Papers*, xlii, 1 (1936).

MARLOWE, C. Legends of the Fenland People (1926).
MARSHALL, W. "On Some Ancient Court Rolls of the Manor of Little-port." *Proc. Camb. Antiq. Soc.* iv, 97 (1881).
MAWER, A. and STENTON, F. M. The Place-Names of Bedfordshire and Huntingdonshire (1926).
— — Introduction to the Survey of English Place-Names (1929).
MEM. GEOL. Survey, 1891. The Geology of Parts of Cambridgeshire and Suffolk (a co-operative work).
MUSKETT, J. J. "Cambridgeshire Lay Subsidy Rolls." *The East Anglian*, vols. x–xii (1903–8).
NEILSON, N. Economic Conditions on the Manors of Ramsey Abbey (Philadelphia, 1899).
— Customary Rents (1910).
— A Terrier of Fleet, Lincolnshire (1920).
Nonarum Inquisitiones (Record Commission, 1807).
Oxford English Dictionary.
PAGE, F. M. "Bidentes Hoylandiae." *Economic History*, i, 603 (1929).
— The Estates of Crowland Abbey (1934).
PALMER, W. M. "On the Cambridgeshire Assize Rolls." *Proc. Camb. Antiq. Soc.* iii, 226 (1896).
— Cambridgeshire Subsidy Rolls, 1250–1695 (1912). Reprinted from *The East Anglian*, vols. vii–xiii (1898–1909).
Patent Rolls, Calendars.
PEARSON, J. B. "The Assessments of Cambridgeshire, 1291–1889." *Proc. Camb. Antiq. Soc.* viii, 283 (1895).
— "On the Cambridgeshire Subsidies." *Proc. Camb. Antiq. Soc.* ix, 120 (1899).
PELL, O. C. "On the Domesday geldable Hide." *Proc. Camb. Antiq. Soc.* vi, 166 (1891).
PENNING, W. H. and JUKES-BROWN, A. J. The Geology of the Neighbour-hood of Cambridge (1881).
PETRIE, H. and SHARPE, J. Monumenta Historica Britannica (1848).
PHILLIPS, C. W. "Roman Ferry across the Wash." *Antiquity*, vi, 342 (1932).
— "The Present State of Archaeology in Lincolnshire, Part II." *Arch. Journ.* xci, 97 (1934).
RICHARDSON, H. G. "Note on the Constitution and Records of Com-missions of Sewers." *Report of Royal Commission on Public Records*, vol. ii (pt. ii), p. 98 (1914).
— "The Early History of Commissions of Sewers." *Eng. Hist. Rev.* xxxiv, 385 (1919).
RILEY, H. T. Chronicle of the Abbey of Croyland (1854).
— "The history and charters of Ingulph considered." *Archaeol. Journ.* xix, 32 and 114 (1862).
— Gesta Abbatium Monasterii Sancti Albani (Rolls Series, 12 vols. 1863–76).
ROBERTSON, A. J. Anglo-Saxon Charters (1939).

174   SOURCES AND BIBLIOGRAPHY

ROGERS, J. E. THOROLD. Six Centuries of Work and Wages (1906).

Rotuli Hundredorum (2 vols., Record Commission, 1818).

ROUND, J. H. Geoffrey de Maundeville (1892).

SEARLE, W. G. Ingulf and the Historia Croylandensis (Cambridge Antiq. Soc. 1894).

SEMPLE, E. Influences of Geographic Environment (1911).

SKEAT, W. W. Place-Names of Cambridgeshire (Cambridge Antiq. Soc. 1901).

SKEAT, W. W. "Two Anglo-Saxon Fragments of the Eleventh Century." Proc. Camb. Philol. Soc. (1903).

SKERTCHLY, S. B. J. The Geology of the Fenland (1877).

SMILES, S. The Early Engineers (1864).

SPARKE, J. Historiae Anglicanae Scriptores Varii (1723).

STAPLETON, T. Chronicon Petroburgense (Camden Society, 1849).

State Papers, Domestic Series.

Statutes of the Realm.

STENTON, F. M. Documents Illustrative of the Social and Economic History of the Danelaw (1920).

— "The Road System of Medieval England." Econ. Hist. Rev. vii, 1 (1936).

STEVENSON, D. A. "The Flooded Fens: A Tidal River and its Control." Scot. Geog. Mag. liii, 171 (1937).

STEVENSON, F. S. "St Botolph (Botwulf) and Iken." Proc. Suffolk Inst. Arch. and Nat. Hist. xviii, 29 (1924).

STEWART, D. J. Architectural History of Ely Cathedral (1868).

— Liber Eliensis, Books i–ii (1848).

STREATFIELD, C. G. Lincolnshire and the Danes (1884).

STUBBS, C. W. Historical Memorials of Ely Cathedral (1897).

SUTTON, A. F. "Churches visited from Wisbech." Lincs. Associated Architect. and Archaeol. Soc. Reports and Papers, xxvii, 245 (1904).

SWINNERTON, H. H. "The Post-Glacial Deposits of the Lincolnshire Coast." Quart. Journ. Geol. Soc. lxxxvii, 360 (1931).

TAYLOR, ISAAC. Words and Places (1902).

THORPE, B. Codex Exonensis (1842).

TURNER, G. J. Select Pleas of the Forest, 1209–1334 (Selden Society, 1901).

Victoria County Histories: Cambridgeshire, Huntingdonshire, Lincolnshire, Norfolk, Northamptonshire.

WARNER, G. The Guthlac Roll (Roxburghe Club, 1928).

WARNER, R. H. History of Thorney Abbey (1879).

WEBB, S. and B. English Local Government: Statutory Authorities for Special Purposes (1922).

WELLS, S. The History of the Drainage of the Great Level of the Fens called Bedford Level. 2 vols. (1830).

WHARTON, H. Anglia Sacra sive collectio historiarum de archiepiscopis et episcopis Angliae ad annum 1540. 2 vols. (1691).

WHEELER, W. H. A History of the Fens of South Lincolnshire (2nd edition, 1896).

WHITE, C. H. EVELYN. "The Aldreth Causeway, its Bridge and Surroundings." *Proc. Cambs. and Hunts. Archaeol. Soc.* i, 12 (1904).

WILLARD, J. F. "Inland Transportation in England during the Fourteenth Century." *Speculum*, i, 361 (1926).

WRÉTTS-SMITH, M. "Organization of Farming at Croyland Abbey 1257–1321." *Journ. of Econ. and Business History*, iv, 168 (1932).

WYLIE, J. H. History of England under Henry IV (1894).

APPENDIX

A COMMISSION OF SEWERS HELD AT WISBECH IN 1438

Public Record Office, Chancery Miscellanea (c. 47), 7/5

Inquisitio capta apud Wysebech in Comitatu Cantebrig' die Sabbati proximo ante festum Sancti Jacobi Apostoli Anno Regni Regis Henrici sexti post conquestum sexto decimo coram Johanne Colvyle milite Gilberto Haultofte & sociis suis tam Justiciariis domini Regis virtute cujusdam commissionis ejusdem domini Regis eis directi quam domini Ludovici Archiepiscopi Rothomagensis administratoris perpetui in spiritualibus & temporalibus ecclesie & episcopatus Eliensis virtute litterarum Patencium eiusdem domini Ludovici eis factarum ad omnia Wallias Fossata Gutturas seweras pontes calcetas & gurgites per costeram maris & marissi in fines & limites per omnes Comitatus Lincoln' Northt' Hunt' & Cantebr' & Trenchias aquarum dulcium per diversa loca in Comitatibus predictis ad mare descendentes supervidendum & defectus eorum audiendum & terminandum assignatis per sacramentum Johannis Bytham Johannis Howsold Johannis Masse Johannis Thruston Richardi Lombe Willelmi Halman Martini Thomson Roberti Algoode Willelmi Gybbe Johannis Derby Johannis Mannyng senioris Johannis Drewe Willelmi Russhforth Johannis Barker Draper Johannis Edwarde Johannis Grene Nicholai Bateman & Galfridi Reynald qui dicunt super sacramentum suum quod fossatum maris incipiens apud Tyddegote in Tydde Sancti Egidii juxta Comitatum Lincoln' usque ad Bevys Crosse in Wysebech predicta tenetur esse in altitudine quinquaginta pedum & in latitudine in superiori parte dicti fossati sex pedum Et quod omnes terrarum sive tenementorum tenentes in dicta villa de Wysebych & in villis de Leveryngton Tydde Sancti Egidii & Newton quilibet eorum pro rata tenure sue usi fuerunt a tempore cujus contrarii memoria hominum non existit ad reperandum sustentandum ac faciendum dictum fossatum ac illud tam per dictam consuetudinem quam per judicium & assignacionem quorundem Justiciariorum progenitorum domini Regis nunc quondam Regum Anglie ad omnia Supradicta audiendum & terminandum assignatorum redditum & factum reperare sustentare ac facere tenentur & obligantur secundum quantitatem tenure sue.

Super quo pro eo quod videtur Justiciariis predictis tam per veredictum Juratorum predictorum quam per supervisum eorundem Justiciariorum in hac parte habita comparentibus omnibus in hac parte convocandis & consencientibus ac visis intellectis statutis in hiis casibus editis de Romneymerch predicti Justiciarii statuunt & ordinant pro salvacione omnium villarum predictarum quod omnes terrarum seu tenementorum tenentes in dictis villis videlicet quilibet eorum pro rata tenure sue seu tenementorum suorum reperet sustentet & de novo faciet tociens quociens necesse fuerit predictum fossatum per eum aut per eos in quo vel in quibus defectus reperacionis sustentacionis sive de novo reperietur ad opus reperacionis sustentacionis sive de novo factionis fossati predicti & hoc tociens quociens continget in futuris hujusmodi defectus vel defectum reperiri.

Item presentant quod tenentes terrarum sive tenementorum in veteri mercato de Wysebech predicta usi fuerunt a tempore cujus contrarii memoria hominum non existit ad reperandum sustentandum & de novo faciendum quoddam fossatam [sic] maris de Bevisecrosse usque ad magnum pontem de Wysebech ex parte occidentali ripe de Wysbech predicta videlicet quilibet erga terras seu tenementa sua Et quod dictum fossatum tenetur esse in altitudine x pedum & in latitudine superiori parte dicti fossati xij pedum.

Super quo pro eo quod videtur Justiciariis predictis tam per veredictum Juratorum predictorum quam supervisum eorundem Justiciariorum in hac parte habita comparentibus omnibus in hac parte convocandis & consencientibus ac visis intellectis statutis in hiis casibus editis de Rumney Merch predicti Justiciarii statuunt & ordinant pro salvacione omnium terrarum seu tenementorum predictorum in veteri mercato de Wysbech predicta quod omnes predictarum terrarum seu tenementorum in veteri mercato de Wysbech predicta tenentes videlicet quilibet eorum erga terras seu tenementa sua reperet seu sustentet ac de novo faciet dicta fossata tociens quociens necesse fuerit Et quod nullis eorum jactet fimum nec aliquod aliud in dictam Ripam nec faciet Stampes in dictam Ripam nec ponet segerekes nec sterquilinium videlicet a Geyherne usque mare super litore dicte Ripe per quod aqua artetur vel obstupetur Et hoc sub pena xxs domino Episcopo solvenda per eum aut per eos in quo vel in quibus defectus reperacionis sustentacionis sive de novo factionis fossati predicti sive aliorum ordinacionum vel statutorum predictorum imposterum reperietur & hoc tociens quociens continget in futuro hujusmodi defectus vel defectum reperiri.

Item dicunt quod terrarum & tenementorum tenentes de le

Townehende de Wysbech ex parte boriali Ripe usi fuerunt a tempore cujus contrarii memoria hominum non existit ad reperandum sustentandum & de novo faciendum quoddam fossatum vocatum le Eebryncke a magno Ponte in Wysbech usque Soreldyke Et dicunt eciam quod terrarum sive tenementorum tenentes in le Fenhende de Wysbech usi fuerunt a tempore predicto etc [sic] ad reperandum sustentandum & de novo faciendum quoddam fossatum vocatum le Newdyke videlicet a Sorelsdyke usque Gyehirnum et aliud fossatum vocatum le Fendyke quod se extendit a Gehyrnum predictum usque Piggesdrove Crosse Et dicunt eciam quod terrarum & tenementorum tenentes in le Fenhende de Wysbech non sunt sufficientes ad reperandum predictam fossatam [sic] de le Newdyke videlicet a Sorelsdyke usque Gehirn' & le Fendyke a Gehirn' usque Piggesdrove Crosse.

Super quo pro eo quod videtur Justiciariis predictis tam per veredictum Juratorum predictorum quam supervisum eorundem Justiciariorum in hac parte habita comparentibus omnibus in hac parte convocandis & consencientibus ac visis intellectis statutis in hiis casibus editis de Rumpney merssh predicti Justiciarii statuant [sic] & ordinant pro eo quod terrarum & tenementorum tenentes in le Fenhende de Wysbech non sunt sufficientes ad reperandum sustentandum & de novo faciendum predictum fossatum vocatum le Newdyke videlicet a Sorelsdyke usque le Gehirn' & fossatum maresci videlicet a Gehirn' usque Piggesdrove Crosse [?] tam terrarum & tenementorum tenentes de le Townehende ex parte boriali Ripe de Wysbech quam terrarum & tenementorum tenentes de le Fenhende de Wysbech de cetero reperabunt sustentabunt & de novo facient predicta fossata videlicet fossatum Marys vocatum le Ebryncke ex parte boriali ripe predicte videlicet a magno ponte de Wysbech usque Sorelsdyke & le Newdyke videlicet a Sorelsdyke usque Gehirn' & le Fendyke videlicet a Gehirn' predicto usque Piggesdrove Crosse videlicet quilibet pro rata tenure sue tociens quociens necesse fuerit.

Item presentant quod terrarum & tenementorum tenentes in Leveryngton usi fuerunt a tempore cujus contrarii memoria hominum non existit ad reperandum sustentandum & de novo faciendum quoddam fossatum maresci in Leveryngton videlicet a Piggesdrovecrosse usque le Clouse que est divisa inter Leverynton & Sutton quilibet pro rata tenure sue secundum antiquum agistamentum.

Super quo pro eo quod videtur Justiciariis predictis tam per veredictum predictorum Juratorum quam supervisum eorundem Justiciariorum in hac parte habita comparentibus omnibus in hac parte convocandis & consencientibus ac visis intellectis statutis in hiis casibus editis de Rumpneymerssh predicti Justiciarii statuant [*sic*] & ordinant pro salvacione tocius villate predicte quod predictum fossatum maresci in Leveryngton videlicet a Pyggesdrovecrosse usque le Clouse predictam de cetero reperetur sustentetur & de novo fiat per predictam villatam de Leveryngton tociens quociens necesse fuerit quilibet pro rata tenure sue.

Item presentant quod terrarum & tenementorum tenentes in Leveryngton usi fuerunt a tempore cujus contrarii memoria hominum non existit ad reperandum sustentandum & de novo faciendum quod fossatum vocatum Shoffendyke quod se extendit a clusa predicta usque le Goredyke in Newton et quilibet pro rata tenure sue.

Plus in dorso

Super quo pro eo videtur Justiciariis predictis tam per veredictum Juratorum predictorum quam per supervisum eorundem Justiciariorum in hac parte habita comparentibus omnibus convocandis & consencientibus ac visis & intellectis statutis in hiis casibus editis de Rumpney merssh predicti Justiciarii statuant [*sic*] & ordinant quod omnes terrarum & tenementorum tenentes in Leveryngton reperabunt sustentabunt & de novo facient predictum fossatum videlicet a clusa predicta usque le Goredyke in Newton videlicet quilibet pro rata tenure sue tociens quociens necesse fuerit.

Item presentant quod omnes terrarum & tenementorum tenentes in Newton usi fuerunt a tempore cujus contrarii memoria hominum non existit ad reperandum & sustentandum & de novo faciendum quoddam fossatum vocatum le Shoffendyke incipientem apud le Goredyke de Newton & extendit usque Tydthredyng videlicet quilibet pro rata tenure sue tociens quociens necesse fuerit.

Super quo pro eo quod videtur Justiciariis predictis tam per veredictum predictorum Juratorum quam supervisum eorundem Justiciariorum in hac parte habita comparentibus omnibus in hac parte convocandis & consencientibus ac visis & intellectis statutis in hiis casibus editis de Rumpney merssh predicti Justiciarii statuant [*sic*] & ordinant quod omnes terrarum & tenementorum tenentes in Newton predicta reperabunt & sustentabunt & de novo facient predictum fossatum videlicet le Goredyke predicto usque ad Tyd Thredyng predicta videlicet quilibet pro rata tenure sue tociens quociens necesse fuerit.

Item presentant quod omnes terrarum & tenementorum tenentes in Tyd Sancti Egidii usi fuerunt a tempore cujus contrarii memoria hominum non existit ad reperandum sustentandum &

de novo faciendum quoddam Fossatum vocatum Shoffendyke quod se extendit a Tydthredyng usque le Egreyndes in Tyd Sancti Egidii videlicet quilibet pro rata tenure sue tociens quociens necesse fuerit.

Super quo pro eo quod videtur Justiciariis predictis tam per veredictum Juratorum predictorum quam per supervisum eorundem Justiciariorum in hac parte habita comparentibus omnibus in hac parte convocandis & consencientibus ac visis intellectis statutis in hiis casibus editis de Rumpney merssh predicti Justiciarii statuunt & ordinant quod omnes terrarum & tenementorum tenentes in Tyd predicta reperabunt & sustentabunt & de novo facient predictum fossatum a Tyd Thredyng usque Tyd Egreyndes predicta videlicet quilibet pro rata tenure sue tociens quociens necesse fuerit.

Item dicunt quod a tempore cujus contrarii memoria hominum non existit debent & solent esse duas clusas in Leveryngton unde una clusa debet esse apud Rotespype in eadem villa ad Costas & expensas omnium qui habent terras a Newebriggedrove in Wysebech usque le Seedyke & alia apud Meysland in eadem villa ad Costas & expensas omnium illorum habentium terras a Soreldyke in Wysebeche usque Newebriggedrove in eadem villa.

Item presentant quod Prior de Ely & Thomas Tuddenham Miles debent & solent facere a tempore cujus contrarii memoria hominum non existit unam Crestam in Tholymersedrove in Wysbech incipientem apud le Fendyke & extendit usque Tolymers in eadem villa altitudine quatuor pedum & latitudine octo pedum.

Item dicunt quod terrarum & tenementorum tenentes de Gehirn feld de Wysbech a tempore cujus contrarii memoria [sic] non existit debent facere & reperare unam Crestam que se extendit a Blakesdyke usque Mariottesbrigge in eadem villa altitudine quatuor pedum & latitudine octo pedum.

Item dicunt quod omnes terrarum & tenementorum tenentes de Gehirnfeld de Wysbech a tempore cujus contrarii memoria hominum non existit debent facere unam Crestam a Mariottysbrigge usque Tolymersdrove juxta communem Seweram ex parte occidentali altitudine quatuor pedum & latitudine octo pedum.

Item dicunt quod terrarum & tenementorum tenentes de Gyhyrn Crosse in Wysebech usque Sorelsdyke in eadem villa debent facere & reperare unam Crestam super Blakedyke a Gyhyrn Crosse usque Sorelsdyke predicto altitudine iiij pedum & latitudine octo pedum.

Item dicunt quod terrarum & tenementorum tenentes in Gyhyrnfeld simul cum terris & tenementis Willelmi Cause in Tolymersfeld in Wysebech debent facere & reperare unam

Crestam A Mariottesdrove in Wysebech usque Doddesbrigge in eadem villa juxta communem Seweram ex parte boriali altitudine iiij pedum & latitudine octo pedum.

Item dicunt quod omnes terrarum & tenementorum tenentes in Gyehyrnfeld simul cum terris & tenementis Willelmi Caus in Tolymersfeld & terrarum & tenementorum tenentes de Mundeforth Felde debent facere & reperare unam Crestam a Doddesbrigge usque ad antiquam clusam ad terras Ricardi Benet altitudine iiij pedum & latitudine octo pedum.

Item dicunt quod omnes terrarum & tenementorum tenentes de Recheysfeld debent facere & reperare unam Crestam a dicta clusa usque Belymylle Brigge juxta communem Seweram ex parte orientali in altitudine iiij pedum & latitudine viij pedum.

Item presentant quod Thomas Hyptoft & tenentes sui debent facere & reperare unam Crestam in Ratrowe ex parte orientali dicte vie a Tolymersdrove usque Ratrowe Brigge altitudine iiij pedum & latitudine viij pedum.

Item presentant quod terrarum & tenementorum tenentes Hugonis Sorell in Willelake & terrarum & tenementorum tenentes de Mundeforth Felde debent facere & reperare unam Crestam in Gawyldrove A Doddesbrigge usque Blakedyke altitudine iiij pedum & latitudine viij pedum.

Item presentant quod omnes terrarum & tenementorum tenentes de xxix acras terre in le Tounehende in Wysebech debent facere & reperare quoddam Fossatum vocatum Belymylledyke videlicet a Belymylle Brigge usque terram nuper Willelmi Beteyns altitudine iiij pedum & latitudine viij pedum.

Item presentant quod omnes terrarum & tenementorum tenentes de Sayersfeld in Wysebech predicta debent facere & reperare unam Crestam in Walysgate incipientem apud Belymylle Brigge usque Robynsbrigge in eadem villa altitudine iiij pedum & latitudine viij pedum

Adhuc de Wysebech.

Item presentant quod omnes terrarum & tenementorum tenentes in Briggefeld in Wysebech ex parte boriali prope abuttantum super Brigge Drove versus orientalem debent facere & reperare unam Crestam in Brigge Drove in Wysebech in altitudine iiij pedum & latitudine octo pedum.

Item presentant quod omnes terrarum & tenementorum tenentes villate de Wysebech debent facere & reperare unam clusam in Sewera de Wysebech ad quendam Pontem in Newton juxta le Fytton Gole ad obstupandum aquam ibidem quando necesse fuerit.

Item presentant quod ubi tres pipe de novo facte in quoddam Campo vocato Smalemedowes in Wysebech videlicet prima pipa per Episcopum Eliensis & parcenarios suos secunda per dominum de Coldham & parcenarios suos & tercia per tenentes terrarum & tenementorum ex parte Australi ripe de Wysebech sunt facte nimis large in latitudine & contra presentacionem Et modo presentatum est quod emendantur.

Super quibus pro eo quod videtur Justiciariis predictis tam per veredictum Juratorum predictorum quam per supervisum eorundem Justiciariorum in hac parte habita comparentibus in hac parte convocandis & consencientibus ac visis intellectis statutis in hiis casibus editis de Rumpney merssh predicti Justiciarii statuunt & ordinant pro salvacione villate de Wysebech quod Episcopus Eliensis & successores sui Prior de Ely & successores sui Thomas Todenham Miles Thomas Hyptoft Willelmus Caus & heredes sui Dominus de Coldham & parcenarii sui & omnes alii supradicti ac omnes dictarum terrarum & tenementorum tenentes infra villatam de Wysebech ut predictum de cetero solentur ad faciendum reperandum & sustentandum omnia & singula in forma prout in presentacionibus predictis specificantur quilibet pro rata tenure sue tociens quociens necesse fuerit.

Item Justiciarii predicti statuunt & ordinant pro salvacione villate de Wysebech quod fossatum maresci vocatum Wysebech Feldyke barretur in certis locis ubi necesse est pro averiis ibidem transeuntibus Et quod Haffe[?] essentes infra maresce ibidem [?   ] fossatum maresci in diversis locis ubi necesse fuerit Et quod omnes terrarum & tenementorum tenentes de Oldefeld in Wysebech abuttantum super seweram de Coldham obstupandi debent fines fossati [?   ] apud Tybyry-lane usque Coldham Pipe.

Item Justiciarii predicti statuunt & ordinant quod omnia Kedella stampes damys [sic] & alia ingenia in Ripa de Wysbech [?   ] per que Aqua in aliquo artatur seu obstupatur amovantur & deponantur & quod nullus de cetero faciat in dicta Ripa hujus Stampes damma [sic] kedella seu alia ingenia vide-licet a Gehirn' usque ad mare sub pena Centum solidorum Episcopo Eliensis qui pro tempore fuerit solvenda Et quod unus custos pro salvacione patrie deputetur ad custodiendum & super-videndum aperiendum & claudendum lez iiij Gates annuatim de Wysebech Leveryngton Newton & Tyd Sancti Egidii ad Costas & expensas videlicet quilibet pro rata porcione terrarum suarum.

Item Justiciarii predicti statuunt & ordinant quod omnes esseweras cujuslibet villate de Wysebech a fossato maresci usque ad fossatum maris bene & in omnibus partibus fodiantur &

mundantur certis temporibus anni per illos per quos ex antiquo fodere mundare hac [?] consueverant Ita quod aqua habeat cursum suum sine ullo impedimento usque ad mare & quod omnes Pontes clusae pipae & gutturae infra omnes villatas hundredi predicti reperentur & mundentur bene & sufficiente in omnibus [?] necesse fuerit per illos per quos ut supradictum est Ita quod nullum dampnum per defectum ejusdem reparacionis aliquibus partibus ullo modo eveniet Et quod omnia Fossata vocata Wardyches inter omnes & singulas villatas hundredi predicti exaltantur reperentur & sustententur bene & sufficienter per illos etc. ut supradictum est in latitudine xvj [?] pedum & quod [?] sufficiente in latitudine ad obstupandum aquam cujuslibet villate ab altera Ita quod nullum dampnum alicui villate per defectum hujusmodi reparacionis per aquam alterius villate ullo modo eveniet sub pena xls Episcopo Eliensis qui pro tempore fuerit solvendorum Ac eciam quod omnes Creste tam inter omnes Campos quam juxta omnes Seweras omnium & singularum villatarum hundredi predicti exaltentur reperentur & sustententur bene & sufficiente latitudine & Spissitudine per illos etc [sic] ut supradictum est Ita quod nullum dampnum aliquibus partibus per defectum hujusmodi reparacionis ullo modo eveniet sub pena viginti solidorum Episcopo Eliensis pro tempore fuerit solvenda Ac eciam quod nullus de cetero [?] faciet aliquam Wardech seu Crestam infra aliquas villatas hundredi de Wysebech predicti sub pena xls Episcopo Eliensis qui pro tempore fuerit solvenda tociens quociens [?] Et quod Ripa de Wysebech fodiatur & elargatur in locis defectis videlicet a Gyehern usque mare tociens quociens necesse fuerit per omnes terrarum & tenementorum tenentes in dicto hundredo de Wysebech videlicet quilibet eorum pro rata tenure sue.

Item presentant quod Fossatum vocatum Grenedyke de Welle quod incipit ad Crucem lapidiam in Welle & ducit usque Sewaleslote in Welle exaltetur & reperetur altior quam nunc est in altitudine ij Pedum & latitudine xij Pedum per tenentes terrarum & tenementorum in Budbeche videlicet quilibet pro porcione sua ac eciam quod abbas de Bury debet reperare unum fossatum in Welle quod ducit ad Sewaleslote in Welle usque lake brigge & quod fiat altior quam nunc est in altitudine duorum pedum & latitudine & summitate octo pedum Et quod tenentes terrarum & tenementorum in Sayersfeld in Welle debent reperare quoddam fossatum in Welle vocatum Thorndych videlicet a Lowndesdrove usque ad Crucem lapidiam in eadem villa Et quod fiat altior quam nunc est in altitudine ij Pedum & latitudine viij Pedum Et quod quedam drava in Welle vocata Meisdrove que ducit ad

Grenedyke usque Piysdrove fiat altior quam nunc est in altitudine trium Pedum & latitudine xij Pedum per tenentes terrarum & tenementorum in Budbech infra predictam dravam Item Jurati predicti presentant quod est & ex antiquo fuit quedam Cresta in Uppewelle vocata Piysdrove quod ducit ad Grenedyke in Uppewelle usque magnam Ripam de Welle predicta Et quod Cresta predicta debet ex antiquo fieri & reperari per tenentes terrarum & tenementorum villate de Uppewelle predicta Et dicunt quod oportet pro salvacione porcionum ibidem adjaciencium quod predicta Cresta fiat integre & altior quam nunc est in locis bassis in altitudine trium pedum Et quod eadem Cresta habeat in summitate sua latitudinem octo Pedum Et dicunt quod omnes habentes terras seu tenementa in Campo vocato Rudbech in Owtewelle & Upwelle debent reperare quendam gutturam prope mesuagium Simonis Kyng in Owtewelle predicta per quam Aqua de Rudbech incurrere potest in [?] Ripa de Outewelle Et dicunt quod oportet pro salvacione terrarum seu tenementorum in predicto Campo de Rudbech quod predicta Guttura fiat de novo ex lapidibus per homines habentes terras seu tenementa in predicto campo de Rudbech.

Super quibus pro eo quod videtur Justiciariis predictis tam per veredictum Juratorum quam per supervisum eorundem Justiciariorum in hac parte comparentibus omnibus convocandis & consencientibus ac visis & intellectis statutis in hiis casibus editis de Rumpney merssh predicti Justiciarii statuunt & ordinant quod predictum Fossatum vocatum Grenedyke ac eciam predictum fossatum quod ducit a Sewaleslote usque latebrygge Ac eciam predictum fossatum vocatum Thornedyck ac eciam quedam drava vocata Meisedrove Ac eciam predicta [sic] vocata Pyisdrove exaltentur & reperentur in latitudine altitudine & summitate in forma superius specificata per partes predictas videlicet quilibet pro rata tenure sue tociens quociens necesse fuerit Ac eciam quod predicta Guttura que jacet prope mesuagium Simonis Kynge fiat de novo ex lapidibus per partes predictas ut predicitur.

Item presentant quod fossatum vocatum Elmsendiche quod incipit apud Kekysmylle & ducit usque Benestdehyrn & de inde usque Tylneyhyrn & de inde usque Mareysdam in Elme debet exaltari & reperari secundum Antiquum agistamentum altior quam nunc est in altitudine trium Pedum & latitudine summitate sex pedum Item presentant quod fossatum vocatum Redmoredyke in Elme incipiens apud Coldham Clouse & ducens usque Frydaybrigge in eadem villa debet reperari & sustentari bene & sufficienter per omnes tenentes terrarum & tenementorum in Campo de Redmoresfeld & Walysschefeld per novum agista-

mentum faciendum Et quod dictum fossatum debet exaltari altior
quam nunc est in altitudine quatuor pedum & latitudine summitate octo pedum Item presentant quod fossatum quod incipit
apud Frydaybrigge predicto ex parte occidentali Ripe usque
Mareysdam debet exaltari & reperari Altior quam nunc est in
altitudine trium pedum & latitudine summitate octo pedum Item
presentant quod fossatum vocatum le Eebrynke in Elm ex parte
orientali Ripe de Elm quod incipit ad dravam Sancti Egidii &
ducit usque Frydaybrigge & de inde usque Mareysdam debet
exaltari & reperari altior quam nunc est in altitudine trium Pedum
& latitudine in summitate duodecim Pedum per tenentes terrarum & tenementorum in Oldefeld & Nedham secundum
agistamentum inde faciendum.

Item presentant quod Fossatum vocatum Nedhamdyche in
Elme quod incipit apud Thorndyche in Welle & ducit usque
Coldham Kyrse [sic] in Elme debet exaltari & reperari altior quam
nunc est in omnibus locis bassis & fiat equipollens & equale in
altitudine & latitudine fossato Johannis Blewyk jacente super
dictum Fossatum. Item presentant quod omnes homines habentes
terras abuttantes super quendam Seweram in Elme que ducit
per capita terre in Nedham a Frydabrygge usque Knytysdyk in
eadem Villa & deinde Capella Sancti Christoferi in Outewelle &
deinde usque clusam apud Crucem lapidiam in Outewelle debent
& solent reperare & mundare predictam predictam [sic] juxta
capita terrarum suarum Ita quod Aqua de Nedham habeat
cursum suum usque Welleschooll Et quod omnes homines
habentes terras inter Frydabrigge in Elme & Grenedyk in Welle
& inter Bysshopisdyk & Nedhamdyk in Elm predicta debent
facere & reperare unam Clusam meliori modo quo poterit & fiat
integre & sufficienter ad obstupandum aquam de Owtewelle
tempore yemalis.

Super quibus pro eo quod videtur Justiciariis predictis tam per
veredictum Juratorum quam per supervisum eorundem Justiciariorum in hac parte habita comparentibus ac visis intellectis
statutis in hiis casibus editis de Rumpneymerssh predicti Justiciarii statuunt & ordinant pro salvacione villate de Elm quod
Episcopus Eliensis & successores sui & Willelmus Venour ac
omnes terrarum & tenementorum tenentes infra villatam de Elm
ut predicitur de cetero onerentur ad faciendum reperandum
exaltandum & sustentandum omnia & singula in forma predicta
prout in presentacionibus predictis specificantur videlicet quilibet
pro rata tenure sue tociens quociens necesse fuerit.

Item Justiciarii predicti statuunt & ordinant quod ubi aqua
Campi de Oldefeld in Elme ex parte orientali Ripe de Elm solebat

habere cursum suum & evacuare per unam pipam jacentem
subter Ripam de Elme vocatam Massinghams Pype et de inde
solebat cadere & evacuare in Ripam de Wysebech apud
Devyse pro eo quod Ripa de Wysebech per plures annos elapsos
continue exaltari & obstupari cum ejeccione zabule maris per
fluxum & refluxum maris sic quod predicta aqua de Oldefeld per
nullam possibilitatem cadere seu evacuare potuerint nec possunt
Et Ideo Justiciarii predicti statuunt & ordinant pro salvacione
predicte ville quod aqua predicti campi de Oldefeld de cetero
evacuare & sewerare debet per pipam predictam vocatam
Massynghamspype jacentem subter Ripam de Elme inter messuagium Johannis Blythe ex una parte & messuagium Nicholai Rateles-
den ex parte altera & de inde linealiter per antiquam Seweram
inter terram Johannis Tosty ex una parte & terram Johannis
Westbroke ex altera parte usque dravam vocatam Toundrove &
de inde per dictam dravam ex una parte & capitibus terrarum
Johannis Westbroke Johannis Edryche & Bedylacre usque terram
Willelmi Gryswell ex altera parte & de inde per dictam dravam
ex una parte & terram Johannis Conysbury & Willelmi Gryswell
ex parte altera usque seweram vocatam Coldham seweram apud
Crumdykbrigge & de inde in dictam Seweram de Coldham usque
pipam jacentem subter Ripam de Wysebech vocatam Coldham
Pype & de inde in predictam Seweram de Coldham usque
Gurgitam in Leveryngton vocatam Dieugard & de inde usque
Mari [sic] & quod aqua de Redmorefeld & Welysschfeld de
cetero non currant nec habeant cursum suum per dictam Seweram
de Coldham set [sic] predicta aqua de Redmorefeld & Walyssch-
feld debent de cetero evacuare per pipam vocatam Redmore
Pype jacentem apud finem ville de Elm & de inde inter fossatum
vocatum Hillarydyk ex parte una & capita terrarum Johannis
Walpoll usque terras Willelmi Beston ex parte altera & de inde
inter dictum Hillarydyk ex una parte & dictam terram dicti
Willelmi Beston ex parte altera usque terras Johannis Walpoll &
de inde ibidem extransverso dictum Fossatum vocatum Hillaridyk
in Seweram vocatam Waltersee seweram & de inde in eadem
sewera de Waltersee usque Gurgitem in Leveryngton vocatam
Dieugard & de inde usque mare & quod omnes habentes terras
in predicto campo de Oldefeld & omnes quo per evacuacionem
aque ejusdem Campi [?] habentes de cetero sunt onerati ad
predictam Pipam vocatam Massynghampype & dictam seweram
de inde ducentem usque Coldham seweram apud Cromdykbrigge
ut predicitur bene & sufficiente faciendas & reperandas imperpetuum pro porcione terrarum suarum Et quod sint onerati &
contribuarii simul cum Willelmo Venour domino manerii de

Coldham ac dictam Seweram vocatam Coldham Seweram a dicto
Cromdykbrigge usque mare & ad crestam ejusdem & ad dictam
pipam vocatam Coldhampype faciendas reperandas & susten-
tandas pro porcione terrarum suarum prout predictus Willelmus Venour & parcenarii sui ante haec tempora illas facere
reparare & sustentare solebant juxta ordinacionem inde ex antiquo
factam Et quod Creste dicte Sewere de Coldham sint sufficientes
Ita quod predicta aqua de Oldefeld currat in dictam seweram de
Coldham infra Crestas. Et quod non currat altior quam terre
sunt que abbutantes super dictam Seweram Item presentant quod
omnes habentes aliquam foveam abbutantem super dictam
Seweram de Coldham de cetero debent obstupare dictam foveam
cum uno dammo [sic] & uno clote desuper sito. Ita quod dictum
dammum sit in latitudine duodecim pedum & in altitudine
equipollens capitibus terrarum adjacientum. Ita quod nullum
dampnum per aquam dicte seweris terrarum adjacientum ullo
modo eveniat prout ex antiquo ordinacione existit. Item presentant quod omnes habentes terras in Redmorefeld & Wallysschfeld
de cetero sint onerati & contribuarii simul cum dicto Episcopo
Eliensis ad predictam Seweram de Waltersee A predicto loco in
Hillarydyke ubi aque de Redmorefeld & Walysschefeld cadunt in
dictam Seweram de Waltersee & ad Crestam ejusdem Sewere
de Waltersee simul cum predicta pipa vocata le lordyspype
faciendum reperandum & sustentandum imperpetuum pro
porcione terrarum suarum.

Item presentant quod terrarum & tenementorum tenentes de
Leveryngton debent & solent facere & reperare unum Fossatum
in Leveryngton vocatum le Wardyk altior quam nunc est in
optimo loco per tres pedes Item presentant quod villata de
Leveryngton de toto tempore predicto debet & solet facere &
reperare octo pontes in Newton adjacentes in locis ut in antiquis
Evidenciis domini Regis continentur & prout ex antiquo de jure
feceretur Et dicunt quod octo pontes in Newton jacentes videlicet
primus pons versus australem ad clusam que clusa est reparanda
Et alius pons jacens versus frontem Andrae Cok due [sic] apud
Leveryngton Pype in Newton unus apud Lordyslane unus apud
Childesgrave unus apud Grendyk & unus apud Startesgate Et
requisitum fuit toto Inquisitioni si unquam viderint seu aliquis
eorum viderit aliquem pontem dictorum octo pontium ac in aliquo
loco nisi ubi jacentem nunc qui dixerunt coram Justiciariis quod
non Item presentant quod villata de Leveryngton de toto tempore
predicto debet & solet facere reperare & exaltare unam Crestam
in Leveryngton predicta incipientem apud Neuton Gordyk &
ducentem usque Bondesgate in Leveryngton & ab inde usque

Rechemound in eadem villa in altitudine quatuor pedum & latitudine octo pedum. Item presentant quod Tenentes terrarum de Harpfelde in Leveryngton de toto tempore predicto debent & solent facere reperare & exaltare unam Crestam in quodam loco vocato Towlanes incipientem apud Shoffendyk in Leveryngton & ducentem usque Blaklane in eadem villa in altitudine quatuor pedum & latitudine viij Pedum. Item presentant quod Tenentes terrarum de Southhinham in Leveryngton de toto tempore predicto debent & solent facere reperare & exaltare unum Fossatum vocatum Overdyche in Leveryngton predicta incipientem apud Belymyllebrigge & ducentem usque Persondroveshende in eadem villa Et tunc ab inde usque Meyesbrigge per Tenentes terrarum de Northhinham etc. Et ab inde usque Blakelanefeld per Tenentes terrarum de Fenhalfeld etc. Et ab inde usque Bondysgote per Tenentes terrarum de Blakelanefeld altior quam nunc est in optimo loco per ij pedes & latitudine xij pedum Item presentant quod Tenentes terrarum de Fenhalfeld in Leveryngton de toto tempore predicto debent & solent facere reperare & exaltare unam venellam vocatam Polylane incipientem apud Shoffendiche in Leveryngton & ducentem usque Meyesbrigge in eadem villa in altitudine quatuor pedum & latitudine octo pedum.

Super quibus pro eo quod videtur Justiciariis predictis tam per veredictum Juratorum quam per supervisum eorundem Justiciariorum in hac parte habita comparentibus omnibus convocandis ac visis intellectis statutis in hiis casibus editis de Rumpneymerssh predicti Justiciarii statuunt & ordinant pro salvacione ville de Leveryngton quod omnes predictarum terrarum & tenementorum Tenentes infra villatam de Leveryngton ut predicitur de cetero onerentur ad faciendum reperandum exaltandum & sustentandum omnia & singula in forma predicta prout in presentacionibus predictis specificantur videlicet quilibet pro rata tenure sue tociens quociens necesse fuerit etc. [sic]

Item presentant quod una Sewera debet fieri in Fenlondfeld in Neuton latitudine sex pedum & profunditate trium pedum inter terram Martini Thomson & terram Johannis Mendham de Custagiis & expensis omnium terrarum & tenementorum inde proficua habentum. Item presentant quod fiat alia sewera in eodem Campo latitudine sex pedum & profunditate trium pedum inter terram Johannis Rogerson & terram Alicie Pope ad custagia & expensas omnium terrarum & tenementorum inde proficua habentum. Item presentant quod alia sewera fiat in longefeld in Neuton in latitudine sex pedum & profunditate trium pedum juxta terram Johannis Derby vocatam Barowsdyk inter terram Simonis Thomson a Millane usque Medowelane ad custagia &

expensas omnium terrarum & tenementorum inde proficua
habentum Item presentant quod alia Sewera debet fieri in medio
Campi de longefeld predicto a terra Johannis Colvyle militis
juxta terram Johannis Godeknape usque ad predictam Seweram
proximam presentem latitudine sex pedum & profunditate trium
pedum ad custagia omnium terrarum inde proficua habentum
Item presentant quod omnia capita terrarum de Fytton Croftes
fodiantur a Doddyk usque Medowlande latitudine octo pedum
& profunditate iiij pedum ad custagia & expensas omnium
terrarum inde proficua habentum. Item presentant quod omnia
capita terrarum de Fytton croftes fodiantur in latitudine octo
pedum & profunditate quatuor pedum a Lowynysfendyke usque
Doddyk ad custagia & expensas omnium terrarum inde proficua
habentum Item presentant quod [sic   ] fiat una Sewera
per capita terre in medio Campi de Oldefeld videlicet a Fytton
Croftes usque terram Johannis Colvyle militis vocatam Worthey-
nyscroft latitudine sex pedum & profunditate trium pedum ad
custagia & expensas omnium terrarum inde proficua habentum.
    Plus in dorso de eodem Recordo.
    Item presentant quod fiat alia Sewera juxta Wortheynyscroft
predictam ex parte australi Doddyk ad custagia & expensas
omnium terrarum & tenementorum inde proficua habentum
latitudine sex pedum & profunditate quatuor pedum Item
presentant quod villate de Neuton a tempore cujus contrarii
memoria hominum non existit debet & solet facere exaltare &
reperare quoddam Fossatum vocatum Lowynysfendyke incipientem apud Fytton & ducentem usque Tydde Syddyk altior quam
nunc est in optimo loco per ij pedes & latitudine duodecim pedum
Item presentant quod Johannes Symondson de Neuton de toto
tempore predicto debet & solet facere & custodire unum dammum [sic] ad finem orientalem terre sue in Newfeld ad custodiendum aquam de Newfeld predicta Ita quod non descendat
infra proximum campum vocatum Rolsesfeld Item presentant
quod villata de Neuton de toto tempore predicto debet & solet
facere reperare & exaltare quoddam fossatum in Neuton vocatum
le Gordyk incipientem apud Blakkyslane & ducentem usque
Shoffendyche in altitudine sex pedum & latitudine duodecim
Pedum etc [sic].
    Super quibus pro eo quod videtur Justiciariis predictis tam per
veredictum Juratorum quam per supervisum eorundem Justiciariorum in hac parte habita comparentibus & consencientibus
omnibus convocandis ac visis intellectis in [sic] hiis casibus editis
de Rumpney [?   ] predicti Justiciarii statuunt & ordinant
pro salvacione villate de Neuton quod omnes predictarum

terrarum & tenementorum tenentes infra villatam de Neuton ut
predicitur de cetero onerentur ad faciendum reperandum exaltandum & sustentandum omnia & singula in forma predicta prout
in presentacionibus predictis specificantur videlicet quilibet pro
rata tenure sue tociens quociens necesse fuerit etc [sic].
Item presentant quod omnes terrarum & tenementorum
tenentes in Newfeld in Tyd Sancti Egidii debent & solent facere
& reperare unam Crestam in quodam Campo vocato Beesland-
feld in eadem villa incipientem apud Tyd Syddyk usque Brounesbrigge altitudine iiij pedum & latitudine octo pedum Item presentant quod omnes terrarum & tenementorum tenentes in
Southfeld in eadem villa incipientum apud Tyd Syddyk usque
Brounesbrigge altitudine quatuor pedum & latitudine octo pedum Item presentant quod Tenentes terrarum & tenementorum
in Southfeld in eadem villa incipientum ad terram Johannis
Honfeld abbuttentum super quendam mancionem vocatum
Beesplase usque Tyd Syddyk a tempore cujus contrarii memoria
[sic] non existit predicti debent & solent facere unam Crestam
super Syddyk incipientem apud Beeslandend & ducentem usque
Avereystrese in eadem villa altitudine quatuor pedum & latitudine
octo pedum Item presentant quod Tenentes terrarum & tenementorum in Southfeld predicto abbuttentum super Brodgate de
toto tempore predicto debent & solent facere reperare & exaltare
unam Crestam juxta communem Seweram ex parte Australi
altitudine quatuor pedum & latitudine octo pedum Item presentant quod omnes Tenentes terrarum & tenementorum in
Bradeste abbuttentum super Hascroftlane versus occidentem de
toto tempore predicto debent & solent facere & reperare quemdam Seweram incipientem apud Seweram juxta terram vocatam
Stokwelleslond usque Brossebrygge latitudine octo pedum & profunditate quatuor pedum. Item presentant quod omnes tenentes
terrarum & tenementorum in Halcrofte de toto tempore predicto
debent & solent facere & reperare bene & sufficienter communem
Seweram in Halcrofte usque Welmanysflete extransverso communem viam vocatam Crossegate & sic per terras nuper Thome
Rethirwyk & Johannis Mayner usque terram nuper Johannis Bee
modo Johannis Hunston & sic inter terras dicti Johannis Hunston
& Isabelle Rethirwyk usque Sondylane & ibi fiat unus pons
latitudine unius pedis & profunditate unius pedis & sic inter
terram Johannis Lambard & terram nuper Galfridi Cosyn usque
Sedyklane & terram cujusdam Campi vocati Blohevede usque
Gurgitem Item presentant quod omnes tenentes terrarum &
tenementorum in Edykfelde a Blakkeslane usque Mosseslane
abbuttentum super Edyk de toto tempore predicto debent &

solent facere & reperare unam Seweram ad capud borialem
terrarum & tenementorum de Edykfeld predicto latitudine octo
pedum & profunditate quatuor pedum. Item presentant quod
omnes tenentes terrarum & tenementorum in Edykfeld de toto
tempore predicto debent & solent facere unam Seweram ad
capites boriales terrarum & tenementorum de Edykfeld predicto
abbuttentem super Edyk a Blakkeslane usque Barowsgrene
latitudine octo pedum & profunditate quatuor pedum Ita quod
aqua dulcis habeat cursum suum juxta Blakkeslane usque
magnam Seweram & sic ad mare Item presentant quod omnes
tenentes terrarum & tenementorum in Hornfeld de toto tempore
predicto debent & solent facere reperare & exaltare unam
Crestam in Brodgate in Tyd sancti Egidii ex parte australi sewere
a Marteynysfendyk usque ad angulum ubi Willelmus Hoberd
modo manet altitudine quatuor pedum & latitudine decem pedum.
Item presentant quod omnes Tenentes terrarum & tenementorum in Cokeleyfeld de toto tempore predicto debent & solent
facere & reperare bene & sufficienter unam Crestam in Bottelles-
lane a Bottellesbrigge usque le Gedyke altitudine quatuor pedum
& latitudine duodecim pedum Item presentant quod omnes
Tenentes terrarum & tenementorum in Fendykfeld & Northlane-
feld debent & solent facere & reperare unam Crestam in Blakelane
in Tyd predicta a Botellesbrigge usque Tubbesbrigge & a terra
Johannis Ingleth usque Gedyk altitudine quatuor pedum &
latitudine octo pedum Item presentant quod omnes tenentes
terrarum & tenementorum in Carrowfeld abbuttentum super
Gegate a Gotebrigge usque Northlane de toto tempore predicto
debent & solent facere & exaltare unam Crestam in Gegate in Tyd
predicta ubi necesse est altitudine quatuor pedum & latitudine
duodecim pedum Item presentant quod omnes tenentes terrarum
& tenementorum villate de Tyd de toto tempore predicto debent
& solent facere & exaltare unum Fossatum vocatum Bysschopys-
dyk a Tubbesbrigge usque le Gedyk altitudine quatuor pedum &
latitudine duodecim pedum Item presentant quod villata de Tyd
Sancti Egidii de toto tempore predicto debet & solet facere &
reperare bene & sufficiente unam clusam de novo vel unum
Dammum [sic] in commune Sewera de Tyd juxta terram Simonis
Cauchon & Hascroftlane ex parte occidentale & aliam clusam
vel unum Dammum in commune sewera apud Brownysbrygge
Et aliam clusam vel unum Dammum in Commune Sewera apud
Wesynghambrigge & aliam Clusam vel unum Dammum apud
Boteleslanebrigge & aliam clusam vel unum Dammum in
commune Sewera apud Tubbesbrigge & aliam Clusam vel unum
Dammum apud Mannynggysbrigge & aliam clusam vel unum

Dammum in Commune Sewera apud Beeslanebrigge & aliam clusam vel unum Dammum in commune Sewera apud le Stonbrigge in Kirklane Item presentant quod villata de Tyd de toto tempore predicto debet & solet facere reperare exaltare & manutenere bene & sufficienter duo Fossata vocata Wardyches in Tyd predicta videlicet le Suddyk & Thredyk incipientes apud Avereystrees in Tyd predicta & ducentes usque Newfendyk in eadem villa altior quam nunc sunt in optimo loco per sex pedes & latitudine duodecim pedum Item presentant quod dicta villata de Tyd de toto tempore predicto debet & solet facere exaltare & manutenere bene & sufficienter unum Fossatum vocatum Marteynysfendyk in Tyd predicta incipientem apud Avereystrees & ducentem usque Wesynghambrigge in eadem villa altior quam nunc est in optimo loco per sex pedes & latitudine duodecim pedum.

Super quibus quod videtur Justiciariis predictis tam per veredictum Juratorum predictorum quam per supervisum eorundem Justiciariorum in hac parte habita comparentibus & consencientibus ac visis intellectis statutis in hiis casibus editis de Rumpneymerssh predicti Justiciarii statuunt & ordinant pro salvacione villate de Tyd quod omnes predictarum terrarum & tenementorum tenentes infra villatam de Tyd ut predicitur de cetero onerentur ad faciendum & reperandum & exaltandum & sustentandum omnia & singula in forma prout in presentacionibus predictis specificata videlicet quilibet pro rata tenure sue tociens quociens necesse fuerit.

Item Justiciarii predicti statuunt & ordinant pro salvacione villate de Tyd predicte quod una Sewera fiat de novo a Brownesbrigge usque Kyrklane ex parte Boriali de Newgate latitudine decem pedum & profunditate ut decet Ita quod aque de Gletesfeld Fendykfeld Cokeleyfeld Hornefeld & Rylondsfeld habeant cursum suum usque ad dammum nuper Willelmi Noche modo Willelmi Hobert ex parte boriali de Brodgate & sic extransverso le Brodgate usque Brownesbrigge predicto ex parte australi de Brodgate & sic usque predictam novam Seweram Et tunc extransverso Kyrkland et ibi fiat unus pons in latitudine & profunditate ut decet & sic per capites terre de Somerleswe abbuttentes super Kyrkland versus occidentem usque Thorgereslane & sic per Thorgereslane ex parte boriali usque Hascroft Dyke juxta le Thestilbrigge & a Thestelybrigge ad finem de Thorgereslane usque Harcroft Mille Hylle extransverso Hascroft Dyke & sic usque ad antiquam seweram vocatam Brossobrigge & sic usque mare per omnes terrarum & tenementorum Tenentes villate de Tyd predicte & quod due Sewere ex utraque parte de

Brodgate & Kyrkgate a domo Willelmi Hobert & Brownesbrigge obstupantur cum necesse fuerit. Et quod una Sewera reperetur & fodiatur ad capud Australem de Southyraftefeld juxta le Syddyk videlicet a Childesgrave usque le Gorys & sic usque Thestelybrigge in latitudine & profunditate ut decet per omnes terrarum & tenementorum Tenentes in Southgraftefeld predicto Et quod omnia capita terrarum de Southgraftefeld predicto versus Thorgareslane obstupantur per Tenentes terrarum ibidem sub pena cujuslibet eorum xxs domino Episcopo Eliensis qui pro tempore fuerit solvenda Ita quod Aqua de Southgraftefeld predicto habeat cursum suum usque ad mare sine ullo impedimento Et quod quilibet qui tenet terras vel tenementa in Tyd predicta capiat terram & solum ad reperandum & faciendum le Shoffendyk de communa juxta Ripam que est inter Tyd predictam & Tyd beate Marie que est divisa inter Comitatum Cantebrig' & Comitatum Lincoln' Et quod le Shoffendyk predicta barretur in tribus locis pro Carectis ibidem transeuntibus Et quod quedam Venella in Tyd predicta vocata Beeslane barretur pro Carectis ibidem transeuntibus videlicet a festo Sancti Michaelis Archangeli usque festum Sancti Petri vocatur ad vincula per tenentetes [*sic*] terrarum in Newfeld.

Item presentant quod Thomas Floore de Okham in Comitatu Rotl' reperare & sustentare debet in Fossato maresci vocato Wysebechefendych quandam porcionem continentem vi [crossed out] xx pedum per viginti & quatuor acras terrae in Wysebech [?].

Plus in Dorso

die lune in Festo Sancti Wulstani Episcopi & concessa Anno regni dicti domini Regis decimo septimo dicte porcionis Fossati predicti dirupte & fracte fuit prefato Thoma present [*sic*] & prepositi Fossatorum predictorum premuniebant eundem Thomam quod dictam porcionem Fossati predicti faciendam & emendam [?] idem Thomas recusavit per quam aqua maresci predicta dictam porcionem ejusdem Fossati fregit ac diversae porciones dicti fossati Galfridi Lambard & aliorum adjacentes dictae porcioni fossati predicti Thome fractae & disruptae extiterunt in veresimilem distruccionem tocius patrie super dictam fraccionem M^1. M^1. M^1. M^1. CCCC. acrarum terre villate de Wysbeche M^1. M^1. M^1. M^1. DC. acrarum terre villate de Leveryngton M^1. CCCC. acrarum terre villate de Neuton & M^1. M^1. acrarum terre villate de Tyd submere & inundate fuerunt & ad huc existunt.

INDEX

New drains, 149, 153, 166
Newton, 59, 77, 151
Nomansland, 53 n., 68 n., 86 n.
Norfolk, 1, 11, 18, 28, 29, 33, 34 n.,
40, 57, 58, 61, 67, 69, 99, 124, 131,
133 ff., 141. *Also see* Marshland
North Walsham, 132
North Witham, 37
Northampton, 11, 98 n., 104
Northee, 81
Northumbria, 12
Norwich, 131, 133 ff., 150, 162

Oats, 53 n., 55
Occupations, chap. 2 *passim*
Offoldfal, 51
Old Wellenhee, 98 n., 99
Oolitic rocks, 107
Ouse, R. *See* Great Ouse, R., *and*
Little Ouse, R.
Outwell, 70, 96, 99, 158 n., 168. *Also
see* Well
Over, 50

Parish boundaries, 17 ff., 68, 69
Pasture, 22, 24, 48, 52, 55, 61, 66 ff.,
120, 121, 142 n., 150. *Also see*
Cattle, Common rights, Inter-
commoning
Peacocks, 36 n.
Peat-lands, 2, 5, 7, 15, 16, 18, 52, 141
Perch, 28
Peterborough, 2, 3, 7 n., 8 n., 10,
11 ff., 16, 21, 24, 31, 36, 50, 54,
57 n., 87, 88, 92, 94, 99, 104 n.,
105 n., 113, 118 n., 158, 168. *Also
see* Medeshamstede
Phisshesilver, 31
Pickerels, 28
Pidley, 78
Pike, 30
Pinchbeck, 76, 77, 89, 131, 137, 148,
152, 154
Place-names, 8, 10, 11, 29, 94 n.
Plough-teams, 122 ff.
Podike, 79 n., 160, 167
Population, 122 ff.
Purprestures. *See* Enclosure, Re-
clamation

Quadring, 39, 131, 137 n., 148, 151
Quaternary deposits, 1, 2, 4 n.
Quaveney, 103
Quy, 3

Radfield hundred, 130
Ramsey, 12, 14, 29, 30 ff., 34 n.,
36 n., 48, 51, 53, 54, 59, 72, 75 n.,
77, 78, 80, 81, 101, 102, 104, 105,
110, 113, 144, 145 n., 149, 150, 162
Raveley, 68, 78, 150 n.
Rebellions, 119, 143 ff.
Reclamation, 4, 43–52, 61, 66, 67,
79 ff., 141, 142. *Also see* Division of
fens, Enclosure
Reeds, 8, 22, 32 ff., 42, 92
Rhine, R., 1
Roach, 28
Roddons, 6, 94 ff.
Roman period, 3 ff., 20, 95 n.
"Roman" Bank. *See* Sea-bank
Romney Marsh Custom, 164, 165
Rout-penny, 103 n.
Rushes, 22, 32 ff.
Rutland, 11, 98 n.

St Albans, 13
St Ives, 29 n., 51, 94
St Neots, 36 n., 70
Salter's Lode, 158 n., 167. *Also see*
Well Creek
Salt-pans, 21, 37 ff., 51, 121
Sawtry, 14, 49, 56 n., 75 n., 100,
104 n., 150 n.
Scandinavians, 10 ff.
Scrane, 11
Scrivelsby soke, 75, 76
Sea-bank, 3, 4 n., 41, 100, 152, 160
Sedge, 32 ff.
Sedgeford, 132
Sefare, seesilver, sesilver, 103
Segsilver, seggesilver, 33
Sheep, 68, 121, 131
Shippea, 103
Ships. *See* Boats
Sibsey, 115
Silt-lands, 2, 4 n., 5, 15, 16, 18, 28,
39, 55, 128, 130, 131, 137, 140, 141
Skidbrook, 137 n.
Skirbeck, 11, 116
Skirbeck wapentake, 11, 38, 124, 137,
138, 140, 151
Smeeth, 67
Smithdon hundred, 132, 136
Snettisham, 131
Soham, 23, 107, 108, 109, 111, 130 n.,
144
Somersham, 62, 78, 80 ff., 101, 102,
148 n., 150

Wilton, 28
Wisbech, 23, 57, 77, 81 n., 82 n., 94,
 96, 98, 99, 101, 105, 115 n., 151,
 156 ff., 165, 166, 168
Wisbech hundred, 7, 130, 141, 162
Wissey, R., 94 n., 96
Wistow, 32, 62, 68 n., 78
Witchford hundreds, 110, 130, 141
Witham, R., 2 n., 11, 38, 46 n., 93,
 94, 101, 104, 153, 159, 165

Wolds, 140
Wopenny, 162, 163
Wood Walton, 49, 56 n., 101 n.,
 104 n., 150 n.
Wooton, 39
Wraggoe wapentake, 138
Wrangle, 41, 151

Yarmouth, 131, 133 ff.
Yaxley, 73 n., 82, 98